CREATIVE INTERIORS

CREATIVE INTERIORS

A complete practical course
in interior design

WREN LOASBY

David & Charles

A DAVID & CHARLES BOOK

© Wren Loasby 1992

First published 1992
Reprinted 1993
Reprinted 1994

A catalogue record for this book is available from the British Library.

ISBN 0 7153 9935 7

Typeset by XL Publishing Services, Nairn, Scotland
and printed in Singapore by
CS Graphics Pte Ltd for
David & Charles plc
Brunel House Newton Abbot Devon

CONTENTS

INTRODUCTION

The ever-increasing sales of books and magazines showing stylish, beautifully decorated houses, both large and small, give some indication of the continuing interest in, and appeal of, interior decoration; but, for various reasons – location, family commitments or cost – it is often impossible for people seriously interested in learning more about interior design to attend a specific training course. This book intends to present that knowledge in an easily digested form, and to set projects, just as they might be presented in a course, to enable you to build up your very own design portfolio.

Of course it is impossible for any book to turn its reader into a fully fledged interior designer – but we hope this one will nurture and expand perhaps half-formed feelings about interior design, and give the aspiring designer confidence in his or her own flair and ability. The projects which are suggested at the end of each chapter start with the basics of room design and then cover one specific subject at a time. Not only should these projects be fun to do, they will also allow the compilation of a really professional-looking portfolio of work which will be a pleasure to show to anyone, be they friends or possible future clients. Remember, a good-looking and interesting portfolio could well be your passport into the exciting world of interior design!

In reading through each chapter think carefully about the things which are discussed – make the projects come really alive by basing some of them on rooms in your own home. Each project is designed to provoke constructive thinking about the specific subject just discussed, and how to deal with certain areas or potential problems. And it cannot be over-emphasised how important it is to read as many books and magazines as possible which show and discuss the interiors of all types of homes, from the simplest thatched cottage to the grandest of mansions. Try to look at any surrounding with fresh eyes, and think carefully about various aspects of interior design and decoration. Be perceptive about the furnishings, floor coverings, wall finishes and furniture layouts. You can always learn something, and reading and observing will help form your own opinions as to why – or why not – a scheme works. Become a squirrel, *keep* cuttings of everything you like, or which has a particular application. Turn a simple concertina file into an invaluable reference source with leaflets and cuttings filed under appropriate headings.

No particular equipment is needed to complete the projects; but it is important to remember that each one is adding to your very own design portfolio: the more effort and care put in, the more impressive the portfolio will look. Think about layout and presentation, finish designs with an edging to hold them together and – unless your handwriting is very stylish – consider using instant lettering as headings.

We hope above all that this book and its projects will bring great pleasure, and that one of its results will be a glorious portfolio of which anyone would be truly proud.

CHAPTER 1

INFLUENCES OF THE PAST

Everyone with a real interest in interior design needs to have some background knowledge of the basic elements that go into the make-up of a room; so, what are these elements?

In Britain, surprisingly, there are still about six million houses which were built before 1920, and a quarter of these would have been built in the Victorian era. And even for a house which is post-1920, it is still relevant to know how various influences from the past affect things today; and for those living in a period house, these influences will be of particular interest. However, unless you are a purist, it would be a mistake to try slavishly to attain authenticity in every particular: after all, a house is meant to be a home, not a museum, and over the years even a very old house will have been modified as the owners' needs and, indeed, ideas and fashions have changed.

Let us take a look at the historical backgrounds of the basic structures – floors, walls, ceilings, doors and windows – and see how things have evolved over the centuries.

FLOORS

SOLID

For centuries the only flooring was bare earth which was either worn down or beaten into a firm surface; by medieval times, however, things became a little more sophisticated. Initially the bare earth was covered with rushes or laths which were bound together by a primitive form of plaster, usually made from lime, and this flooring was then strewn with rushes not only for warmth but also to keep the dust down.

People then discovered that if they combined earth and clay and mixed it with a liquid – very often ox blood was used – they could bake it in their fires and, when cool, it would have a hard smooth surface which made an ideal flooring. Naturally enough this method, too, was adapted and soon the stiff mixture of earth and clay was being cut into squares and then baked in a kiln, the end result

being bricks and paviors which were very like the quarry tiles we know today.

If an area was rich in a suitable stone this was often quarried and then cut into large flagstones to make enduring floors. People in places such as Cornwall and Wales found their local slate was ideal for floors and, indeed, this material became so popular that it was often carried to other parts of Britain. In many regions handsome marbles in a large variety of colours were to be found – although then, as now, it was an expensive material and so was only used in the finest of houses. Portland stone was also much sought after as a flooring material for grand houses and looked particularly well when laid in the traditional diamond pattern intersected with small squares of black marble, an enduring style which is still as elegant today as when it was first used in the seventeenth century.

By Victorian times marble and other polished stones had become widely available; this resulted in a huge upsurge of interest in their decorative possibilities, which in turn led to often complicated mosaic and tessellated floor patterns. Patterned ceramic tiles grew in popularity, and areas such as porches, hallways and passages most frequently received the attentions of creative tilers, their work still being appreciated today by many owners of Victorian houses.

WOODEN

Crude wooden floorboards were first used in the upper part of a house, to divide up the height and to create more living space. These first boards were roughly hewn and varied in width and thickness, but most were of a generous size, and of a solidity which still endures today. For centuries the most common materials used were oak and elm, and it was not until about the seventeenth century that a cheaper alternative was found. This was fir wood, sometimes known as deal – and not only was it cheaper, it could also be supplied in ready-cut boards, so reducing the carpenter's time and effort; by the early eighteenth century deal floorboards had become commonplace.

Herringbone work – a traditional design for wooden and other flooring

During the fourteenth and fifteenth centuries aromatic herbs were also strewn on top of the rushes as they not only sweetened the atmosphere but were believed to have antiseptic properties.

FAR LEFT: *A modern-day recreation of the woven rushes which would have covered stone floors in the Middle Ages*

LEFT: *An ancient flooring technique brought bang up to date using modern vinyl tiles*

This kitchen shows quarry tiles and a batten door, which have not altered in style since medieval times

RIGHT: *A floor painted with red and green strips to add interest to the plain floorboards. Note how the colours are echoed on the sides of the bath and in the accessories.*

BELOW RIGHT: *An intricate parquet flooring pattern, demonstrating the attractive effects which can be achieved*

A cloth soaked with a mixture of malt vinegar and paraffin will get rid of dust, and when a soft dry cloth is used to buff up, will leave a wonderful shine on wooden floorboards.

Black-painted wooden beams can be restored by first removing the paint with a paint-stripper and then sanding off the remaining traces. In really bad cases a plane can be used instead of a sander.

Naturally the gentry did not find it acceptable to have 'common' floorboards, so craftsmen, working on a smooth base floor, evolved a method of inlaying blocks of differently coloured woods into various patterns; this method became known as parquetage, now more commonly known as parquet. The results were very attractive, and with loving care and attention over the years, a parquet floor would mellow to a soft, gleaming surface which showed off expensive rugs to perfection.

Of course, rugs had been available from the early part of the seventeenth century, but along with tapestries, they had more usually been hung on walls or used as table covers; it was not until the eighteenth century that someone was inspired to place them on floors instead, thus softening the expanse of floorboards and adding a feeling of comfort to all manner of rooms, hallways and

corridors. Not everyone could afford woollen rugs, but other coverings were gradually being introduced – one of the most popular was an oiled floorcloth made from canvas covered with many layers of paint, decorated with a pattern and then sealed with several coats of varnish. This floorcloth was the forerunner of linoleum.

Some people preferred simply to paint their floorboards, either in a single colour or more elaborately with borders and central patterns. It is interesting that this method of decorating a floor is regaining popularity, and some very interesting results can be achieved – everything from bold geometric patterns to delicate, subtle stencilled floors can now be seen.

CEILINGS

The wooden floors which were first used in the upper part of a house also served as ceilings to the rooms below. When they were first introduced, the living area below must have seemed rather cramped and this is probably why people first thought of trying to create more light by painting the boards with several coats of a white lime solution. And as time went on, they found they could stop the draughts whistling through the floorboards by sealing the areas between the joists with a thick plaster; the joists themselves were left bare, and the net result provided both a warmer bedroom above and a decorative ceiling below. The bare joists mellowed into a lovely honey shade as the years went by; occasionally they may have been given a light limewash, but they most certainly would *not* have been painted in the horrendous black which is seen in so many 'olde worlde' buildings today.

For a long period the timber beams and joists were left untouched; then shortly before the reign of Henry VIII, craftsmen began to see their decorative possibilities and started to embellish them with all kinds of carving, often carrying a particular theme down into carved wooden friezes to echo the beams above. The Tudor craftsmen were also adept at plasterwork and soon it became

A neat example of a pre-cast ceiling rose

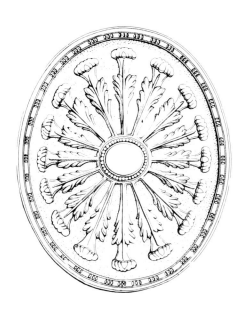

Some examples of classic designs for ceiling roses

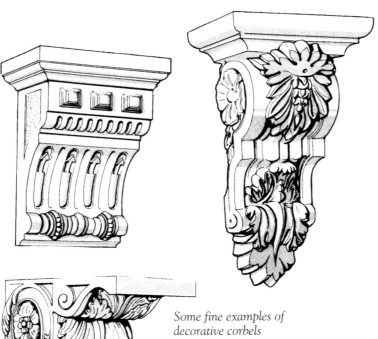

Some fine examples of
decorative corbels

ABOVE RIGHT: *Various
mouldings have been used to
unite these interconnecting
rooms*

RIGHT: *Two very different
friezes, but both are based on
Adam-style designs*

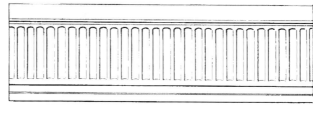

FAR LEFT: *An example of a simple modern pre-cast moulding design*

LEFT:*There are designs for cornices to suit almost every style of room*

usual, in the houses of the well-off, to apply deep plaster friezes to the tops of walls and to ornament the ceilings themselves with Tudor roses and lattice or strapwork designs.

By the early seventeenth century it was fashionable for ceilings to be coved, smoothly plastered, and decorated with mouldings which were often painted or gilded. Inigo Jones was the great innovator behind this now classical style and his influence continued until well into the eighteenth century; then the brothers Adam introduced their beautifully restrained designs, inspired by the Grecian architectural style. Of course not everyone wanted, or could afford, decorative plasterwork, but during this period most houses had at least a simple cornice below a plainly plastered ceiling. This is a device which endures to this day and is one which, however simple its character, can add immeasurably to the appearance of many rooms.

The Victorians loved decorative plasterwork, and by the nineteenth century it was possible to cast cornices, friezes and ceiling roses in moulds, a cheaper process than hand-plastering and which brought these desirable and decorative pieces within the means of far more people. Many examples of mould-made plasterwork still exist in houses built during the 1800s, some very ornate and some elegantly restrained, but all adding to the general ambience of their surroundings. The ever-inventive Victorians also developed a method of pressing thick paper into moulded plasterwork shapes. This was sometimes used on ceilings but most often was applied to walls below the dado rail – today, we know this paper as Anaglypta and Lincrusta.

INTERNAL DOORS

The earliest doors were very primitive affairs and were made from solid, vertical wooden planks placed edge to edge and joined together by oak or iron 'pegs' which would be hammered through to similar horizontal planks set across the back of the door. Not unnaturally these early doors were known as plank doors and were hung from wooden posts which were an integral part of the building structure. What we now know as a batten door is a variation of this style, having diagonal braces set between the horizontal planks and giving great stability to the whole structure.

Adaptations of both these styles continued well into the sixteenth century when doors made with two panels surrounded by a frame began to make their first appearance. Mostly these panelled doors were left unadorned, although in richer homes they were sometimes heavily carved or embellished with mouldings. It was not until the mid-seventeenth

century that the more elegant four- and six-panelled doors began to appear – these simple, classic doors, ideally twice as high as they are wide, have certainly survived the test of time, being as popular today as they were then.

By the time these doors were first introduced, the posts on which they were hung had also developed, and were no longer an integral part of the building but a separate structure set into the wall; the join between wall and post was disguised by an architrave which formed a frame, or case, to the door. Whilst most people were content to leave these simple door frames just as they were, the fashionable preferred to embellish the frames with elaborately carved medallions and swags, and to surmount the whole by pediments. Often the treatment of the door frame would be echoed in panel work on the walls and chimneypiece, a practice which further emphasised the fact that the owners could afford to have everything 'designed' to suit a particular room.

BELOW LEFT: *A typical plank door design;*
RIGHT: *A board-school Gothic door*

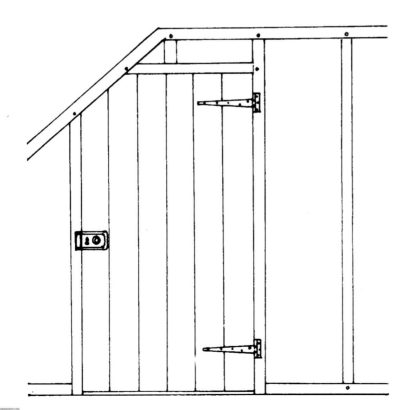

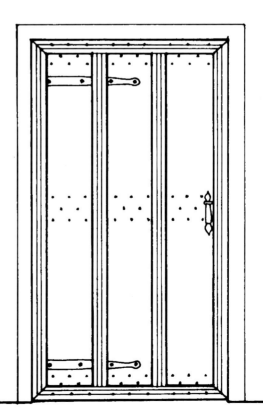

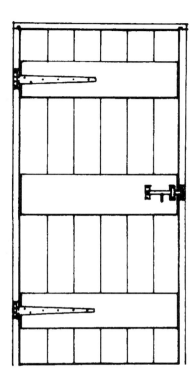

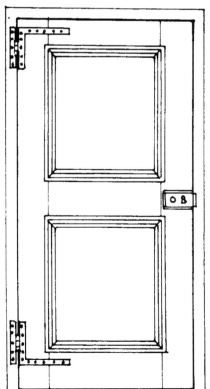

WINDOWS

The word 'window' derives from the words 'wind-eyes' or 'wind-holes' – literally holes cut in the exterior walls of a house, through which smoke could escape and light and air could enter. Frames or lintels were used to support the structure around the hole, and vertical posts known as mullions were used, not only to support the lintel but to deter intruders, because in those early days there was no other means of closing the wind-hole. A solution was eventually found to this problem and for many centuries thereafter window openings were closed by wooden shutters or by using linen, waxed paper, parchment or, in very poor houses, sacking stretched onto frames and criss-crossed with thin pieces of wood. To allow more light into a room it was common to have splayed reveals, both inside and out, and this simple solution must certainly have helped to increase the available light.

Although glass had been made in Britain since the thirteenth century, it was not until two hundred years later that the wealthy began to use it – and even then, all they did was adapt the custom of using criss-cross frames, so that instead of thin pieces of wood, lead strips were used to hold the pieces of glass (or 'quarries') in place. Many of these old leaded lattice windows still survive today (see photograph on p19), so in a house where a quarry needs repairing, it is worth seeking out a source of old glass rather than using new.

As glass became more readily available, even smaller householders started to use it, and the existing window openings were fitted with a frame which could hold the glass in place. The frame became known as a 'casement' and was usually made from iron in stone-built houses and from wood in timber-framed houses. Naturally enough, the windows themselves became known as 'casement windows', and by the latter part of the seventeenth century it was possible to glaze them with larger quarries made from glass which had been blown and then spun into a flat disc. The glass disc, which had quite considerable variations of thickness, would be cut into quarries and the

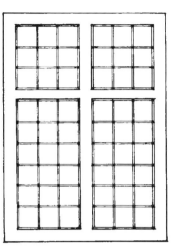

A mullion window

LEFT ABOVE: *A batten door*
BELOW: *An early two-panelled door*

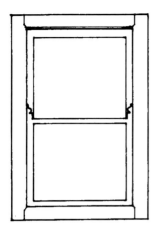

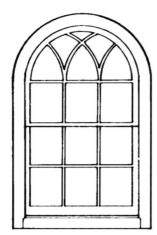

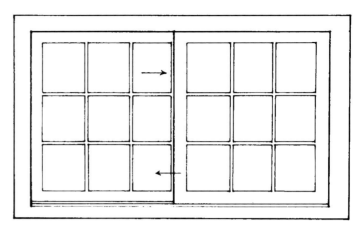

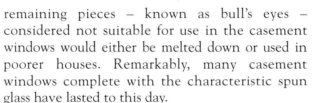

ABOVE LEFT: *A typical sash window*
CENTRE: *A Regency-Gothic sash window*
RIGHT: *A horizontal sliding sash window*

remaining pieces – known as bull's eyes – considered not suitable for use in the casement windows would either be melted down or used in poorer houses. Remarkably, many casement windows complete with the characteristic spun glass have lasted to this day.

It is believed that the Dutch may have introduced sash windows towards the end of the seventeenth century, and there can be no doubt that they were an elegant addition to the houses of the Georgian period. In the early sash windows the panes were 'pegged', that is, held in position by an iron pivot which fitted into notches; but before long a simple, weighted sash window evolved, followed soon after by the more sophisticated boxed frame construction in which pulleys and weights were concealed. Such was the popularity of sash windows that a method was devised to replace smaller casement windows by fitting a sideways-sliding sash window into the space available – perhaps an early case of 'keeping up with the Joneses'?

These lovely new sash windows were usually set in from the outer wall of the house (London boroughs insisting on a minimum retreat of 4in, on the grounds that it would reduce the fire risk!), and inside would often be dressed with shutters which folded back into wall recesses to reveal an elegant window seat. And, of course, not all Georgian windows were oblong; just look around in places such as Bath and Cheltenham, where many beautiful additions and variations to the original

can be seen (see photograph on p20). Three-sectioned Palladian or Venetian sash windows, with the side sections proportionally narrower than the central one, were popular, and often the central window would have a curved top – the softening effect this had on an otherwise classic-style building was remarkable. Bay windows, too, became popular during this period, not only because they extended the size of the room but because they allowed in even more light.

The introduction of commercially available glass in about 1840 meant that small glazing bars were no longer necessary, and sadly many of the elegant multi-paned windows of the earlier Georgian era were replaced by four-paned sashes. And even these were superseded by two-paned windows, consisting of one large pane of glass in each half of the window – it does not take a great leap of the imagination to see how today's 'picture' windows developed.

In conclusion, this short history has only touched on the basic structural developments of a room; however, it is hoped that even such a brief introduction will prompt you to look with fresh eyes at the various elements which go into the making of an interior. To a would-be interior designer it is most important to have a basic knowledge of these things, to expand that knowledge by continually looking at, reading about, and working with these various aspects and seeing what can be achieved. (Walls have not been mentioned here as they are discussed in more detail later, see Chapters 4 and 5.)

A magnificent mullioned and latticed window, flanked by an elaborately carved corbel

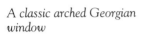

A classic arched Georgian window

PROJECT PAPERS

These first two projects are designed to make you look beyond the decorative possibilities of a room, and to make you think about the 'nuts and bolts' of its basic structure. Moreover they could well form the foundation of your portfolio, and will really help when undertaking those projects which are more concerned with the decorative aspects of a room.

PROJECT 1

From your files or magazines cut out examples of rooms showing:
- A window with mullions
- A casement window
- A sash window

Arrange the cuttings attractively onto one or more sheets of A4 paper, and beside each explain briefly your reasons for choosing these particular examples and why you feel they are both in keeping and in sympathy with the particular rooms in the photographs. Imagine that these will be shown to a prospective client, as it will help you to be both informative and concise.

Finally, think about which style of window you personally prefer and jot down just what it is that so much appeals to you. It would be worth illustrating your ideas in some way, either by a simple sketch or another cutting, as a permanent record of your views at this time. In a few years you may well be surprised how much your ideas have changed!

PROJECT 2

(a) Think about and then write down what you feel are the advantages or disadvantages of a solid floor as opposed to a wooden one. With cuttings taken from magazines or trade brochures, show examples which will clearly illustrate these advantages/disadvantages.

(b) Illustrate by examples and then discuss the properties of oak, elm and fir floorings. Find out as much as possible about each wood, such as when it was first used as a flooring, if it is still used today, and where you feel it would most properly be used.

The excellent free leaflets and brochures produced by the Timber Research and Development Association will help you with this project. They are packed with really useful and interesting information and are available from TRADA Publications, Hughenden Valley, High Wycombe, HP14 4ND.

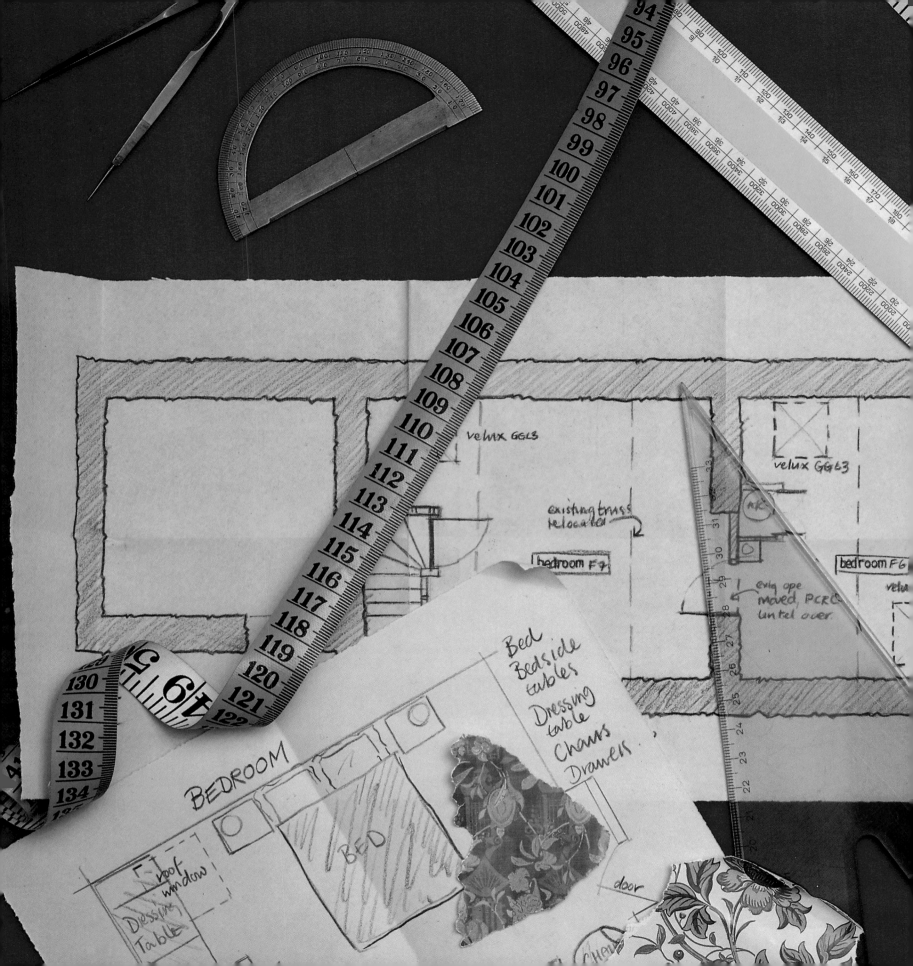

CHAPTER 2

PLANNING AND MEASURING A ROOM

IN THE INTRODUCTION it was suggested that it might be best to choose projects which could be based on rooms in your own home: so before doing anything else, sit quietly in the room you have chosen and really look at it – pretend you have never seen it before, and try to see it as a stranger would.

First of all, what is its function? Nowadays it is rare to have rooms which only have one use, such as dining or sitting, and even the kitchen is seldom the sole domain of the cook. Think how the room has to work for you – is it a sitting-room where you watch TV, or will you need to eat in it, too? Is a study or working area needed, and if so, could a desk be better placed in a bedroom instead of taking up valuable space downstairs? If it is a kitchen, is the eating area for quick meals or for young children? It is quite amazing how much space can sometimes be squeezed out of the most unlikely rooms.

There are several other things to think about and to consider carefully, too, and it helps to draw up a check-list so that none of the aspects which need to be taken into account are missed. The following list should cover most of the relevant questions:

1 Is the shape pleasing?
2 Is it possible to remove part of a wall to improve the space or visually improve the room?
3 Are the doors sound?
4 Are the doors faced in hardboard?
5 Could the door style be improved?
6 Are there wall lights?
7 Are there centre or other ceiling lights?
8 Are the windows in proportion to the room size?
9 Can the windows be altered or disguised?
10 Does the room appear small, the right size or cavernous?
11 Are the walls straight and in good condition?
12 Is the ceiling in good condition, or cracked?
13 Are there gaps between the skirting and the walls?
14 Does the fireplace function properly?
15 Is the fire surround pleasing/acceptable/terrible?
16 Are there mouldings, cornices, dados etc, and are they in good condition?
17 How many radiators are there?
18 Are the radiators in the right positions?
19 Are there enough power points?
20 Are the power points in convenient positions?

The questions which might be asked can be endless, but this list should help you to be objective about the structure of the room and its present fixtures and fittings (although not its furniture, fabrics and so on – that comes later). Do not feel overwhelmed if some of the problems the list throws up seem to be insuperable: they are not. Everything can be resolved, and something which may at first appear to be a handicap and impossible to alter may well turn out to be the basis or the starting point from which a room reflecting your individuality and character can be created.

Learn to work with space, see potential in everything, and be imaginative in the use of individual areas of space. A door moved to the centre of a room can make all the difference; a dividing wall removed could open up untold possibilities for the space created; a small window overlooking a garden could probably be turned into a full-length glass-door not only letting in more light but helping to bring the garden indoors, too. Think not only of how you want the particular room to be used, but also how it will work in relation to the others in the house. Perhaps a room which has always been thought of as a rather dark sitting-room because it faced east could become a delightful breakfast-room simply because it *does* get all the early morning sun. Some of the suggestions will not, of course, be applicable to your own situation; but nonetheless it is imperative to keep both eyes and imagination open to the possibilities which abound.

One of the most useful ways of focusing on a particular room is to sketch a plan of it and measure all the dimensions. You may think that you know the room intimately, but could be surprised at how much more you will discover about it in the course of incorporating all the salient points on a sketch plan. For instance, had you realised that the depth of the recesses on either side of the fireplace varied quite so much? This could be vital when ordering shelves or cupboards to fit the space, because the discrepancy may mean that you will not achieve the effect you had in mind. And maybe the electricians have put power points in the most convenient place for *them*, but will they suit *your* lighting requirements? Drawing power points and TV aerial points on a plan will help pinpoint any areas which might be a problem when the time comes to put the furniture in place.

Radiators are often a source of annoyance, so show them on the plan too, and consider if they could, or should, be moved to make the arrangement of furniture easier and more logical. How often have you been into a room where the radiator is either hidden by a sofa, thus losing the effect of its heat output, or else seems to dominate the room because it was installed in the wrong place to start with? There are solutions to all these problems, however, and a sketch plan will help highlight the awkward areas.

MEASURING UP

Having looked at your room thoroughly, and assuming that you want to be as proficient as possible, the next few pages will show, stage by stage, how a professional interior designer would go about measuring up a room. You will learn how to turn the rough sketches into a room plan drawn to scale, from which not only you but your decorator, carpet-fitter, curtain-maker and electrician can work with confidence, knowing that the measurements are exact. This can be a fascinating exercise, and with a little time and care, really professional-looking results can be achieved. Remember, too, that some of the future projects can be based on these plans so it is worth spending time on them.

Measurements can be taken in inches or centimetres but the metric scale will help when the kitchen and bathroom planning stages are reached. The sample sketches which follow have all been measured in centimetres; notice that they require no great detail, but the more clearly the measurements are shown the easier they will be to work from, so mark them like this:

60cm

Note that a figure accurately taken but drawn to an unmarked destination will only confuse. It may seem as if the sketches incorporate too many measurements, but as you work through the projects you will be glad that all the necessary information is at your fingertips. Bear in mind, too, that if ever a potential client asks you to measure up a room it would appear very unprofessional if you had to return to take more measurements.

Take measurements in the following order and remember to write them on the *outside* of the plan, except the first set which should be written inside:

1 Front wall to back wall; side wall to side wall.
2 Wall to window.
3 Width of window.
4 Window to wall.
5 Width of window architrave; NB window and door architraves should be included in the wall measurements, *not* the door or window openings.
6 Wall to door.
7 Width of door (excluding architraves).
8 Door to wall.
9 Wall to fireplace.
10 Depth of fireplace recess.
11 Overall width of fireplace wall.
12 Fireplace to wall.

Carry on in this fashion until all the horizontal measurements have been taken, and do not forget to include the radiators and the areas each side of them too. When the measurements are complete it is useful to check that the various individual measurements add up to the overall dimensions. Do not worry if the figures are not exactly the same – although if there are significant differences something has gone wrong and it is worth checking again. The sketch plan should look something like the drawing overleaf.

If you are used to working in inches the following may help you to visualise the *approximate* metric equivalent:
3in = 7·5cm; 6in = 15cm; 1ft = 30cm

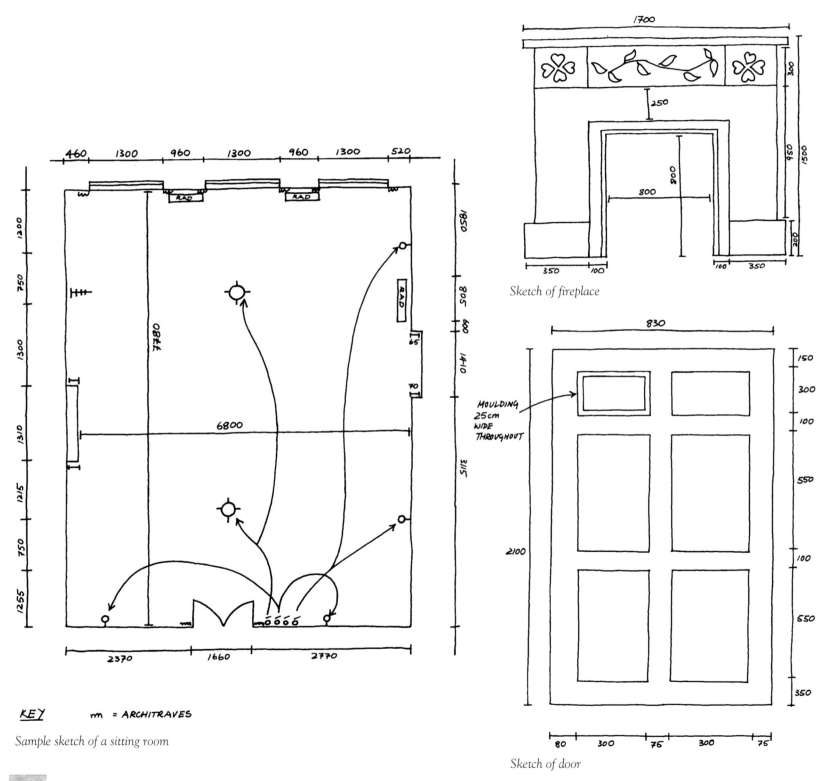

460 1300 960 1300 960 1300 520

1200

750

1300

1310

1215

750

1255

0880

6800

RAD

RAD

RAD

1850

805

600

1410

3115

65

70

2370 1660 2770

KEY   m = ARCHITRAVES

Sample sketch of a sitting room

1700

300

1500

250

050

800

800

200

350 100 100 350

Sketch of fireplace

830

150

300

100

MOULDING
25cm
WIDE
THROUGHOUT

550

2100

100

550

350

80 300 75 300 75

Sketch of door

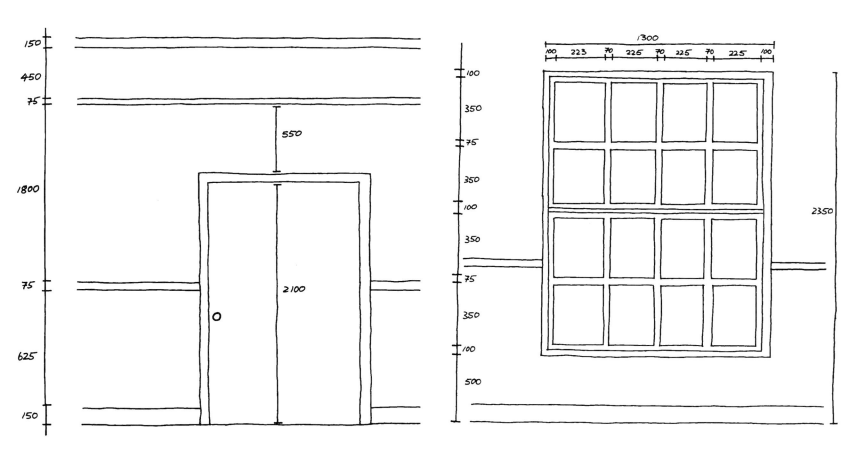

Sketch of wall elevation

Sketch of window elevation

When the horizontal figures are complete, take the vertical ones, and for these a sketch of a section of the wall elevation is necessary – see the drawing above. The measurements needed are:

1 Overall height from floor to ceiling.
2 Depth of skirting board.
3 Skirting board to bottom of dado (if any).
4 Depth of dado.
5 Top of dado to bottom of picture rail (if any).
6 Depth of picture rail.
7 Top of picture rail to bottom of cornice (if any).
8 Depth of cornice to ceiling.
9 Overall height of door, omitting architrave.
10 Top of door architrave to bottom of picture rail, cornice or ceiling.

To complete the room sketch, make elevations of the radiators, doors, fireplace and windows as well (they will look rather like the sketches on these pages), and if there are any special features in the room such as alcoves or archways, sketch these in too and add the relevant dimensions to the drawings.

When all the measurements have been taken, note on the sketches the positions of electric sockets and TV points and with dotted lines, show which switch turns on which light source (see how they have been marked on the sketch plan opposite). Finally, take a careful look at the room again to make sure that everything has been noted on your sketches, and then you will be ready to start the scale drawing.

It is a good idea to mark on the plan where the north compass point can be found. This could be relevant when deciding upon a colour scheme.

27

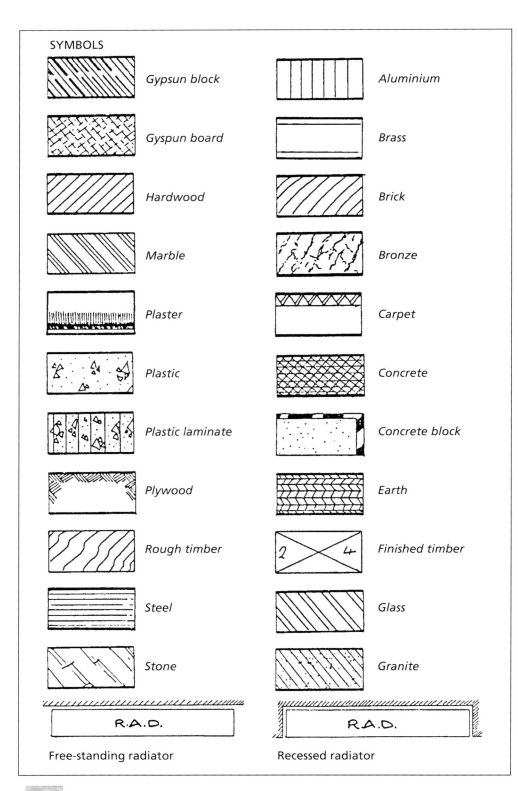

SYMBOLS

Gypsun block	Aluminium
Gyspun board	Brass
Hardwood	Brick
Marble	Bronze
Plaster	Carpet
Plastic	Concrete
Plastic laminate	Concrete block
Plywood	Earth
Rough timber	Finished timber
Steel	Glass
Stone	Granite
R.A.D.	R.A.D.
Free-standing radiator	Recessed radiator

SCALE DRAWING

EQUIPMENT AND MATERIALS

It is quite possible to use just a ruler, a pencil and graph paper to make a scale drawing, but it is well worth investing in a scale rule to help draw the lines, as counting the tiny graph squares can be an eye-boggling exercise! Ideally, too, you should have a large drawing board, T-square and a set-square, but any firm, smooth board large enough to hold the graph paper will do.

Graph paper comes in many sizes and scales, but the one most commonly used by interior designers has large squares of 1cm and small squares of 1mm. It is worth investing in one large sheet of graph paper rather than trying to stick sheets of the A4 size together. Attach the graph paper to the board by using a strip of low-tack masking tape at each corner, making sure that the paper is absolutely straight on the board.

For drawing the lines a finely pointed pencil is necessary, and you may find that a 0.5mm propelling pencil is the best for ensuring a continuous supply of fine lead points.

GETTING STARTED

Start the scale drawing by lightly outlining the overall room dimensions on the centre of the graph paper, leaving sufficient space above, below and on either side of the room plan to draw on the wall elevations.

DIMENSIONS

When drawing to scale you may feel that it is not necessary to put the dimensions on the drawing; however, not only will this make it look more professional, it will also provide an easy reference guide for later working. Always put the overall dimensions farthest from the drawing, with the line showing the breakdown of measurements set between the overall dimensions and the drawing.

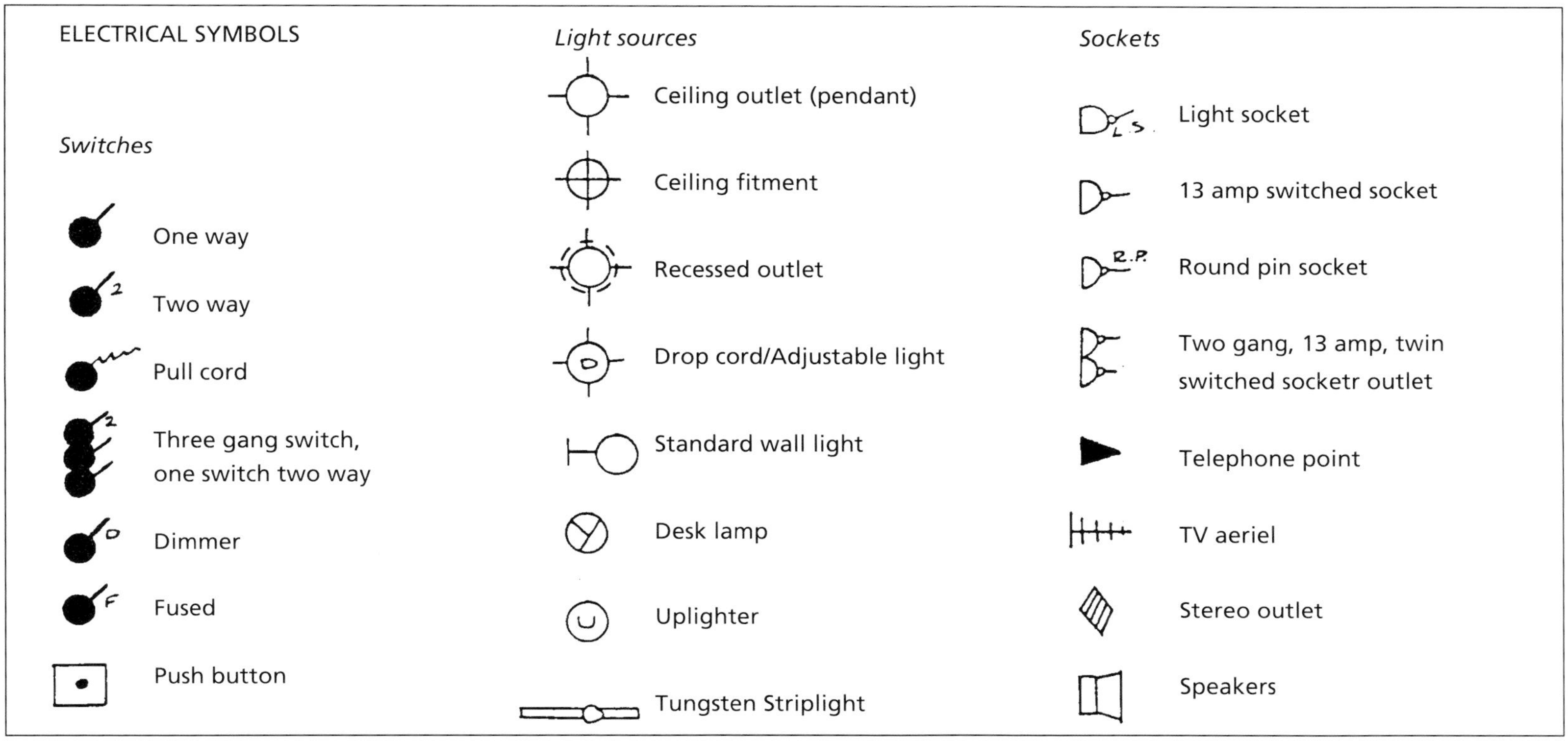

ELECTRICAL SYMBOLS

Switches

⬤ One way

⬤ Two way

⬤ Pull cord

⬤ Three gang switch, one switch two way

⬤ Dimmer

⬤ Fused

▢ Push button

Light sources

Ceiling outlet (pendant)

Ceiling fitment

Recessed outlet

Drop cord/Adjustable light

Standard wall light

Desk lamp

Uplighter

Tungsten Striplight

Sockets

Light socket

13 amp switched socket

Round pin socket

Two gang, 13 amp, twin switched socketr outlet

Telephone point

TV aeriel

Stereo outlet

Speakers

ELEVATIONS

Elevations are drawn so that they line up with the corners of the plan and look as though the upright walls have fallen flat. They are easy to draw and give an immediate visual impression of the room with its doors, windows, skirting boards, architraves and mouldings all clearly shown.

SYMBOLS

There is a range of commonly used symbols which are useful to indicate various things on a drawing: these are shown in the diagrams on these pages.

On the plan overleaf you will see how the rough sketch has been translated into a finished plan, and this is the kind of result you should be aiming for. See how the electrics are shown, and note that the centre drawing is outlined with 'hatch' markings to indicate the depth of the brick and plastered walls. Accuracy may be difficult for these particular measurements, but some can be obtained by

measuring the depth of the door and window openings. It is not always necessary to show wall depths, but they will be needed if structural changes are to be made to the room.

COMPLETED PLAN

When completely happy with the drawing, go over it all again with either a special permanent ink drawing pen, or place tracing paper over the master drawing and, with a drawing pen, go over all the lines again. When inking over it is useful to start at the top horizontal line and work downwards until every horizontal line has been drawn. Then move over to the left-hand side of the board to draw all the vertical lines until reaching the right-hand side (or vice versa if left-handed). When all the lines have been inked over you will have a permanent record which will not smudge and which, if necessary, can be photocopied to give to the various tradespeople who may be employed.

To help line up the graph paper on the drawing board, mark the board 2·5cm (1in) down from the top on both the left- and right-hand sides. Line the paper up with these markers and then carefully attach to the board with pieces of masking tape. Finally, check alignment once more with a T-square.

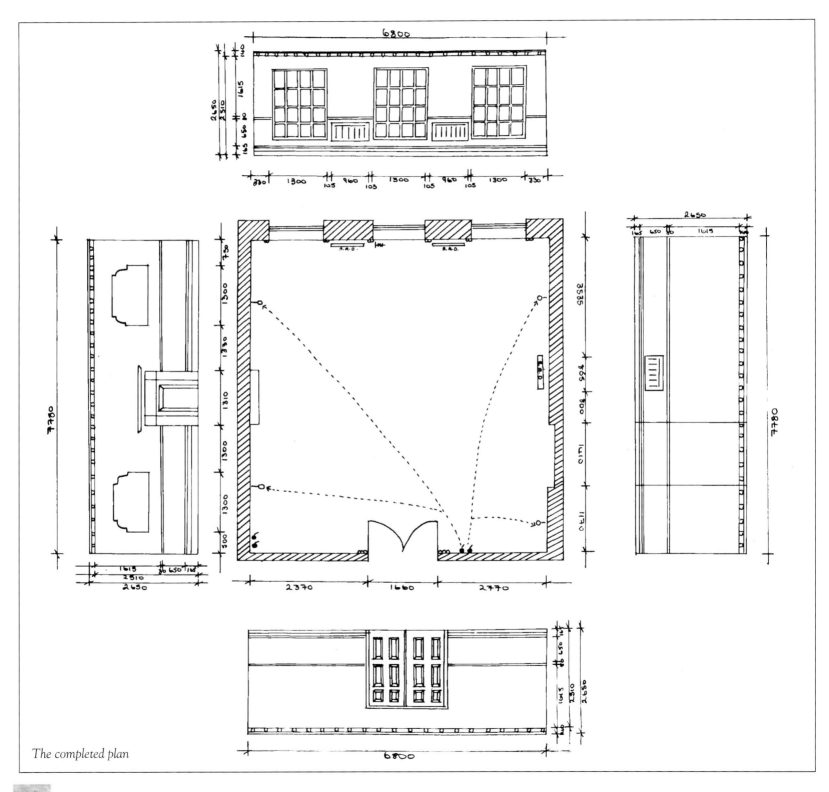

The completed plan

PROJECT PAPERS

Drawing up a room plan to scale is a time-consuming exercise, but a most important one. Firstly, it is very satisfying to produce a professional-looking document – and it does become easier the more confident and adept you become. Second, it cannot be over-stressed that a good scale plan is a vital document for an interior designer: trying to design a room without a plan showing all the relevant measurements is like trying to build a house without foundations.

   The following two projects are intended to provide more practice in drawing sketches and scale plans; and three such layouts in a portfolio cannot fail to look impressive.

PROJECT 3

Sketch another, completely different room in your own home and then draw up the flat floor plan to a scale of 1:50 or, if using imperial measurements, to a scale of $\frac{1}{4}$in:1ft. As before, show all the relevant measurements and electrical details. Do not do the elevations at this stage, but pretend this plan will be photocopied to give to a carpet fitter who only needs a flat floor plan. In a legend box at the side fill in any details the fitter may need: which room it is, to which scale it has been drawn, the date, and so on.

PROJECT 4

By this stage you should be getting to know at least two rooms very intimately – how the floors and walls have been constructed, the window style, whether the doors are modern or period. Also the room plans will have revealed all the good and bad points which will need either emphasising or playing down in the general decorating scheme.

   For this project pretend you are working for a client, using the floor plan above. To get a complete picture a client would need to see wall elevations, so first trace over the floor plan in Project 3 and then add these elevations, together with all the relevant measurements and electrical details. In one legend box give details of the client, which room is shown, the scale and what the present colour scheme is and which pieces of furniture have to be retained. In a second legend box state what, if any, structural changes you suggest, your proposed colour scheme and where you would place the retained furniture.

   Finally, think of a word or phrase which will sum up for your client the effect you intend to create.

CHAPTER 3

COLOUR
CONSIDERATIONS

COLOUR IS PERHAPS the most exciting aspect of interior design. Always interesting, the study of colour is an absorbing subject and an enormous one to cover – you never stop learning about it. Always be ready to notice exciting colour combinations, in everything from fashion garments to garden schemes, because they may well suggest or adapt to an interior colour scheme which could become uniquely your own.

But what exactly is colour? In basic terms it is how we perceive waves of light, and even a plain, white light such as daylight is composed of every colour in the spectrum. When the white light is broken up by, say, raindrops which act as a prism we can see the same six colours, always in the same order – red, orange, yellow, green, blue and violet. A person may already have a good feel, or 'eye' for colour, and may use this instinctively when deciding on a decorating scheme; but to understand it properly it is necessary to know at least the rudiments of colour theory, and this is best explained by the colour wheel.

THE COLOUR WHEEL

Sir Isaac Newton first conceived the colour wheel in the seventeenth century, and it was he who placed all related colours near to each other, each with its exactly contrasting or 'complementary' colour directly opposite. His conception of colour has become an invaluable reference, showing which families of colours contrast or harmonise, which are cool and which are warm. The easiest way to understand his theories is to divide the colours into sub-sections.

PRIMARY COLOURS

Red, blue and yellow are called primary colours. This means that they cannot be created by mixing other colours: in other words, they are *pure*. All other colours are produced by mixing these colours; and if red is mixed with blue and yellow in equal amounts the result will be grey. These primary colours are naturally equidistant on the colour wheel, and divide it into thirds as shown in Colour Wheel 1.

SECONDARY COLOURS

Violet, green and orange are secondary colours – each is produced by an equal mixture of the two primary colours on either side of it on the colour wheel. For instance, blue and red produce violet, blue and yellow produce green, and red and yellow produce orange. Violet, green and orange are also known as complementary colours because on the colour wheel, each sits opposite to the primary colour which has not been used in its make-up – see Colour Wheel 2.

TERTIARY COLOURS

A tertiary colour is produced by a further mixing of secondary colours such as green and purple to produce olive, purple and orange to produce russet, and orange and green to produce citron.

The three primary, three secondary and six tertiary colours make up the standard colour wheel as shown in Colour Wheel 3.

When discussing colour the terms 'hue', 'value' and 'saturation' are often used, and are simply ways of expressing colour characteristics. Thus *hue* indicates a colour's position on the colour wheel and gives it its name; *value* tells how much black or white the hue contains; and *saturation* is the measure of colour intensity. Therefore a pinky mauve is low in saturation and high in value, and violet is highly saturated and medium in value. Colour Wheels 4 and 5 will help illustrate these points.

Some other colour terms used in interior design magazines might also need explaining: thus *advancing* colours are warm tones such as red, orange or yellow, and bring a surface visually nearer. *Accent* colours are sharper, contrast colours – when used with discretion, they can bring a whole decorative scheme to life. *Complementary* colours are the shades closest to each other in the colour spectrum,

COLOUR WHEELS

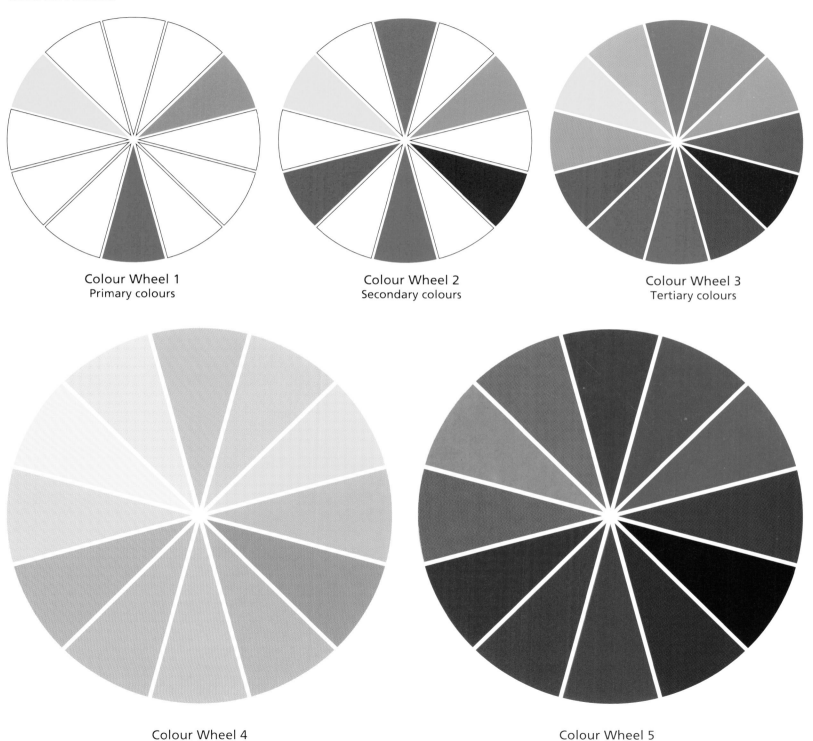

Colour Wheel 1
Primary colours

Colour Wheel 2
Secondary colours

Colour Wheel 3
Tertiary colours

Colour Wheel 4

Colour Wheel 5

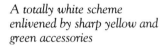

A totally white scheme enlivened by sharp yellow and green accessories

such as gold, yellow, primrose, gradually merging into the palest lime green. Finally, *harmonising* colours have the same intensity, either sharp like bright yellow with emerald green, or mellow as in soft pink with mauve.

COLOUR EFFECTS

The shape and size of a room are constant, but it is possible to change its height, width and length by the way colour is used, and it is this aspect of decoration which is both a constant challenge and a continuing excitement to the interior designer.

Just think what can be done with colour alone. A high ceiling can be lowered by painting it darker than the walls; the walls of a narrow room can be widened by painting them in a pale shade; uneven walls and unsightly pipes can be camouflaged; and a period atmosphere can be created in a modern house by the clever use of colour. The possibilities and delights are endless – but where should one start?

As for the room plan, it is a good idea to have a check-list, with perhaps the following sort of questions:

1 Which is my favourite colour?
2 Which is my least favourite colour?
3 Would my favourite colour look well in this room?
4 Do I enjoy decorating and changing colour schemes frequently?
5 Do I prefer to just freshen a scheme periodically by changing, say, only the cushion covers?
6 What do I normally hang on the walls – photographs, prints, originals, modern or old pictures? Do certain colours recur in these?
7 Have I a favourite picture on which the scheme for this room could be based?
8 Have I a particular collection of favourite objects which would suggest a colour scheme for the room?
9 Do I want to use colours which are smart and fashionable at the moment, or colours with which I feel I can live for years?

10 Do I want a room based on various shades of the same colour, or do I prefer a room of contrasts?

11 Do I prefer a plain or a patterned look in a room?

12 Do I want a dramatic or a comfortable room?

13 Who am I really decorating this room for – myself, or to impress my friends?

14 Do I actually like the present carpet or flooring? If not, can I change it or minimise its effect in some way?

15 When shall I be using this room the most – during the day, the evening, or both? How will it look at night?

No-one can decide instantly on the final appearance of a room, but by asking these questions things will, hopefully, start to clarify. It may be that you already have some kind of basic colour scheme in mind; let us therefore spend a little time considering the impact of various colours and their combinations.

GETTING READY FOR RED

No-one can ignore red; it is the boldest colour in the spectrum and it is hard to have a neutral response to this colour – love it or loathe it.

Red is a stimulating colour, it creates excitement and warmth, quickening both conversation and appetite. Think how often it is used in restaurants and intimate dining-rooms; it is hard to imagine another colour which so instantly sets the anticipatory mood of forthcoming delights.

In the main, red is a sophisticated colour. Some may feel it is more appropriately used in a city setting; but just think of the impact that a jug of scarlet poppies has in a country cottage, red ging-ham cushions on simple pine kitchen chairs, or the effect of red book-spines on a bookshelf. Open your mind to the influence of red. It does, after all, vary from the strongest Chinese lacquer red, through to rich burgundies, warm terracottas, autumn russets and cool corals to the softest of warm pinks.

In China, red is the colour of celebration and happiness and, traditionally, brides were married in red. As China becomes more Westernised the most popular colour for a wedding gown nowadays is pink – a blend of two traditions?

A lovely bedroom with a striking lacquer red wall which emphasises the chinoiserie pieces of furniture

Plain white bathroom fittings in clean blue surroundings. Note how the deeper blue adds warmth to what could otherwise have been a rather cold scheme. Look also at the wall-hung fittings which maximise the available floor space

A group of green plants with variously-shaped leaves add impact to both traditional and ultra-modern rooms. Old favourites such as begonias, ferns and kangaroo vine look well in family rooms and sculptural, dramatic leaves add excitement to modern settings.

THE MOODY BLUES

Blue must surely be the best-loved colour of all, partly because its various shades will flatter nearly everyone, and its tonal range is immense. At one and the same time blue can be romantic, soft and calming, or airy, exciting and dazzling.

Some people say that blue is a cold colour. Not so: it can be just as warm-feeling as pink – so much depends upon the shade chosen. It is an adaptable colour; from the palest misty morning blue to a dark midnight navy, it will tone down hot colours and will give impact to pale shades.

In decorating terms the chalky, soft blues are ideal for large surfaces, whilst the more intense and darker blues can give special dramatic effects or work well as accented colours. Just think how pieces of dark blue and white china give impact when displayed as a collection on a dresser or grouped on a wall.

Almost any room can be decorated in blue. It looks clean in a bathroom, traditional in a kitchen, romantic in a bedroom and spacious in a sitting-room.

GOING GREEN

Green brings the freshness of trees, grass and plants to any interior. There are endless permutations of green deriving from leaves, stems and mosses, and one only has to look at a wooded valley to see how wonderfully all the shades of green harmonise.

Unlike blue, green can be a difficult colour to wear successfully, but in decorating terms it is hard to beat. It is a soothing colour and can be as subtle as the soft greyish-green known almost universally as Adam or Wedgwood green, or as bold as the brightest emerald found in malachite. Like every other colour, green has its fashionable shades – for example, the avocado and olive shades so popular in the 1970s have now given way to cleaner, sharper greens.

A modern room decorated in shades of blue inspired by the dhurrie

Deep green used to dramatic effect, highlighting the white fittings and accessories

Green can form a peaceful background when used with chintzes; it will complement the blues, contrast well with the reds, harmonise with the pastel shades, and create a peaceful oasis in both city and country settings.

YUMMY YELLOW

Did you know that, psychologically, yellow is the happiest colour of all, but that most people find it hard to handle? Its very cheerfulness makes a little seem to go a long way and people can feel overwhelmed with the responsibility of using it well.

Yellow is associated with spring flowers, summer sand, sunlight and warmth, and for these happy

A decorating scheme based on neutral shades, spiced with browns and terracotta

associations alone it is worth using. It need not be employed lavishly – just a dash of it in white emulsion will produce a warm, creamy shade which will certainly take the chill off the dreariest of rooms, and bring a feeling of warmth.

Yellow starts with this warm, creamy shade, then advances through citrusy lemon to the deeper, warm gold shades and, finally, to the earthy yellow ochre which can give such a punch to a neutral colour scheme. Bright orange is a difficult colour to use well, but it does have its place as an accent in a suitable scheme, and should not be ignored.

NATURALLY NEUTRAL

A neutral colour scheme is perhaps the most perennially popular of all. It is extremely practical, easy to live with, exists happily with more dominant shades, and offends no-one.

However, for these very reasons some people may feel that a neutral scheme is too safe, that it lacks personality and is generally boring: but they could not be more wrong, because decorating with neutrals requires both skill and a knowledge of texture. A neutral scheme is mostly a matter of balance between textures and shades, and so long as the tones of both are graduations of the same colour, an overall harmony can be achieved, producing natural and quiet schemes full of subtlety and grace.

Neutral shades range from off-whites such as bone and ivory to beiges and browns, or from white through to greys and blacks; they have an eternal quality which is equally at home in town and country settings. To a large extent, neutrals are the epitome of natural materials – sand, earth, stone and wood – but in the white, grey and black range they can represent the sophisticated man-made world of chrome metal and smoky glass.

Everyone has a favourite colour and it is possible to divide people into spring, summer, autumn or winter groups. Invariably the colours which suit them are also the ones in which they have chosen to decorate their houses. The gems and flowers associated with each astrological sign can also give an amazingly accurate insight into the colours one should use to decorate the main living-room.

COLOUR SCHEMING

When planning a colour scheme the first thing to remember is that there are no right and no wrong colours: if they please you, and you are comfortable with them, then that is all that matters. Planning for other people is another thing altogether and need not concern us here.

As with everything else, colours are influenced by fashion, and moods change all the time, so it is best to choose the colour you like best and complement it with other shades. Perhaps the easiest way to start when planning a colour scheme is to take one large surface area such as the walls, the floor or a large piece of furniture, and decide what your main colour will be.

Here a colour scheme has been built around a carpet which had to remain

WALLS

If the walls are the starting point it is well worth experimenting with different paint colours from the large range of sample pots now available. Paint an area about a metre square either directly on to the wall or on to a piece of lining paper which you can pin to the wall. Look at that colour shade at all times of the day and also in artificial light in the evening to see how it reacts to different lights. Perhaps a dull afternoon makes the colour grey and depressing – or it may hold up well with its sunlit counterpart; artificial light may deaden it and more warmth could be needed. Consider all these things before painting large expanses of wall.

If using wallpaper, get as large a sample as possible, or even buy a whole roll so that you can paste it up and see how it looks and reacts in different lighting. It is well nigh impossible to choose a colour scheme from the small squares of colour in a trade brochure or from a mean little square of wallpaper, so it is worth making the effort to do these experiments at an early stage – it could save both time and money, and more importantly, you will not end up having to live with something you really dislike.

FLOORS

The carpet on the floor could very well be used as a starting point; ideally, it will be chosen with the walls and furniture in mind, but how many times have we all heard people say, 'I hate the carpet but I can't afford to change it'? If this is the case there are things one can do to reduce its prominence. For instance, a brown carpet complemented with other shades of brown, beige and cream could produce an elegant neutral scheme, and a beautiful accent colour will help reduce the carpet's impact. Everything will look as if it was meant to be, and some of the very best schemes have resulted from having to work around something which at first sight seemed a potential horror. Perhaps in an ideal world a uniform pale carpet is best because it increases the apparent size of a room, it can tie a

LEFT: *A scheme based on the sofa material. Note how well the colour-washed shutters blend in.*

BELOW: *A dramatic scheme, again taken from the sofa material*

series of spaces together and, best of all, it forms a good visual background for the rest of the design.

FURNITURE

Sometimes a colour scheme can be built around the largest piece of furniture in the room, say a sofa. If it has a patterned fabric a balanced look can be achieved by matching some of the colours in the print and using them on the walls, cushions and curtains. Using plain shades with a pattern can give a feeling of space, but a sense of harmony can also be achieved by repeating the sofa fabric in matching curtains and, perhaps, in matching wallpaper. In a very large room this treatment will give cohesion and tie everything together; and a small room can be made to look larger by using the same print on the walls and curtaining.

COLOUR BOARD

Getting a colour scheme together is a fascinating process. It is also lots of fun and something which should not be rushed.

Collect lots of pieces of fabric in the shades you prefer. Do not be afraid of mixing textures such as linen with velvet or calico with glazed cotton, for they could all work well together. At the same time collect samples of braiding and fringing which could be used to trim the fabrics and furniture.

Get together as many paint shade cards as possible, as well as carpet and wallpaper samples. Play around with the colours and see what works with what. It may be that more than one scheme suggests itself and, at this stage, it is a good idea to start separating the pieces you like from the mass of samples. If you want to know how, say, a sofa or a chair will look furnished in a particular fabric, you can, on a piece of acetate, trace around a similar shape from a magazine and place the fabric swatch behind it, fastening it with masking tape. The shape

A simple colour board for a scheme built around the shades in the picture

Stencil Border ~ Sponged Walls

Lamps

Sofa

Cushions

will spring to life and you will have a good idea of whether or not that particular fabric will work. Perhaps this tracing and fabric could form the nucleus of a colour board?

To make a colour board, use a stiff piece of card, at least A4 size, and on to it lay the fabric, paper, paint and trim samples which you like. Play around with alternatives and, when you are happy with the selection, stick the samples onto the board with a spot of glue or double-sided tape. Repeat the process if more than one scheme comes to mind. I think you

will be pleasantly surprised to see how a scheme will come together and, at the end of this particular exercise, you will almost certainly be sure which is the right one for both you and the particular room you have in mind.

The colour board does not have to be elaborate, but the time spent on it now will probably save hours in shops and stores later on. It can be slipped into an envelope or manilla folder and will provide an instant reference for the correct shades and fabrics when shopping.

A more sophisticated colour board for a family room overlooking an estuary. The colours chosen reflect the sand, sea and sky, and the trees on the other side of the river

FAMILY ROOM FOR
PATRICK BARNARD ESQUIRE

Easy Chair

Cushions

and Rugs   Braid and Fringes

Checked and plain material used to create a harmonising colour scheme. The padded and plaited tie-backs make interesting use of the materials

PROJECT PAPERS

A well thought-out colour board, together with a room plan drawn to scale, form the basis of all interior design schemes and cannot fail to impress. Not only is a colour board the tangible evidence of your own design skills but it is an invaluable tool for explaining the scheme to a prospective client. Remember that the majority of people have great difficulty in visualising a decorative scheme, but a well-presented colour board will help them grasp what you have in mind and will give them a chance, at this early stage, to suggest any changes or preferences they may have.

The following project is based on a situation in which you may well find yourself.

PROJECT 5

You have recently moved into a late Georgian terrace house and need to decorate, as quickly as possible, a dark basement room with a concrete floor as a den-cum-study for your eighteen-year-old son, and an attic room with wooden floors as a bedroom-cum-study for your twelve-year-old daughter. Both rooms are structurally sound but have not been decorated for years.

Think about the considerations which would have to be taken into account when decorating these very different rooms, and decide on colour schemes for each. Make up two colour boards showing the schemes, and for your own reference attach to them notes briefly explaining the reasoning behind your choices.

PROJECT 6

From a brochure or magazine trace a sofa shape which could be used in your own room plan, mount it on an A4 sheet and beside it place a swatch of material which you consider to be a suitable covering fabric for it. List the fabric's composition, wearing qualities, fire-resistance, yardage needed and price.

On a separate sheet attach samples of a wallcovering, carpet and curtain scheme which you feel would complement the sofa fabric, and jot down notes to explain why you have chosen this particular scheme taking into account the shape and size of the room and its aspect.

These two projects should result in three very different colour boards to add to your portfolio. Try to be as versatile as possible, experiment with colour, be bold and imaginative and, above all, enjoy working on them.

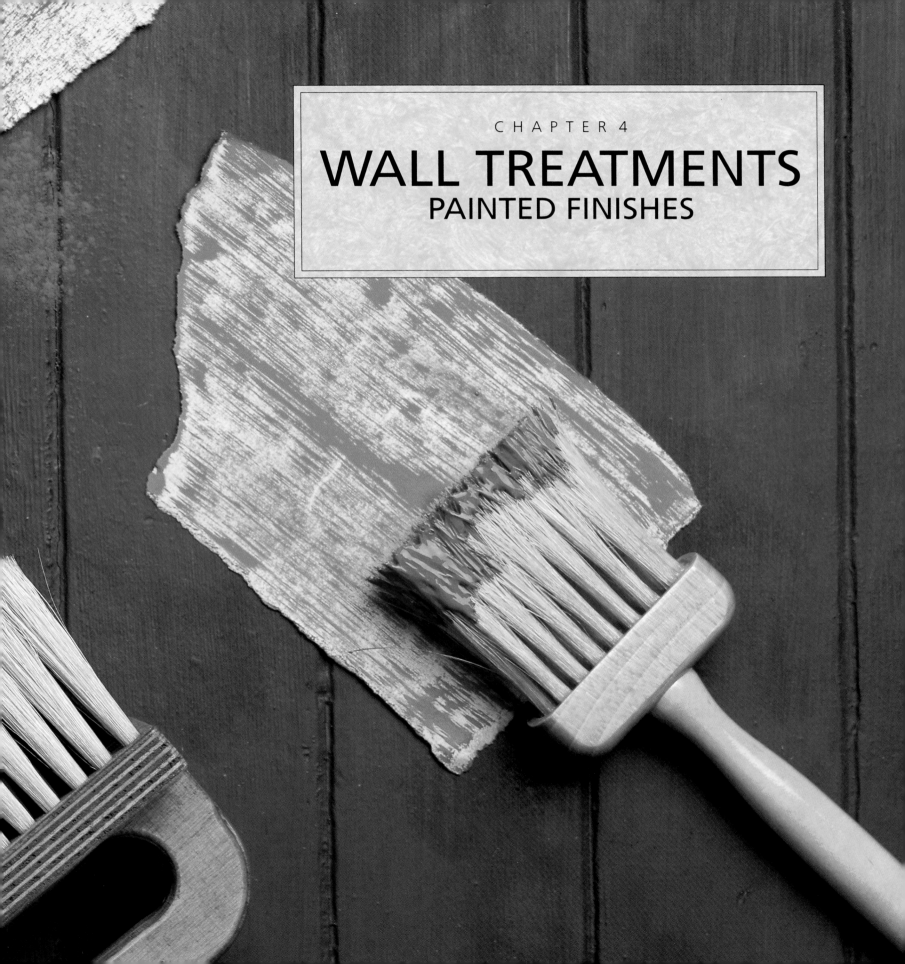

CHAPTER 4

WALL TREATMENTS
PAINTED FINISHES

THERE ARE SO MANY WAYS in which walls can be decorated that this subject could be a book in itself, and indeed there are many books on the various methods; here, however, we shall only look at the most popular and give some guidelines for their application.

If you are lucky enough to have an old house and have found some stone or bricks beneath crumbling plaster, you may decide to clean them up; in fact all you need do is treat them with a clear sealer, and then leave it at that because these natural finishes are very appealing and decorative just as they are.

The same could be said for walls which have had a wooden tongue-and-groove shell applied to them in the past. When stripped of layers of paint the original wood can often be sanded to a smooth, natural finish and then buffed up with a good wax polish. Alternatively, applying a thin wash of emulsion in a sympathetic colour can do wonders to restore the appeal of the wooden boards, and this kind of treatment is becoming increasingly popular.

WHITEWASH

Another old-fashioned treatment which is making a comeback, particularly for rough walls, is whitewash. In fact 'whitewash' should more properly be called 'ceiling white' or 'limewash', and whilst the effect of these two finishes can be very soft and attractive, there can be problems when the time comes for redecorating. Ceiling white is made from a substance called whiting which is bound with glue size, and this holds the whiting particles together very weakly. It is very difficult to paint over a whiting finish, and even the smallest trace of whiting left on a plaster surface will prevent future emulsion or vinyl paints from adhering properly to the plaster.

Limewash is an inexpensive coating which can be used very successfully on brickwork, stucco, stonework and similar surfaces. The base of the material is quicklime and this is made from limestone or chalk and then slaked with water. A wool grease or hot Russian tallow is stirred in to bind the water and quicklime together, and as the coating ages a carbonisation process occurs which hardens the coating and gives it a longer life.

DISTEMPER

You may have heard this word used when decorators talk about old paint finishes, and it is really a term used to describe the types of water paint and oil-bound water paint available before the advent of the emulsion paints we know today.

True distempers were made of whiting bound with glue size which was then tinted, usually with lime-fast pigments such as ochre and similar earth pigments, to give soft, chalky shades. The so-called 'washable' distempers were actually oil-bound water paints and they can be extremely difficult to remove. Distemper is not often used now, but it can still be found on the walls and ceilings of old houses.

EMULSION PAINTS

Emulsion paints are made of plastic-type polymers, they are water-based so they can be thinned easily to give flexibility of application, they give very good coverage and best of all, they are very easy to apply – where would most of us be without them?

The range of shades available is immense – one well-known brand alone has over 1,650 colours in its range, so you would think that if someone could not find something they liked within this kind of colour spectrum they were being particularly choosey.

Even so, it is often the case that we have a colour in our mind's eye that we cannot find in the ranges normally available, and this is when we should consider mixing our own colours. If you are at all interested in colour, you should not be daunted by the prospect of mixing your own; it is pleasing to do and very exciting.

Emulsion paints are water-based and can be tinted with a variety of materials. The most popular are:

Walls colourwashed in a rich red over cream form a perfect background for these vibrant rugs, cushions and fabrics from India

- Poster colours, which are inexpensive and easy to mix; however, the colours are rather heavy and crude.

- Artists' gouache – opaque, concentrated colours in an exciting range, available in tubes.

- Artists' acrylics, which are rather expensive and with a smaller range of colours than gouache, but exceptionally fast drying.

- Powder pigments, which are available in a good selection of strong, clear shades, but do not dissolve as easily as poster colours; ideally, mixed paint should be strained.

- Universal stainers, which are usually used by the decorating trade, but are readily available. These are highly concentrated, clear colours which dissolve easily and can be intermixed to produce more subtle shades.

Whichever pigment is used, it should first be mixed with a small amount of water and then stirred thoroughly into the paint, a little at a time. If a can of white paint is used as the base, all the options are available, but for darker shades it is more sensible to choose a base shade nearer to the colour you want, making final adjustments with very small amounts of pigment. Pigments are usually highly concentrated and a little goes a long way.

One point should be made about emulsioning walls white or pale cream: these should look thick and rich, not pale and wishy-washy, and the only

A simple, country-style kitchen-diner, with colour-washed walls and pretty matching curtains

way to achieve this is to give them about twice as many coats as you feel are necessary – professional decorators recommend at least five!

Despite the range of emulsion colours and the joy of mixing your own, emulsion can be used purely as a base for some very interesting paint effects. Plain emulsioned walls, however pleasing the colour, can sometimes look rather bland and just a simple wash with another colour or a simple glaze can make all the difference between an acceptable finish and one that is far more interesting, even exciting.

COLOUR WASHING

Colour washing must be one of the simplest yet most rewarding of all the decorative wall finishes. It is a semi-transparent film of colour diluted with water, and when correctly applied it can give a luminous quality to otherwise prosaic walls; it is an inexpensive method of producing stunning results.

Distemper can be used over dry, clean paint surfaces to give a translucent quality to the finish.

Thinned emulsion applied with criss-cross brush marks and deliberately leaving some of the background colour showing through will give a 'distressed' finish which cannot be fully appreciated until the wash has thoroughly dried; a second coat of the same or a different shade is then often applied. This is a very good method of disguising a sound wall painted in an unacceptable colour.

For an all-over, nearly matt finish, a well-thinned, flat oil paint is also sometimes used. It is best applied over an eggshell emulsion finish as the brush will work more easily on this surface.

The most translucent of washes is made from pure pigment and water with just a tiny amount of emulsion to give it some body. It is difficult to give hard and fast rules for the proportion of pigment to water and emulsion as so much depends on the required finish, but a rule of thumb recipe is two tablespoons of emulsion to two pints of water, plus a dash of gouache or acrylic, adding more as necessary. The main thing is that the colour should be thoroughly dissolved in the water before adding it to the emulsion; then it can be thinned to the required consistency. Even the tiniest speck of undissolved pigment can become an enormous streak across a wall.

GLAZING

A glaze is a semi-transparent film of oil-based colour. It tends to be richer and more transparent than a wash, but as it does not dry so quickly, it can be worked more easily, and adjustments can be made as one goes along. Many decorative finishes, from woodgraining to marbling, are finished by glazing to give depth and patina to the surface, and professional decorators particularly use glazing for the subtle and sophisticated colour effects much in demand today.

Like colour washing, glazes can help correct an unsuitably coloured wall – they also take a quarter of the time it would take to repaint the wall!

They can be shiny, matt or transparent, depending on what goes into them, but they should not be confused with varnish which also gives a transparent effect.

Glazes can be bought ready-made, requiring only the addition of a tint; these are usually called 'scumble' glazes, and the tinting colours used with them can be universal stainers or artists' oil colours. Unmixed scumble ranges in appearance from thick, runny honey to white handcream, but in all cases it will go transparent when applied to a wall. Ready-made glazes are not easy to buy outside large cities, so the following recipe is given for making your own

scumble glaze. In a suitable vessel mix one part pure turpentine, one part boiled linseed oil and one part drier (all these 'ingredients' are readily available from most decorating suppliers). This is the basic scumble glaze; you may then like to try the three variations shown in the margin, although there are other variations which give differing effects.

Glazes can also be used on woodwork and plasterwork – they look very effective if they are applied all over and then rubbed off with a clean cloth, leaving just a trace of colour in the hollows of the design.

Glazing and colour washes are the basic materials for creating special paint effects on walls and woodwork, and the most usual techniques to achieve these effects are known as stippling, dragging, ragging, bagging and sponging. Obviously, before attempting to apply any of these techniques the surfaces should be fully prepared, and it is as well to sand lightly with wet-and-dry sandpaper,

Scumble glaze recipes

1 part scumble glaze
1 part white spirit
2% flat white paint
Colour to suit.

1 part scumble glaze
1 to 5 parts flat white paint
Colour to suit
White spirit to suit.

1 part scumble glaze
1 to 5 parts of eggshell
  paint thinned with white
  spirit to suit.

Pre-formed panelling given a simple surface glaze

Simple but effective – a beautifully rag-rolled finish

If you do miss patches it is easier to fill in by brushing some glaze directly onto the brush tips, or whatever you are using to stipple with, than it is to brush more glaze directly onto the walls. Do not forget, however, to remove the extra glaze from your brush before moving on.

then wipe with a large damp sponge before finally wiping dry with a tack rag. Tack rags can be bought, but can equally well be made from something like a large handkerchief or a piece of sheeting: this is dampened with warm water, wrung out and then sprinkled with white spirit and three teaspoons of varnish. These should be worked into the cloth with a rubbing action, and the cloth will then pick up all the dust from the working surfaces.

STIPPLING

Stippled walls have been around for generations; decorators have always found stippling an effective way of eliminating brushmarks from painted walls and woodwork, and the resulting finely pitted surface is very attractive.

Professional stippling brushes are large, flat-faced and soft-bristled and give a very fine, mottled texture; however, they are very expensive and it is quite possible to find acceptable alternatives. There is a rubber-tipped brush available, but something like a soft shoe brush, a painter's dusting brush, a wallpaper smoothing brush, an old hairbrush or even a soft broomhead can be very effectively used. It is also possible to use a roller, or bunched-up rags, or marine or synthetic sponges; it all depends on the tool you find easiest to use and the effect you want to achieve.

Stippling is usually done using a transparent or

semi-transparent colour over a white or lightly coloured background; this allows tiny areas of the base colour to show through, producing a soft, mottled effect. For instance, a turquoise glaze over a cream background will appear as the softest aquamarine, and a claret red over white will appear as a deep pink. Do not be afraid to experiment with the glaze colour by mixing, say, two pigments together to produce an interesting colour which will look exciting when stippled over the base colour.

Once the walls are fully prepared, the glaze mixed to the shade you prefer and the floor protected, you are ready to start stippling – and the technique really could not be easier. Brush on a vertical band of glaze about two feet wide and then stipple over it. Roller stippling is fast and easy for one person, but with a brush method it is useful to have two people working at the same time – one can brush on the glaze and the other can stipple, thus keeping a flow going and achieving a more even effect. Always remember to clean the stippler frequently on kitchen paper to avoid a build-up of glaze.

RAGGING AND RAG-ROLLING

Beautiful painted effects can be produced by a method known as ragging or rag-rolling. This is really another version of stippling but is done by using bunched-up rags or chamois leather rolled into a sausage shape, which is then applied to the wall in a rolling movement of the hand. The finished effect looks like crushed velvet or brocade.

First apply the glaze to the wall – because ragging is a much faster process than stippling, quite a large area can be covered with the glaze at one time. The purist would then stipple the glaze to eliminate brush strokes, but it is possible to work directly onto the applied glaze with the loose bunch of material. Either use one hand, and push the glaze about in various directions with a relaxed wrist so as to create an unstructured pattern; or use two hands and roll the bundle of fabric over the glaze in various directions, using the material rather like a rolling pin. The idea is to produce an irregular but

Stippling brushes

fairly uniform pattern, and you will soon discover how much pressure to apply.

The rag will have to be changed fairly frequently. Also, it is important to use the same material throughout the decorating process, as no two materials will give the same effect. Before even starting, it is worth experimenting with several different materials to see the patterns they can produce; then choose whichever seems best, and stick to it. Chamois can be cleaned by dipping it into white spirit, wringing it out and then carrying on as previously.

BAGGING

Bagging is another version of ragging; it uses all the same techniques as in ragging, except that paper or plastic bags are used to achieve the broken colour surface. It is great fun and easy to do and the effect appears rather more casual than ragging.

DRAGGING

Dragging produces a sophisticated paint effect, and John Fowler is credited with making it popular in the 1930s when he used it in English country houses. It looks particularly well in Georgian rooms and makes a wonderful background to a collection

Terracotta sponged over cream. Note how the door frame has been outlined in the same shade

of antique furniture and pictures.

To achieve the effect, a previously prepared and painted wall is covered, strip by strip, with a glaze or wash of a transparent colour; this is then brushed from top to bottom with a dry brush which 'drags' off fine stripes of colour so that the base colour shows through. The appearance is of fine, irregular lines and is very attractive. Once again, professional decorators would probably use a proper dragging brush, but any fairly wide fine-bristled brush, such as a paper-hanger's brush, can be used – and for the adventurous, real variety can be introduced by using worn-out standard paint brushes.

Dragging really is a two-person job, with one applying the glaze or wash and the other dragging it off again. The edge of the band of glaze must be kept 'wet', because if the edge is not wet it is easy to get a build-up of colour at the overlap point and this gives a rather ragged effect. It is a good idea to start dragging where a vertical line such as a door jamb

already exists, as this will make the first strokes much easier. Apply the dragging brush to the wall, making sure the bristles are pressed completely down, and then bring it down through the glaze with as steady and even a pressure as possible.

Again, it is important not to let too much glaze build up in the brush, so keep wiping it on clean rags every two or three strokes. The glaze also tends to accumulate at the top and bottom of the strokes, but any build-up can be feathered out if it is done immediately with a dry brush.

SPONGING

For the faint-hearted who want a broken paint finish but cannot contemplate stippling, ragging or dragging, sponging has to be the answer, for it is very easy to do and achieves fast results. There are two methods – sponging on, and sponging off.

Sponging off is quicker and simpler than

The walls in this pretty kitchen have been sponged in pinks and blues

Three different paint finishes: stippling, dragging and sponging

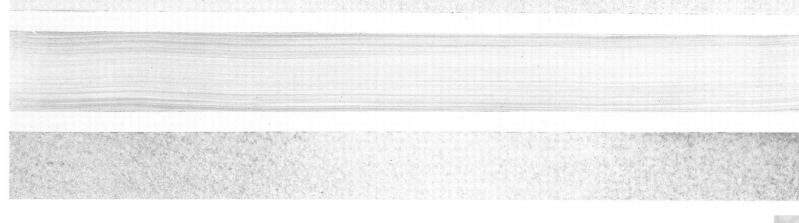

sponging on: the glaze is applied to the wall in approximately 24in (60cm) strips, and then a sponge dampened with white spirit and wrung out thoroughly is dabbed evenly over the glazed area. The white spirit in the sponge removes the glaze, and the result is a very pretty textured finish. Remove excess glaze from the sponge by dipping it in white spirit and wringing it out – and then continue.

When sponging on, pick up the glaze colour – which for ease of use should be on a large flat surface such as a soup dish or tray – dab it on to kitchen paper until a mist of colour appears, and then dab it over the wall in a random fashion. It is possible to obtain a marbled effect by using more than one colour in this way, but each application of colour should dry before the next is applied or the result could be a heavy, smeary mess instead of the light kiss of several complementary colours!

MARBLING

One of the most fascinating painted wall finishes is marbling. Marble has probably been imitated by painters since at least 2000BC, and it provides a constant challenge and delight to the adventurous decorator. However, despite its complicated appearance, copying it involves one technique which can produce extraordinary results with very few tools, and in fact the materials themselves do the work. Marbling can, of course, be used on all kinds of surfaces but it looks particularly well on walls, the area beneath a dado and skirting boards.

Real marble was created by movement, by heat and pressure on limestone which crystallised into a whole spectrum of colours, and by mineral substances which ran through the original molten strata and cooled to form coloured threads, or veins, in the limestone. Thus marble has a luminous, tremulous life of its own: it seems almost possible to look into the heart of it and see diaphanous colours frozen into the stone. It is this translucence, this life and movement which must be re-created in a marbled finish – and the basic technique to do so is actually very simple.

The wall should first be painted with an undercoat of eggshell, and then a translucent oil glaze – tinted with the palest shade possible of the chosen colour – is applied with a brush. The process is known as 'oiling in'. The glaze is then dabbed with a clean piece of lint-free cloth and some areas of glaze actually rubbed away completely to reveal the background colour. The glaze should be left to set for a while, and then a brush known as a 'badger softener' is very, very lightly swept over its surface to give a cloudy effect.

The next stage is to apply the veins: use a small amount of glaze tinted with an appropriate colour, or colours, and apply it with a sable brush or a feather in a meandering, diagonal direction, rather like a bolt of lightning, adding a few 'branches' to give movement. Hold the brush or feather very lightly and twist it as you go along, to give a ragged effect.

When sufficient veining has been applied, dab it with a cloth and then brush with the badger – this will blend and soften the veins with miraculous results: suddenly the surface will resemble marble!

Be warned – marbling can become addictive!

VARNISH

A final coat of varnish can be applied to all the paint effects described here; sometimes the result is good, in other situations varnish is very troublesome.

In an area which will need frequent cleaning or is subject to a lot of condensation, such as a bathroom, a clear, matt polyurethane varnish not only protects the paint finish, but means it can be wiped down as often as necessary. Also, not everyone likes a newly decorated look, and this is where varnish can come into its own, for it too can be tinted to a slightly darker shade and when applied over the paint finish will produce a mellow, older appearance.

On the other hand, even the palest of varnishes has a slightly yellowish tone which will alter the appearance of the paint finish. If someone has spent

Some other effects to try are:
• Pressing a newspaper onto the glazed base to produce little veins.
• Dabbing a sponge into white spirit, squeezing it out well and then dabbing it on the surface to 'open' it.
• Putting a brush in white spirit and then flicking it onto the board, dabbing with a cloth to finish.

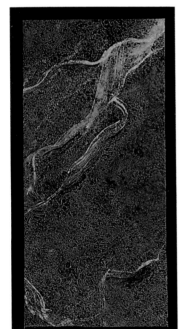

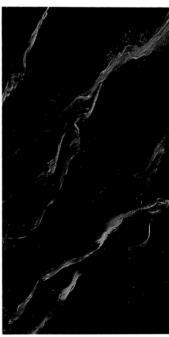

An example of Sienna marbling, and three variations of green marbling

hours getting exactly the right colour on to a wall it is very disappointing if just a single coat of varnish alters – even slightly – the original shade. Furthermore, when the time – or mood – comes for redecorating it is not possible to paint over varnish with water-based paints such as emulsion, and stripping varnish can be a long and extremely messy procedure.

These, then, are the main paint techniques used on walls. You may feel that you would never tackle them yourself but would prefer to employ a professional. Nevertheless, to understand and brief a decorator properly, it is necessary to know the processes involved, what can or cannot be done, and the effects that can be achieved.

The columns and shelf of this decorative archway have been marbled to add substance to the overall decorative scheme

PROJECT PAPERS

No-one who is fascinated by interior design can fail to be aware of the growing interest in many of the paint finishes which have their roots in the past. For centuries skilled craftsmen have used basic materials not only to create subtle paint effects but also to emulate highly expensive materials such as marble and tortoiseshell which were beyond the reach of many people.

Nowadays it is almost impossible to open a home interest magazine and not see wonderful examples of the finishes talked about in this chapter; yet now you will have realised that many of them require no great skill, merely the desire to create them for oneself, and endless practice. The following projects have been designed so that there will be some actual examples in your own portfolio.

PROJECT 7

Using the recipe for home-made scumble glaze (see p53), tint it and then try out some of the techniques described on pieces of shiny white or cream artboard (obtainable from art supply shops). The shiny board allows you to wipe off the results time and time again until you find one you particularly like. Put this aside to dry thoroughly overnight.

Imagine you are going to show this sample board to a prospective client: accompany it therefore with a separate list stating the name of the paint finish, the medium used to create the colour, and where you feel this particular finish could be most attractively used.

PROJECT 8

To accompany the sample board above and to demonstrate even further your knowledge of paint finishes, cut out examples of five different finishes from magazines or trade brochures and mount them on sheets of A4 paper. Label them clearly and add your comments so that if they were shown to someone who knew nothing about them, that person would be able to appreciate the effects which can be achieved.

CHAPTER 5

WALL TREATMENTS
APPLIED DECORATIVE FINISHES

THE VARIOUS PAINTED EFFECTS already discussed are fairly straightforward to achieve; almost everyone is capable of wielding a paint brush or roller and producing a satisfactory finish, and once this has been done, the various bagging, ragging and sponging effects are just further steps along the road. There is no doubt that the painted wall finishes look interesting in themselves, but in fact very often their function is to form the basis of other applied decorative finishes such as stencilling, murals and trompe l'oeil. Other wall finishes which are actually 'applied' should not be neglected either, for they, too, have their place in interior design; and although the most obvious of these is wallpaper, print rooms and walling and tenting should also be considered.

WALLPAPER

The earliest recorded example of European wallpaper is said to date back to the reign of Henry VIII, but it was not until 1692 that the first wallpaper patent was issued. These early wallpapers would have been printed by hand using carved blocks of wood, or hand-stencilled, and although this was obviously a time-consuming and laborious process, the result would have been a highly individual and lasting wallcovering.

Surprisingly, there is still a demand for hand-printed wallpapers produced by the old methods, but it is now more usual to print them by using a silk-screen. It is possible to have modern designs printed by this method but the strength of hand-printed wallpapers lies in the traditional designs which have stood the test of time and have become classics. William Morris and the Victorian architect Augustus Pugin were masters at designing blocked wallpaper and their original designs are still sometimes reproduced by these old methods.

Why should people bother to use hand-printed wallpaper today when there is such a huge range of good machine-printed wallpapers available? Possibly the answer lies in that old maxim 'you get what you pay for'. Those who are prepared to pay the price will have a wallpaper printed on high-quality paper, of excellent design, coloured to individual specification, and produced by skilled craftsmen.

Hand-printed paper is usually made in 10.05m (33ft) rolls and is almost always supplied with the selvages still in place, so accurate trimming is essential. One further point to remember is that, because they are hand printed, it can be difficult to match up pattern repeats; a professional would try to match at the area which immediately attracts the eye, leaving the rest simply to be accepted as it is.

There is a multitude of machine-printed wallpapers, from the cheapest called 'pulps' by the trade because the pattern is printed directly onto raw paper, through to wipeables, washables, even scrubbables. The list goes on – textured papers, flocks, metallic papers, embossed Anaglyptas, and pre-pasted wallpapers of many varieties.

The pulp papers are quite difficult to hang because they are usually very thin and when wet, can over-stretch and so dry out unevenly and look distorted. Better quality papers are mostly coated with a base colour first and then printed. Any paper which has not been especially treated to give a wipeable finish can be given one by using one of the proprietary sealers which are widely available, although it is wise to test the effect of such a sealer on a spare piece of wallpaper first as colours may not necessarily be 'fast'.

Papers which are described as washable have been coated with a thin, transparent plastic film and can indeed be washed with soapy water, but they will not tolerate detergents or being scrubbed with abrasives. Unlike vinyl paper, which has a distinct and not particularly attractive, plastic appearance, washable wallpapers are available in a range of finishes, from matt to glossy.

Vinyl papers are coated, or laminated, with PVC and printed with special dyes which fuse with the surface. They are tough, waterproof, can withstand scrubbing with abrasives and detergents and wear extremely well. A special anti-fungal paste should be used when hanging vinyls because ordinary water-based pastes cannot dry out through the

Washable wallpapers can be removed more easily if the plastic film is scored before a stripper is applied.

LEFT: *A wallpaper called Christchurch, which was designed by William Morris in 1882. Notice how the colours have been reversed in the fabric*

BELOW: *A classic wallpaper, which looks like mattress ticking, blends perfectly with the more complex patterning of the curtain fabric*

laminated surface and therefore have to dry out through the wall, which takes some time, and means that mould could start to form. One disadvantage of vinyl papers is that they are affected by the fumes from such things as gas fires or smoke; the fumes react with the PVC coating and discolour it permanently, so the discoloration cannot be washed away. On the plus side, however, vinyls peel off the walls easily, leaving a paper backing which can be left as lining for the next wallpaper application.

Professionals regard pre-pasted papers as rather a gimmick, but there is no doubt that they do save a lot of time and trouble, not to mention mess, for the home decorator. The back of the paper is coated with an adhesive and only needs dipping into a specially designed water-filled trough to moisten the adhesive; it can then be applied directly to the

ABOVE RIGHT: *Anaglypta pressed into a subtle nursery design*

FAR RIGHT: *A traditional Anaglypta design used beneath a dado rail*

ABOVE: *An Anaglypta design suitable for ceilings*

RIGHT: *A strong Art Nouveau design in Lincrusta*

wall. Once the paper is wet there is about 15 minutes' working time to get it correctly positioned onto the wall. Like the vinyls these papers, too, peel easily off the walls.

The so-called 'wood-chip' papers are often spoken about in derogatory terms but they do, in fact, have their place in certain situations. These papers have had wood chips, small pieces of straw and other fibres mixed into the wood pulp during production, and are available in various thicknesses. They are useful for disguising rough and uneven walls and are usually applied in their off-white state before being painted.

Two other distinctive papers are Lincrusta and Anaglypta. Anaglypta is thick and strong and consists of two layers of paper: the top one is heavy and white, the bottom one is made from ordinary wood pulp. When damp these two layers are pressed together and then embossed, producing high-relief patterns on the paper which remain when it is hung. Again this paper is suitable for covering old and cracked walls and is often used to create panels beneath a dado rail. Some of the embossed designs resemble plaster mouldings and cornices, and even ceiling roses, and although they would not deceive an expert, they are undoubtedly useful for producing the desired effect in certain situations.

Lincrusta is more rigid than Anaglypta and is made from a solid paper backing coated with a pliable mixture of filling and linseed oil. Whilst still soft this is pressed into various textures, relief patterns and other effects which can resemble anything from wall panelling to tiles.

Everyone is familiar with wallpaper which resembles fabric, from simple hessian to flock. And it is just unfortunate that so often 'flocked paper' only brings to mind an Indian restaurant, because with its cut velvet appearance and sense of richness it can look stunning in the right setting. Many other fabric finishes have been imitated by the wallpaper trade – moiré silk, leather, suede, cork, cane and various wood grains – the choice seems endless. Some have been around for a long time, others have endured only briefly.

It is fashionable today to have matching wallpaper and fabrics, and the trend seems to be moving from the safe, smaller designs to something much bolder and more ornate. The matching wall and curtain treatments can then be further embellished by using paper friezes, not only under the cornice or picture rail but around doorways and window frames, at dado level and to outline every vertical and horizontal in a room (see photograph on p68). If this effect particularly appeals to you, cuttings could be taken from both manufacturers' advertising and magazines, and a file built up, thus providing an instant reference to settings which have particularly taken your eye.

Lining paper is also worthy of mention: there are two main reasons for using it – to improve uneven or cracked walls before applying paint or paper, and to provide an even surface with all-over porosity. Lining paper is absolutely essential under delicate wallpapers such as Japanese grasscloths, and is to be recommended under any of the more expensive wallpapers, to produce a really first-class finish. Even 'ordinary' wallpapers will benefit from the use of a lining paper as it will help adhesion, can usually blot out dark wall finishes which could 'grin' through a new surface, and should flatten out uneven and poorly surfaced walls.

There are quite a few varieties of lining paper available. The whitish papers are ideal for normal walls and come in several thicknesses or weights, but the brown-coloured, heavier lining papers should be used on badly cracked or rough walls and under Anaglypta and Lincrusta. Lining paper is always hung horizontally before applying wallpaper so that it goes on smoothly, and also so there is no chance of the vertical joints lying directly on top of each other; for a painted finish, however, it is sometimes hung vertically – it is simply a matter of personal taste in this instance.

There are plenty of books which explain the techniques of actually hanging wallpaper, but the following pointers should be helpful:

• Wallpapers must have sufficient time to expand after they have been pasted, usually at least five minutes, and bubbles and uneven shrinkage are

that these do not appear in the middle of a wall.

- When pasting, do not work with your back to the light as you will not be able to see if the paste has been spread evenly.

- If attempting to do the work yourself, do read up details of wallpapering techniques from a really good manual – it can save hours of frustration.

- Finally, now knowing a little of what to avoid and how things should be done, you are in a very good position to brief a professional!

PRINT ROOMS

The wealthy Georgians were very fond of the 'print room' effect and liked to adorn their studies, libraries and snugs in this manner. It is a decorative effect which is relatively simple to achieve, and the method was to paste, most usually, black and white engravings directly onto a previously painted wall. These engravings would have been of various sizes, and the skill lay in being able to place them in a carefully balanced manner onto the wall. Once the engravings were in situ they were edged with fanciful paper borders of various designs, and then further embellishment added in the form of swags, bows, ropes, lion heads, rosettes and shells, either appearing to suspend the engravings on the wall or simply to decorate the area around them. Some striking examples are in the photographs opposite and on p70, and show the stunning effects which can be achieved.

Specialist shops have a wide range of engravings for sale, and it is also worth shopping around in antique shops and bookshops for old books which even if battered may well reveal untold treasures in the form of suitable engravings to use for print rooms.

Although not strictly suitable for print rooms, there are other paste-on paper motifs available such as cupids, bows, knots and ropes which can look extremely effective in certain situations.

A wallpaper printed to resemble a ragged finish, with complementary borders and three toning fabrics

generally because this simple rule has not been observed.

- Flour or starch-based pastes are the best; either mix your own or buy proprietary brands.

- Starch-based pastes are better for thin or fine wallpapers because they are completely transparent.

- A strong, thin coat of paste is better than a thickly applied weak paste as this will undoubtedly squeeze out between the wallpaper joints and mar the surface of the paper.

- Even from the same dye or printing number there can be a variation in tone between rolls, and it is sensible to unwind each roll a little and compare them in a good light. If variations do occur make sure

Paste-on motifs used to make a Georgian-style feature on a chimney breast

Print rooms are currently enjoying a revival, and the National Trust has a perfect example of this decorative form at its Blickling Hall property, near Aylsham in Norfolk. Such has been the interest in this room that the National Trust now supply sheets of borders, swags, and many of the other traditional designs so that the home decorator can try these effects for themselves.

*Original engravings and motifs
used for print rooms*

*The dramatic effect of this
dining room is greatly enhanced
by the use of paste-on motifs*

WALLING AND TENTING

Lining paper is one way to disguise uneven or badly cracked or plastered walls, but there is another very effective treatment which will not only disguise poor walls but also lift them into the realms of luxury: walling them with fabric. This can, of course, be expensive, but it is possible to create quite stunning effects by using cheap cottons. The important thing to remember is that the material should always be made from a natural fibre such as cotton, linen or wool; man-made fibres are hydrophillic, which means that they will stretch or sag according to the moisture content of the atmosphere. This also applies, unfortunately, to pure silk.

There are three basic methods of walling: fabric wrapped around panels on split battens; fabric stapled directly on to battens already fixed to the wall; and a track system which totally conceals the fixings. Once the battens are in place, the fabric can be stretched flat and fixed with either staples or upholstery tacks covered with braid, or gathered, pleated or hung in dramatic swags. It really is not very difficult to wall a room; it is mostly a matter of time and patience.

Having gone to the bother of walling a room, the final touch should, of course, be a tented ceiling. Nothing else looks quite so luxurious and it will always produce a lot of admiring comments. Although tenting is more difficult than walling a room, mainly because of the all-important fixing to the ceiling centre, it is still relatively easy to do and should not be lightly dismissed. It not only covers bad plasterwork and cracks, it creates a really sumptuous effect.

STENCILLING

Now to the decorative wall finish which, as a professional, is close to my heart. Since childhood I have been fascinated by stencilling, and used to love making potato-cuts, dabbing them in poster

Colourful Indian bedspreads are a cheap but very effective way of walling a room for a really exotic effect.

An attractive stencil with a fruit motif used in a dining room. This example is 1.2m (4ft) wide

Building stencil bridges for a wren (see p74 for full instructions)

paint and then making 'designs'. Learning to mix the basic primary colours in order to produce other shades I became more and more interested, although it was not until later years and working with creative people that the full potential of stencilling was really brought home to me.

Stencilling is a very ancient craft, perfected by the Orientals, and used for centuries as a decorative wall embellishment until the advent of printed wallpaper. Even then, people such as William Morris and Voysey produced wallpaper designs based on stencils. The American settlers from Europe kept the tradition alive, and for the past decade it has been regaining popularity; it is now, in some cases, a highly sophisticated and sought-after decorative finish. It really is extremely versatile, not only for decorating walls, but also floors, ceilings, furniture and fabrics – and for someone seeking something really unique in decoration there are no limits.

Walls which have been prepared with some of the painted effects already discussed make ideal backgrounds for stencilling, but a plainly emulsioned wall is also good as it is possible to stencil panels, dados and cornices onto this, adding interest and depth to a room.

There are many ready-cut stencils available, but it is much more interesting to create your own, or to get someone to create a design which is unique to you. There are two materials used for stencils – a clear acetate film and, traditionally, a brown, waxed, manilla paper which is bought in sheets approximately 20 x 30in (50 x 75cm). Both have their good points and their faults, and it is a matter of individual taste as to which is used. The clear film stencils are useful when doing something like a frieze, as it is easy to see where work was left off and to line up accurately again. However, the paint does build up on them and so obscures the design, and they are not as robust as the waxed card, because the corners of the design can split and cause paint runs. The waxed card is tougher and longer-lasting, but if it is used for something like a frieze, it is essential to use some form of registration mark so that an evenly-spaced, continuous design is

A very large stencil used effectively on a folding screen and door in a restaurant

achieved. This is easily done, however, and as long as you remember that it does have to be registered, there should be no problems. A frieze should not go right into the corners of a wall, but should stop about one or two inches before each corner. It is virtually impossible to stencil into a corner without getting a very fuzzy result, and part of the charm of a stencilled frieze is that it does not look too mechanical. If it is too perfect you might just as well use a pre-printed, paper frieze.

To produce a design of one's own, it is best first to work it out on a piece of plain paper, or to trace something you like from a book or magazine. When happy with the design, attach it to waxed card by masking tape, place a sheet of carbon paper between the design and the stencil card, and then trace over it. If using plastic film, simply put the film on top of the design and trace directly through using a Rapidograph pen.

The next stage is to turn the design into a stencil, and that means leaving 'bridges' or 'ties' to hold the design together; these bridges also give strength to the stencil and form part of the pattern. Shade in the shapes which are to be cut out – it is all too easy to be happily cutting away, and suddenly find that

instead of pretty shapes there is simply a hole! Have a look at the drawings on pages 72 and 75 and you will see what I mean.

When the design will literally hang together, you can then start to cut it out. A piece of hardboard covered with vinyl flooring is a cheap and simple cutting board, although it is possible to buy professional cutting boards, and some stencillers use a thick piece of glass with the edges protected with masking tape. Using a disposable craft knife, cut out the shapes by starting in the centre of the design and working outwards. As you become adept with the craft knife you will find that you can hold the blade at a 45° angle, and this will help prevent the paint from seeping beneath the stencil and causing a fuzzy outline.

Before applying the stencil to the wall it is best to try out various colour combinations and to test different paints so as to establish the colours and the techniques which suit you best. Use lining paper to

Mistakes on an emulsioned wall are easy to paint over, using a hair dryer to speed up the process if several coats of emulsion are needed to blot out the error.

FAR RIGHT: *A selection of stencil brushes*

RIGHT: *A natural sponge, ideal for stencilling and sponging walls*

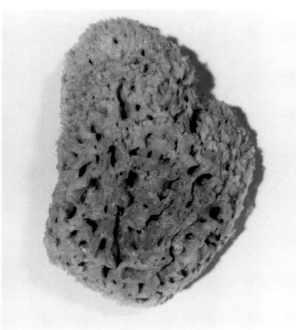

Building stencil bridges for a rose

do this, but remember that if the stencil is to be applied to a coloured background, then it should be tested on a background of the same colour to see the full effect. Always have a small jar of background colour available, or use small sample pots of emulsion. The main requirement of a paint for stencilling is that it should dry quickly. This is especially important if several colours are used, either to merge together or when using multi-stencils.

For walls, the following can be used: artists' acrylics thinned with water or mixed with a little emulsion, flat emulsion paint tinted with the universal stainers discussed earlier, or an oil-based undercoat paint, again tinted with stainers or artists' oil colours. Coming onto the market now are small pots of acrylic paints especially for stencillers, but they are very expensive and a small tin of white emulsion plus a few tubes of acrylic paint will cost much less. Also now available are ozone-friendly spray paints. These certainly save a lot of time and

effort but walls must be carefully masked to prevent the 'fall-out' from spraying the surrounding wall as well as the stencil. If stencilling a large area spray paints are much quicker, but for smaller areas perhaps acrylics mixed with emulsion and applied with a stencil brush are best for the cautious.

The traditional, fat stencil brush gives attractive results and the colour is applied by either a 'pouncing' or a circular movement with an almost dry brush. Dip the brush into the paint and then stamp it up and down on kitchen paper to remove most of the paint; it is surprising how very little is needed to cover quite a large area. Stencil brushes come in various sizes and it is as well to have at least three or four, otherwise you have to keep stopping to wash the brush between colours. It is also possible to use sponges to apply colour, and for very large, simple motifs, even a roller.

The stencil can be attached to the wall either by masking tape or by a spray glue used by graphic designers. The glue is very expensive, but it does

RIGHT: *A stencilled frieze which is in complete harmony with the age of the building*

BELOW: *A bathroom mural combining hand painting, stencilling and sponging*

adhere well to the wall and lessens the chance of smudges; though masking tape should suffice, particularly with the brush method, as long as it isn't loaded with paint. Apply the colour carefully and lightly; it is easier to build up gradually than to have to dampen down too heavy an application of colour. And remember that when the card or acrylic is removed, the colours are always much more pronounced than they appear through the cut-outs – so lightly does it!

The most exciting moment comes when the stencil is removed from the wall – even after years of stencilling and hundreds of different designs, I still get an enormous thrill when I see the finished result.

On walls, friezes are an obvious choice for stencilling, but remember the suggestions made earlier about creating panels, mouldings, dados etc.

These can be used to separate different paint effects, such as marbling inside a stencilled panel with a dragged finish outside. A frieze taken just above a dado and then up and over the doors, with a cartouche over the centre of the door, works very well indeed, and will certainly create interest, for example, in a long corridor lined with several doors. A large, interesting stencil design in, say, the centre of a wall instead of a picture can also work well – have a look at the examples in the photographs. Above all, think creatively and you will be pleasantly surprised at the number of possibilities which are open to an enthusiastic stenciller.

MURALS

To go into precise details of how to create a mural would need a whole book; suffice it that the budding interior designer is fully aware of all the decorative techniques which are available for adorning walls, and just how many possibilities there are to consider. Murals are not very difficult to create and if you have any artistic talent at all it is fun to attempt one. Even though I was dubious about my own abilities I nevertheless enjoyed building up the one pictured in the photograph opposite. It is a combination of hand painting, stencilling and sponging, all done with emulsion paint – it is not marvellous but it did teach me a lot, and the next one will be better.

What exactly is meant by the word 'mural'? It can mean so many different things to different people – a relief carved into a wall, a fabric collage, a mosaic, a large photograph, a painted story, perhaps a very large wall stencil. Even the *Shorter Oxford Dictionary* can get no nearer than to describe it as something 'placed, fixed, or executed on a wall'. Patricia Seligman in her book *Painted Murals* surely gets close to the truth when she says that 'a mural is a work of art that is created for a particular site so that it is incorporated into the architecture; in other words, its composition is influenced by the forces of its surroundings … unlike an easel painting which can be hung anywhere and is appreciated in isolation from its surroundings even though it may enhance them.'

Murals have been around for a very long time; the Egyptians used them in their tombs, the Romans decorated their villas with them, the Minoans painted their important buildings with them, and the Renaissance painters nearly went over the top. True mural painting is simple, stylised and painted in flat colours, and makes no attempt to create a three-dimensional effect such as trompe l'oeil. The Egyptians made no use of perspective, but the Greeks and Romans explore this aspect of the art, and their lively wall paintings were very sophisticated, as can be seen from those preserved by the volcanic eruption which destroyed Pompeii.

Nearly 5,000 years on, murals are still popular and can be seen in the most unlikely places. Perhaps it is because they allow people to express their individuality in these days of increasing uniformity, and invest featureless walls, rooms and corridors with character and life. Murals can be fun in a child's room, grand in an entrance hall, lively in a sports complex and surreal in a bathroom; in cities, murals appear unexpectedly on exterior walls and even in such unlikely places as suburban railway stations. All it takes is imagination, patience and a steady hand!

TROMPE L'OEIL

Trompe l'oeil takes decorative wall finishes to the ultimate extreme, and it would be wrong even to suggest that an amateur could produce the effect with ease. However, it is really surprising what can be achieved by a lay person and it should not be dismissed as too difficult to attempt.

Trompe l'oeil means 'deceive the eye': in appearance it suggests three dimensions where there are, in fact, only two. There is a feeling of fun about trompe l'oeil – its very unexpectedness always causes a reaction, and most people cannot help being intrigued by it. It can also have what could be termed an architectural use. For instance, there is an impressive hall which has a lovely curved alcove

RIGHT: *A wonderful example of trompe l'oeil: it truly could be clouds scudding across the sky as seen through a large window*

BELOW: *This bookcase is another marvellous example of trompe l'oeil*

adjacent to the rather grand doorway – but for some unknown reason there is only one, instead of one on each side of the door, as the architect would surely have planned. This totally destroyed not only the balance of that wall, but also the symmetry of the entire hall. It would have been quite a large building operation to knock out the wall to achieve a matching pair, so the owner of the house employed an artist skilled in trompe l'oeil to reproduce the alcove; now the visitor has to look really hard to detect that this new alcove is, in fact, a very clever deception.

All the decorative wall finishes mentioned in this chapter will help you, as a budding interior designer, to create very individual interiors. Some may be of interest, some intriguing, some totally unacceptable, but the main thing is to realise that there is a life beyond plain emulsioned walls or another layer of wallpaper.

PROJECT PAPERS

Applied decorative finishes are currently very much in vogue, and interest in them shows no sign of decreasing. Indeed the proliferation of courses on the subject show that people are seriously interested in learning more about the techniques employed to create these finishes. Perhaps this is a reaction against the bland uniformity of many of today's houses – or perhaps it is simply that people do have more leisure time in which to expand their own creativity. Whatever the reason, long may it last, and the next two projects should give *you* the opportunity of exploring your own creativity, too.

PROJECT 9

Trace the stencil shape on p72 onto a sheet of clear acetate and then carefully cut out the blocked-in shapes using a craft knife. Attach the cut stencil to a plain piece of paper or board (lining paper is ideal) with pieces of masking tape and then try out several colour combinations using either stencil brushes or sponges.

   When you have found the combination you like, stencil it once more onto an A4 piece of card so that there will be a good example of stencilling in your portfolio to show a possible client. If you wish, list the colours used, suggest a suitable background and the room in which this stencil would be most suitably used.

PROJECT 10

From your growing collection of files and your source of magazines, pick out what you consider to be prime examples of:

- a print room
- a room decorated with matching wallpaper and fabric
- a walled and tented room
- a stencilled room
- a mural
- trompe l'oeil

Paste these onto A4 sheets and imagine that you are a magazine feature writer who has to write an extended caption for each decorative treatment. The captions should explain the merits of each scheme and give the 'reader' some idea of how they were achieved. Be as creative as you wish!

CHAPTER 6

WINDOW TREATMENTS

A WINDOW is one of the main focal points in a room, and choosing a suitable curtain fabric, blind, or some other kind of dressing is quite a challenge – but an enjoyable one.

A window treatment should be in sympathy not only with the furnishing inside the room but also with the exterior style of the house. Nothing looks worse than to see elaborate curtain treatments in small cottage windows, so do consider both aspects before making a final decision on the style of curtaining.

The windows themselves may suggest immediately the right decorative treatment; however by the skilful use of fabric it is possible to create all sorts of illusions, not only to set the mood of the room but also to hide or disguise awkward window shapes. Curtaining can unify windows of different shapes and sizes, and it can enhance pretty window shapes such as bay and bowed windows,

Floral curtains gathered into a simple standard heading

Gothic-shaped windows or roof dormer windows.

So, where to start? A simple check-list could help towards the ultimate solution:

1 What is the size and shape of the window?
2 What are the curtains required to achieve – decoration, privacy, or insulation?
3 Is a simple curtain treatment preferred, or a more elaborate one?
4 Should the curtains be lined or unlined?
5 Should the curtains be hung from a pole or a track?
6 If on a track, should there be a pelmet or valance?
7 What sort of heading is preferred – simply gathered, pencil-pleated, box-pleated, goblet, slot, scalloped or puff-ball?
8 Should the curtains hang straight down, or curve into a tie-back?
9 Should the curtains be combined with either a net or a blind of some kind?
10 Finally, how long should the curtains be? Should they reach just to the window sill, just below it, or right to the floor?

By now you should have some idea of the style of curtain and the kind of heading you prefer, although the various terms used may need more detailed explanation.

CURTAIN HEADINGS

Curtain styles are usually created by heading tapes with a gathering cord and those most commonly used are the ones below.

STANDARD

This is made using one-inch tape, gathered into an even, narrow heading. It is suitable for basic, informal curtains and for use under pelmets and valances. A synthetic tape is available for very lightweight, sheer and net curtains. This type of uncomplicated heading is suitable for cottage windows or for dormers, and uses the least amount of material – usually one and a half times the width of the track.

PENCIL PLEAT

This is a neat, slim and unobtrusive heading which will suit most decorating styles, particularly modern ones, but it is important to allow about two and a half times the track width of fabric to enable the pleats to stand up nicely. This type of heading does not require a pelmet or valance.

TRIPLE PLEAT

Sometimes called a French pleat, this heading is very popular for use on fabrics such as velvet and is often used with a buckram stiffening to produce regular, full folds in a fabric. Again, ample material – usually two and a half times the track width – is needed to achieve the essential fullness. The pleats can be fanned out and finished with a button sewn at the base of each.

GOBLET

This is sometimes called cartridge pleating and is a more formal heading for heavier, floor-length curtains. The pocket, or goblet, formed by the pleat can be stuffed with tissue paper or a polyester filling to sustain the shape.

SLOT

This is a cased heading which can be simply fed onto a pole. Alternatively a more elaborate effect can be achieved by forming a channel and leaving fabric above the seamed case to stand free. At least two or three times the pole width is needed to achieve a satisfactory finished appearance.

BOX PLEAT

The description speaks for itself, and here again ample material must be allowed, usually at least three times the track width. With patterned fabrics care should be taken to ensure that even patterning runs across the width of the fabric.

PUFF BALL

This is a spectacular heading, easily achieved. It is basically a slot heading, but above the seamed case an allowance of at least 12in (30cm) should be made. The fabric needs to be about two or three times the pole width, and when threaded onto the pole, the fabric above the casing is pulled and 'scrunched' into puffy shapes.

SCALLOPED

This style of heading is used for the so-called 'café curtains'. For slight fullness an allowance of 50 per cent more than the pole length should be made.

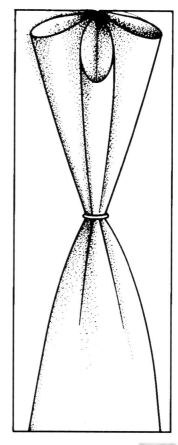

BELOW LEFT: *A goblet heading*

BELOW: *A pencil pleat*

An elaborate valance which has been gathered, scalloped and frilled

The height of a tall window can be reduced by a deep, draped valance.

Valances come in all sorts of styles – pencil-pleated, simply gathered into a frill, gathered onto a stiffened band, French pleated, looped in Austrian blind style and, most elaborate of all, swagged and tailed. Swags and tails are difficult to get right and it is worth making a toile to determine the exact pattern before cutting into expensive fabric. Swags should always be cut on the bias of the material and tails look more dramatic if lined with a contrasting fabric.

ADAPTATIONS OF BASIC CURTAINS

Basic curtains can be trimmed in various ways to produce different styles – smart and sophisticated, frilly and feminine, grand and theatrical. Some of the methods used to create these effects are as follows:

BORDERS

Borders of contrasting braid can be attached to plain curtains, or complementary fabric borders can be inset along the leading edges of the curtains. In both cases it is important to get the dimensions right, and a good rule of thumb is that the width of the inset or braid should approximately equal the width of the border. Borders may be taken along the bottom and outer edges of the curtains if desired but, if this is done, the corners must be correctly mitred to produce a professional effect.

LEADING EDGES

The central, leading edges of curtains can be trimmed in various ways. One of the most usual is to trim the edge with a frill of matching or contrasting material. A variation of this is to add two frills, sometimes one plain and one patterned, the top frill being narrower than the bottom. Frills can also be extended on rounded corners to the base of the curtains, and sometimes a piping is added between the frill and the leading edge of the curtain.

Two smarter leading edges are fan pleats, with the

PELMETS AND VALANCES

Although not strictly curtain headings in that they are not made from the curtains themselves, pelmets and valances are devices used to hide a curtain track or a simple, gathered heading and are thus 'heading' a curtain treatment.

A pelmet is usually a fixed shape formed from plywood or thick buckram, both of which can be covered with a wadding or a cotton bump before the final curtain material is applied. Valances are sometimes known as 'soft pelmets' and are usually adaptations of various types of curtain heading with trims added to emphasise shape or specific detailing. A point to remember is that padded, fabric-covered pelmets are difficult to clean, so it is advisable not to use them in kitchens and bathrooms, where a pelmet painted or papered to match the walls might be more appropriate.

The clever use of red borders and edgings on all the soft furnishings in this delightful children's room adds emphasis and brings it totally alive

pleats running down the leading edge so that the dust does not settle into the pleat pockets, and picot edging. Picot edging can be formed by using a picot braid, or by creating triangles from fabric, slightly overlapped and then attached to the leading edge. This method certainly looks very elegant, but is best left to the professional curtain-maker.

Leading edges can be trimmed with bullion fringing, which is often dyed to match the fabric, and further embellished by the use of tassels. An important point to remember is that the weight of the fringing should be in proportion to the weight of the curtain fabric.

Curtains can also be looped and tied in various ways to create quite theatrical effects; one of the easiest to achieve is called 'bishop's curtains'. These are fully gathered curtains, best made with stiff silk which will hold its shape, which are then tied in two places at approximately one-third intervals to give a puffed or 'balloon' effect. They are, of course, used as dress curtains. A method known as Italian or theatre stringing can also be used – this is achieved by stringing the curtains diagonally through rings sewn at approximately 4in (10cm) intervals. The lining will be visible, so a patterned contrast lining is often used and looks very attractive.

A swagged and tailed valance
lined with a contrasting fabric

TIE-BACKS

Tie-backs make a very attractive and professional finish to your curtain treatments and come in many styles. They can be straight-edged and simple, or curved and piped. Some have bound edges, some pleated edges, frilled edges or scalloped edges. One effective treatment is to back a piece of fabric with a curtain heading which can then be pulled up to form pleats or frills, depending on the heading used. Another which is very popular at the moment is to plait three lengths of fabric which have been padded with wadding, to form a plump, expensive-looking tie-back.

Of course, tie-backs need not be made from fabric, and corded rope tassels can look very elegant. It all depends on the type of curtain fabric used, the effect desired, and which treatment looks best in a particular room.

FABRICS SUITABLE FOR CURTAINS

Provided it drapes or folds well, almost any material can be used for curtains – although that does not mean that, in practical terms, every fabric is suitable. Obviously a fabric must complement the colour scheme of the room, but such things as the fabric weight and whether it is resistant to fading should also be considered. Nothing is more heartbreaking than to find exactly the right shade, to make it or have it made up into a particular curtain style, and then to find that after a relatively short while, the edges and folds have started to fade. There are, of course, solutions to most problems: to help prevent fabric fading, the curtains can be lined, or sheer curtains or roller blinds can be used to act as a sunscreen and bear the brunt of strong sunlight.

Unless a particularly diaphanous look is desired, it is best always to line curtains. It can make a tremendous difference to even the cheapest of fabrics, making the curtains hang better and last longer; and expensive curtains should not only be lined, but interlined with bump to enhance their

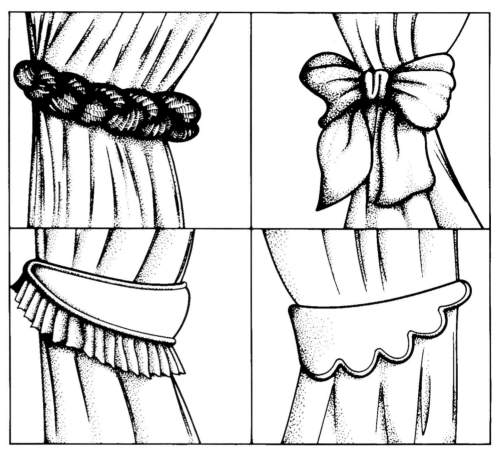

Tie-back suggestions

appearance. An added bonus is that lined curtains will help to insulate the room.

Fabric weight is important too – a thick fabric used for sill-length curtains could look bulky and stiff, whereas used for floor-length curtains it would hang better and add importance to the window. Whichever fabric is decided upon, I would suggest that it is worth investing in a metre of it first, and bringing this home to see how it works with the existing furnishings and colour scheme. Once again, look at it in both artificial and natural light – gather it into folds and see if the effect is good.If it is patterned, check that the design is proportional to the size of the room, or whether it is too dominant. Such a short length of material will not be wasted as it can always be made into a cushion cover or used to make a tie-back, or as a cloth for a round table or cut into strips to make a bias edging.

Quick and easy tie-backs can be made by using broad strips of matching or contrasting fabric tied into a large bow. Trim the edges diagonally to create a softer shape.

RIGHT: *A beautifully draped set of curtains, complete with matching tie-backs*

BELOW: *A collection of richly coloured curtaining fabrics*

The following fabrics are those most commonly used for curtaining. The fibres from which the fabric is woven determine how well it will hang, wash and wear, and the yarns used can be animal, vegetable or man-made.

COTTON

Cotton is a vegetable fibre and is one of the most useful fabrics in the interior designers' range. At its simplest it can be bought as **calico**: an unbleached, plain woven cotton of medium weight. It has a matt finish, is relatively cheap, so can be used lavishly to create dramatic window treatments, and is very strong. However, it does tend to shrink, so it should be washed before being made up into curtains.

Muslin is also a basic material made from cotton.

It is very loosely woven and fine, and can be used for sheer curtain treatments. It drapes well, is cheap, and it can therefore be used quite lavishly to create unusual and decorative window treatments. It is a fabric not to be ignored or lightly dismissed.

Gingham is a lightweight cotton fabric woven into a checked pattern by using yarns in two colours. It has always been popular and still is today, moving out of the kitchen into the bedroom, the dining-room and even the sitting-room. A more sophisticated look is created by Madras cotton checks; these are woven from yarns of many colours, and are increasing in popularity, used as counterpoints to both plain and patterned materials.

Chintz, also known as **glazed cotton**, has been popular for many years, deriving its name from the early Indian-inspired chintz prints which were finished with a glaze. Its attractive shiny finish has an ageless appeal and it is suitable for curtains in almost any room. The cotton from which it is made is fairly lightweight, but is tightly woven so it accepts both dyes and glazing very well. The glazing can either be very light, which gives a soft sheen to the fabric, or heavy, which produces the familiar shiny, crisp effect.

Easy-care cotton is a name given to cotton which has been given a polished, easy-care finish. The fabric is quite soft and silky to touch and drapes and washes very well indeed, so is easier to care for than a chintz.

Cotton satin was developed as a cheaper and more practical alternative to satin, which was made from pure silk. It is closely woven, hard-wearing and has a gentle sheen which is very attractive. It is available in various qualities but a heavy version will make up into beautifully soft curtains which will drape well and look extremely elegant in, say, a sitting- or drawing-room.

Sateen is not unlike cotton satin but is a much

Cheerful gingham and matching stripes are used here to decorate a nursery

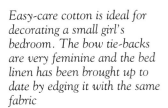

Easy-care cotton is ideal for decorating a small girl's bedroom. The bow tie-backs are very feminine and the bed linen has been brought up to date by edging it with the same fabric

lighter-weight fabric mostly used for curtain linings. It is available in a wide range of colours and is a most useful fabric.

Printed cotton is exactly what it says – a base cloth made from cotton, sometimes cotton satin, which is then printed with a wide variety of colours and designs. It makes up well into curtains and its price depends on the number of colours used in the design and also the quality of the base cloth.

Seersucker is familiar to everyone. Its characteristic puckered and flat striped effect can be created either by a special heat process, or by alternately weaving one group of threads tightly, the next loosely. It can be made into lightweight curtains, but is now most usually used to make festoon blinds.

The king of the cottons has to be **velvet**, and apart from expensive silk, cotton velour is the best quality velvet to use for sumptuous curtains. Although it is a heavy fabric it drapes beautifully,

and is available in an enormous range of colours. When making curtains the pile can run either up or down; the important thing to remember is that the same direction must always be followed, as the variation in colour can be quite dramatic. Generally the colour is richer when the pile runs upwards, so it is worth taking some time to look carefully at the velvet to see which appearance is most suitable. Velvets can also have the pile cut to form patterns, or crushed, to create yet another effect.

LINEN

Linen is made from flax which is perhaps the strongest fibre known. The fibre is smooth and straight and is very resistant to rubbing and dirt. The name which is most familiar is **linen union**, a blend of cotton and linen to which small quantities of nylon have been added to give even more strength. Linen union is mostly used for upholstery,

This Spartan room is softened by the use of sheer curtains, draped simply over a white pole

but it is also used for full-length curtains because it is heavy and drapes quite well.

Linen is sometimes also used to create brocade and damask.

MAN-MADE FIBRES

Versatile man-made fibres mimic everything from silk to lace, and undoubtedly have their place in today's furnishing schemes. The most popular for curtain treatments are dupion, moire, and sheers and voiles.

Dupion is the fabric which most resembles silk and was introduced as a cheaper alternative. It can be heavily slubbed to resemble the alternate thick and thin threads of raw silk but it is basically a lightweight cloth which needs lining and, preferably, interlining. It is suitable for both short and full-length curtains as it drapes well. Its drawbacks are that, unless the synthetic fibres are

mixed with cotton or linen, it has to be dry-cleaned and it is also subject to fading.

Moire, or **watered silk**, is another fabric which is now usually made from man-made fibres. The distinctive wavy appearance of watered silk can now be applied by machine to a plain, lightly ribbed cloth which is sometimes overprinted with stripes or a classic design. Note that moire can react to humidity and temperature changes by expanding and contracting, so it should be sewn very loosely to allow for this.

Sheers and **voiles** are now usually made from polyester or nylon woven very closely to produce a fluid, flimsy appearance. We are all familiar with sheers, and voile is the name given to sheers which have been overprinted with a design, often to co-ordinate with a printed curtain fabric, the same design repeated on both fabrics. Both are used to give privacy or to filter strong sunlight so that the main curtains are protected from fading.

RIGHT: *Extravagant use of roller blinds in a garden room. The fabric has been carefully chosen to echo the shades of the garden flowers, and is also used as cushions on the Lloyd Loom chairs*

BELOW: *Smart Roman blinds decorate a traditional sash window*

These are therefore the main fabrics used today as curtaining, but two others are worthy of mention – **brocade** and **damask**: both fabrics can be made from silk, linen, cotton or synthetic fibres so it is hard to categorise them as animal, vegetable or man-made. The main difference between them is in the weaving; brocade is a woven fabric with a raised design which looks like embroidery, whilst damask is woven to produce patterns which appear matt against a shiny background.

BLINDS AND SHUTTERS

Another popular window treatment, and one often used with curtains, is to fix blinds. There is a wide choice, and several factors should be borne in mind when trying to decide on the type most suitable for a particular window. For instance, in which room is it to be used – bathroom, kitchen, sitting-room? Is its main function to provide privacy, to filter sunlight instead of a sheer curtain, to soften an ugly window, to create a really sumptuous effect, or to clothe a window where curtains would be a problem to hang? Once the answers to some of these questions have been established, look at the types of blind which are readily available.

AUSTRIAN BLINDS

These are softly gathered blinds with fullness in the gathered width. The familiar deep swags are made by pulling the fabric up by cords which are threaded through tapes sewn at regular intervals down the length of the fabric. When completely lowered the blind looks like a straightforward curtain. Often the blinds have frilled edges and they can be shaped in various ways by making adjustments to the cords. They are best made from light or mediumweight materials which will hang well and look attractive when gathered into the swags.

FESTOON BLINDS

There is often confusion about the difference between festoon and Austrian blinds, and they do indeed look very similar when swagged into position at a window. However, festoon blinds are usually made from a lightweight, unlined fabric which is permanently gathered into ruched swags. This means, of course, that they are purely decorative, whereas Austrian blinds can be adjusted to filter sunlight or add privacy.

ROLLER BLINDS

Roller blinds create a more tailored look at a window and are made from a stiffened fabric attached to a spring-loaded roller. Tightly woven cottons, treated with a stiffener, are ideal, but do remember that the fabric needs to be flexible enough to roll up. I once tried to make a blind from a plastic-coated, tablecloth material and it did not work at all.

This photograph shows clearly the effect of Roman blinds when fully extended

ROMAN BLINDS

Roman blinds are very elegant and more sophisticated than straightforward roller blinds. They should be made from closely woven fabric and the pleated effect can be 'hard-fold' or 'soft-fold'. Hard-fold blinds are made with horizontal slats of wood which hold the pleats in place; soft-fold blinds simply fold upon themselves without the use of slats.

VENETIAN BLINDS

Venetian blinds have been in use for years. The slats are usually made from wood, plastic or metal and these are manipulated by vertical cords which angle the slats to a fully opened, partially opened or fully closed position. All Venetian blinds collect dust, but the newer so-called 'micro-blinds', which have

The mellow pine shutters in this bedroom are unadorned by curtains, but note how the ceiling colour has been used to create interest around the window frame

very fine slats, are easier to maintain and are often used for privacy.

These work on the same principle as Venetian blinds but are hung vertically instead of horizontally, and are controlled by chains at the top and bottom. The slats are usually made from a semi-stiffened fabric, so they give a softer look than Venetian blinds; they are particularly used in modern settings.

SHUTTERS

Many old houses are still lucky enough to have the original shutters intact, and these are both attractive and useful. When drawn over the window at night they perform the double function of security and double glazing and undoubtedly add charm to a room. Even with shutters, curtains are

sometimes still hung, but shutters can look very stylish if left unadorned – a simple edge of colour on the surrounding window frame, which echoes the furnishings of the room, is often the most effective way of highlighting their attractiveness.

CURTAIN TRACKS AND POLES

Before actually measuring a window and calculating how much fabric will be needed, it is worth having a look at the various tracks and poles which are available and which can determine the curtain heading. The positioning of these tracks is an important calculation when measuring up a window, and it will also be necessary to decide where the pelmet board, or lath, to carry these tracks or poles will be situated.

POLES – WOODEN AND METAL

Plain wooden poles look good in country or traditional settings and, for a more decorated look, they can be painted to match a particular scheme or embellished with stencilling. The pole ends are usually a simple ball shape, although elaborately turned ends are available. Brass poles suit a more formal setting and are usually more elaborately finished. For instance, the poles themselves are often reeded, and the ends shaped into finials representing urns and pineapples.

More recently nearly every magazine has photographs of decorative metalwork, everything from chairs to gazebos; some of the most interesting products, however, are the curtain poles with ends shaped into spear heads, dolphins and fantastical animals. In the right setting they look wonderful, and it is good to see more of these imaginative but useful products.

Normally curtains are visualised as being attached to the pole by means of large rings, each with an eyelet at the bottom to hold the fabric. However, poles are available which have a concealed track so that only the face of the pole is visible; this gives a cleaner line to a window treatment.

TRACKS

There are many tracks available and it is sometimes quite a problem to decide which is the right one for a particular curtain treatment. There is a straightforward, basic track which is suitable for light and mediumweight fabrics and sheers. It is flexible, so can be fitted within a recess, it is easily cut to size, and is best used under a pelmet or valance.

The next step up is a rail which has a track concealed behind it, and again, this is suitable for

A narrow window will look wider if the pole is extended beyond the window frame.

A simple wooden pole looks just right in this pretty pink bedroom

light to mediumweight fabrics. The advantage of this track is that it is unobtrusive and can be left plain or papered or painted to match the wall.

Ideal for small windows is a ceiling-mounted track which can be fitted to the underside of the window or perhaps recessed into plaster; there is even a track which combines a valance rail. So, whatever the window treatment required, there should be a suitable track. Apart from the very basic track, most have cording sets so it is easy to draw the curtains.

Plastic-coated curtain wire is still an easy way of hanging sheer and lightweight fabrics, and is a simple solution to rooflight windows where fabric is stretched between two curtain wires either to diffuse the sunlight or darken a room for sleeping purposes.

MEASURING WINDOWS

The next most important stage in a window treatment is measuring up the window and calculating the amount of material needed.

Before doing anything, take a careful look at both the window itself and the area surrounding it. Are there any awkwardly placed heating pipes or power points in the way? Is there sufficient space between the window and the wall for a curtain to hang, or should some other treatment be considered? On which side should the pull cord be placed? Is the floor uneven? (This could affect the appearance of full-length curtains.) How far should the pelmet board project?

Once all these aspects have been considered, look at the diagram opposite and take the following measurements:

1 Inside recess depth.
2 Inside recess width.
3 Outside width of window.
4 Outside depth of window.
5 Sill to floor.
6 Ceiling/coving to top of window frame.
7 Width of lath or pelmet board.

8 Drop from lath to floor (for full-length curtains).
9 Drop from lath to below sill (for sill-length curtains).
10 Depth of lath/pelmet board.

To work out the total amount of fabric needed, the following calculations should be made:
1 Take width of curtain track.
2 Multiply this by one-and-a-half, two, or even three, depending upon the curtain heading finish.
3 Add side hem allowances (and centre overlap if applicable).
4 Allow a further 3in (7.6cm) for curtain heading and 6in (15cm) for curtain hem, ie a total of 9in (22.8cm) for each fabric width.
5 Divide this figure by the width of curtain fabric to give the number of widths needed. If pattern repeats are involved, add the depth of one pattern repeat to each fabric width. This calculation may not work out to a whole number of widths, so round the figure up to the next full width.
6 Multiply the number of widths by the length of curtain to give total fabric requirements.
7 Divide this total by the number of curtains.

NB If sheers are being calculated, remember to double the heading and hem allowances.

AWKWARDLY SHAPED WINDOWS

There are other things to take into consideration when measuring and dressing windows of more complicated shape, for example a deep attic dormer, a windowlight in a roof, a bay window, or an oddly shaped window which may have some architectural merit. A bay window is one of the most common to have to deal with, and the depressing sight of sad lengths of fabric hung at each 'division' in such a window is frequently encountered. Bay windows became very popular after the abolition in Britain of the Window Tax in 1851, and the Victorians loved

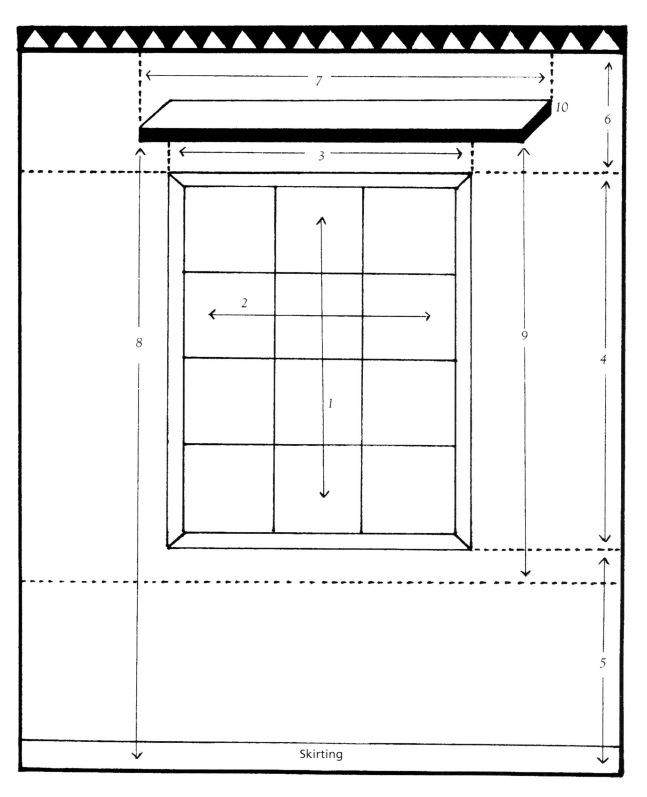

Sequence for taking measurements

Skirting

97

them. A bay window will let in more light than a flat window and will give character to a room, so do make the most of it and treat it sympathetically.

Because of their shape, bay windows do pose certain problems as tracks and poles need to fit their angles; but tracks can be bent to shape or made to measure, whilst wooden poles can be joined by connection joints and metal poles can be shaped to order.

Make the most of the light by keeping the bay clear of curtains during the day and only pulling them at night. It makes it easier to close them if a drawstick is used, which is attached to the top of the leading edge of each curtain; during the day this is hidden behind the curtain edge. For privacy, hang sheers in the bay or use Venetian blinds.

Very large bay windows can take elaborate treatments, and curtains with valances, poles swagged with fabric, or pelmets swagged and tailed will all come into their own in such a setting. Do be imaginative: don't always settle for the easiest option!

Dormer windows can be treated in several ways. It is possible to buy swivel rods which are fixed to either side of the window so that curtains can be swung out of the way during the day and pushed back at night. Café-type curtains also look good in dormer windows. Consider using two layers to create a pretty effect. Shutters, too, could be used, as they will also swing flat against the wall when not in use. Another solution is to ignore the dormer recess completely and hang curtains from a pole close to the ceiling, then hold them back with another pole fixed at the angle where the bottom wall meets the sloping ceiling.

Venetian and vertical blinds can be made to measure for all kinds of awkwardly shaped windows; and something like a Velux rooflight can have a blind sandwiched between two layers of glass.

For their full beauty to be shown off, arched windows really call for professional treatment, with curtains fitted on to a curved track to emphasise the arched shape. However, shutters are another solution; or a curtain track could be fitted about 4in (10cm) above the arch and extended beyond the

window so that, during the day, the curtains clear the window completely and leave the shape revealed.

Often windows are positioned close to a door, fireplace, wall or some other obstruction, and there is not sufficient room to complete the desired curtain effect. One solution to this problem could be to use Roman, Austrian or roller blinds, made from the same fabric as the other curtains in the room; or hang just one curtain, held back with a tie-back during the day, and released at night.

A round window can be made to look very important by using a pole positioned about 9in (22.8cm) above it and then swagging it with fabric wrapped around the pole in a seemingly casual manner; or give it a more formal appearance with swags and tails.

The main thing to remember is that there is a solution to everything – all it needs is imagination!

USEFUL TIPS FOR CURTAIN TREATMENTS

- A window will look taller if the track is positioned about 9in (22·8cm) above the frame to create extra height. The gap can be filled with a pelmet or valance to maintain the illusion.

- The height of a window can be reduced by fixing a pair of curtains together at centre top and then scooping the sides back, holding them in place with tie-backs.

- When deciding on a curtain style, remember that sill-length curtains look informal, whereas floor-length ones will look more elegant.

- Floral printed cotton curtains look pretty when held in place with a length of broderie anglaise with narrow ribbon threaded through the eyelet holes.

- A straightforward curtain heading attached to a pole can be given interest by tying contrasting bows to the curtain rings.

PROJECT PAPERS

Window treatments can make or mar the whole appearance of a room. It is better to use an economical roller blind than to have skimpy, mean-looking full-length curtains – so if economy is necessary, try not to fall into the trap of believing that a conventional window treatment is the only answer.

The following two projects are based on typical problems encountered in older houses. So often French doors were put in with no thought of either the existing window style or the proportions of the room, and the second project covers a very common situation.

PROJECT 11

Imagine a room which has a large modern French door, leading to the garden, at one end. Unfortunately the door is not set in the centre of the wall but to the left of centre, leaving very little wall space on the far left side. An additional problem is that there is a small window of sill height immediately to one side of the door. At the other end of the room, a window is placed centrally in the wall and is a classic Georgian-style sash window.

Think of a curtain scheme which would unify the different windows, and sketch how you would dress them, eg simple, gathered headings or something more elaborate. Make appropriate notes by the side of the sketch to explain your ideas.

PROJECT 12

A friend who has just moved into a flat in an Edwardian house has asked you to suggest an appropriate window treatment for her large sitting-room. The room is rectangular in shape and has three large sash windows along the wall which faces the street. These windows look directly into the flat across the road and there is a great deal of traffic noise.

Sketch two alternative window dressings for this room, and alongside them briefly explain what you are trying to achieve and why you feel the scheme would work.

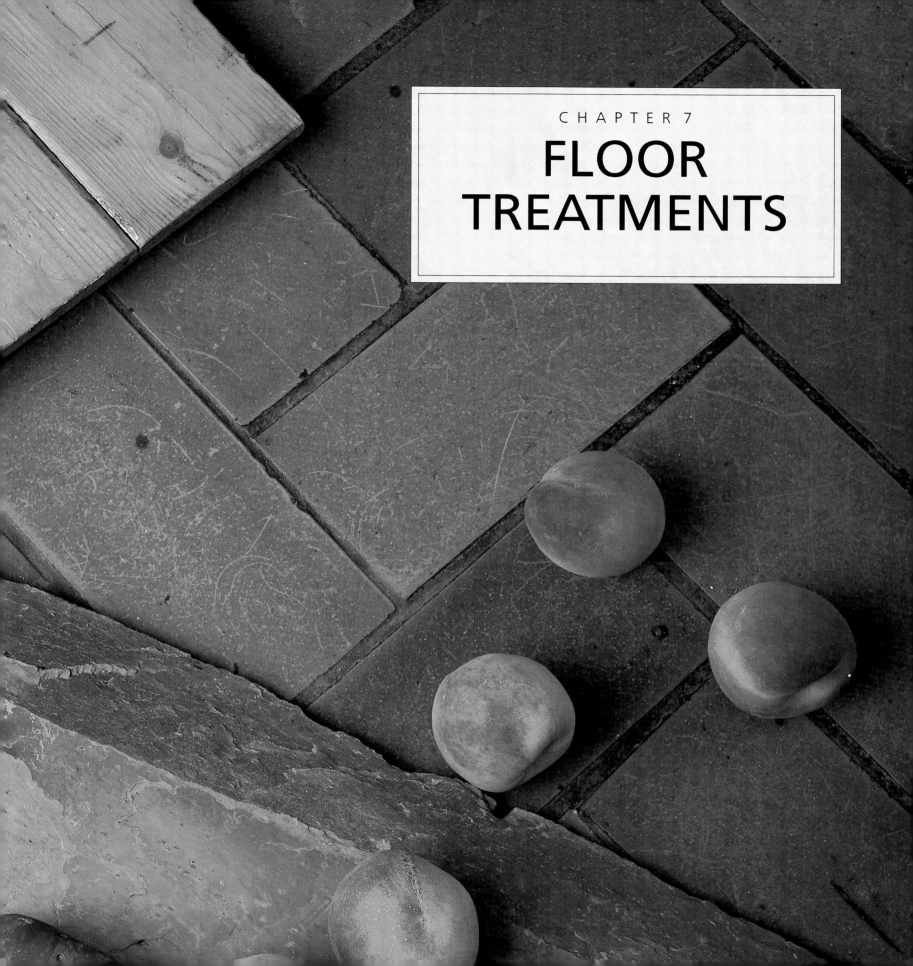

CHAPTER 7

FLOOR TREATMENTS

It is important to appreciate that the floor is, literally, the basis of any interior scheme, both aesthetically and practically. Floors take a lot of punishment, not only having to withstand the constant abrasion of feet, perhaps both human and animal, but also having to bear the weight of furniture and resist dirt and spills. Furthermore the budding interior designer will be particularly aware of the floor as a setting for furniture and personal possessions, and the choice of colour, texture and finish will have an important and dominant effect on the overall decorative scheme.

Whether the floor space is covered by carpet, tiling, vinyl flooring or by some other method, there are some facts which remain constant. First of all, plain surfaces will increase the impression of space; this also applies to small patterns and light colours. Heavily patterned surfaces and dark colours will make a room look smaller, as will bordered edges.

Before anything else it is important to look at the subfloor to make sure that it is in good condition and damp-proof; it is pointless spending money on any type of flooring if, say, a suspended timber floor is uneven, or not strong enough to support the weight of something like terrazzo or marble tiles laid on top. Solid concrete floors laid over the foundations can crumble and become uneven, and so might need to be screeded before any top finish can be applied. And do not forget that plumbing and central heating pipes run under floors, so any change in position of a radiator or a washbasin should be done before the flooring is put down.

Again, a quick check-list is a good idea, particularly if several different tradespeople will be employed to carry out alterations such as rewiring or plumbing. Ask the following questions:

1 What is the room used for – living, eating, bathing, library or music room, home office or any combination of these things?
2 Which activities take place on the floor – sitting, playing, exercise or simply lying?
3 Are there areas which will receive lots of wear?
4 Will pets shed hairs or come in with muddy paws?
5 Is there direct access to the outside?
6 How long has the flooring to last?
7 How much cleaning and maintenance will it require?
8 Has the flooring to provide sound insulation?
9 Has the flooring to suit an existing decorative scheme or should the decoration be planned around the floor?
10 Can other areas with different floor coverings be seen from the room concerned?

From the original room plan you will know the area to be covered, and by now will probably have an idea, too, of the preferred floor treatment. Let us consider what is available.

HARD FLOORS

BRICKS

Early flooring methods employed bricks which were made from a mixture of earth and clay combined with ox blood. Bricks are still used today as they give an immediate warm, rustic feel to an interior, and they are practical in ground-level rooms leading to the outside. Many shades of brick are available so it is possible to create a variety of patterns from these, one of the most traditional being the herringbone shape illustrated below.

Nowadays bricks are usually laid on a damp-proof course and set into a bed of mortar, whereas old bricks would have been laid directly on to the earth. Although bricks are porous, they do have the advantage of being non-slip and are often stain- and grease-resistant. Some can be sealed, in which case they can be simply mopped over with warm water to clean them and, easier still, a good sweep over with a brush will clean unsealed bricks.

CERAMIC TILES

The main thing to remember when using ceramic tiles as flooring is that they should actually be of flooring strength. All tiles are heavy so they must be laid on a solid floor, either concrete or reinforced suspended timber, and this subfloor must be perfectly flat or the tiles will crack when walked on.

There are three types of ceramic tile available today – matt-finished tiles, glazed tiles which are shiny and smooth, and unglazed tiles, usually in natural earth shades. There is a huge range of styles available and whatever your preference is, be it for geometrics, abstracts or flowers, it should be easy to find what you want without too much difficulty. Collect brochures and styles you like from magazines, and these will be a constant source of inspiration for particular interiors. Sizes vary from tiny mosaics to at least a foot square, and it is possible to buy hexagonal, rectangular and inter-locking shapes as well as the more usual squares.

Increasingly, tiles are being imported from abroad, particularly Europe, and many of these have a naive charm, with little figures of people working, simple flower motifs and child-like drawings of animals and birds. Do not forget, however, that domestic tile manufacturers continue to flourish and produce some really excellent designs. Just look at the photograph showing the wonderful Art Nouveau Selection, based on the designs of Charles Rennie Mackintosh (see photograph on p 104). The Victorians were particularly fond of tiled hallways and it is still possible to get reproductions of many of the original designs and colourways.

Ceramic tiles have many advantages: they stand up well to heavy wear; they are impervious to water and most chemicals; and they are cool to the feet. The disadvantages are that they can be slippery when wet, dishes will break when dropped on them, they can crack or chip if heavy objects fall from working surfaces, they are noisy, and some people find them tiring to the feet. Also, if they are used where there is a lot of glass and where temperatures are likely to fluctuate or be extreme, make sure they are frost-proof.

A modern version of the classic old herringbone pattern (see p10)

seaside cottage, and they certainly give instant ageing. However, they do have a very uneven surface and are quite difficult to keep clean – though like bricks, they can be sealed, or treated with a mixture such as linseed oil and wax which will heighten their colours, rather like pebbles in a water-filled glass jar.

COBBLES AND PEBBLES

Cobbles and pebbles make an interesting floor for something like a porch or lobby in a country or

CONCRETE

Concrete, with its rather cold and unsympathetic surface, is usually thought of as a base for other floor

Some exciting new tiles based on Charles Rennie Mackintosh designs

treatments, but it is an extremely flexible material and its appearance can be altered according to the mixture of cement, aggregate and water used in its composition. Also, wet concrete can be imprinted with all sorts of textures and patterns, and smooth, dry concrete can be given a lively treatment with special floor or boat paints; so do not dismiss it out of hand.

MARBLE

Marble is an extremely expensive flooring but it does look supremely elegant. Like slate, marble is 'metamorphic', which in this case means that it is produced from limestone crushed under natural pressure or affected by moisture or heat, sometimes a mixture of all three. The name 'marble' comes from the Latin for 'shining stone'.

Marble is an extremely hard-wearing surface which is impervious to water and, allegedly, to stains – though beware of believing this wholeheartedly. Marble has an in-built lustre, but it can also be polished after laying, and is available in many beautifully veined shades. Obviously it is a heavy material to use, so once again, the subfloor should be sound and very strong to bear its weight. For ease of laying, it is increasingly available in thin sheets, strips, square blocks and shaped forms from which many patterns can be created.

Once in place, marble is very easy to look after and clean, but it is cold to touch and rather noisy when walked on.

MOSAIC

Mosaics can be made from a variety of hard materials – ceramics, glass and marble – and the individual pieces are usually no larger than an inch with slightly irregular edges. Mosaic is an ancient floor treatment and unique and wonderful designs can be created by the tiny pieces in a myriad of colours. There are still craftsmen who specialise in mosaic work and who will create individual designs, either on site or in a workshop first. It is also possible to buy sheets of mosaics with peel-off backings to make laying them easier, but this does limit the design possibilities.

Mosaic floors tend to be rather rough to walk on and need to be laid on an absolutely flat subfloor, usually of concrete or a specially treated latex. They are easy to clean and are very hard-wearing and cool but, like most hard floors, they can be noisy and rather hard on the feet.

QUARRY TILES

Quarry tiles are traditionally associated with country houses and come in a variety of colours ranging from buffs to browns and from reds to purply-blue. Like bricks, they are made from unrefined clay and can be used both inside and outside as they are resistant to frost.

Quarries are an attractive but basic flooring and are usually square or rectangular in shape. They have all the characteristics of ceramic tiles, standing up to heavy wear extremely well and being impervious to water, but they are a little softer to the feet than ceramics and look best when treated in a straightforward and unsophisticated manner. They are easy to maintain but, like some of the other hard floors, they can be cold and noisy, and things dropped upon them will break.

SLATE

Although rather brittle and heavy to handle, slate is a beautiful floor finish with its slightly uneven surface and its range of colours from light and dark greys to bluey-greys and greeny-greys to purples and reds. It is immensely heavy so needs a strong subfloor and should be professionally laid but, once down, it does look surprisingly elegant and can be treated with a mixture of linseed oil and turpentine to add a lustre and bring up its colour (see photograph on p106).

Slate is also extremely hard-wearing, is easy to maintain and impervious to water, but it can feel rather cold unless dressed with rugs. Rugs in fact look particularly well on slate floors, adding a feeling of richness to this natural material.

Avoid using soap when washing slate floors because it can form an unattractive scum which will be difficult to remove.

Slate has been used as flooring in this unusual and effective bathroom

STONE

A stone floor actually takes some living up to and is not used all that often nowadays. It seems to have a medieval, even ecclesiastical feeling – just think of churches and cathedrals – and is a perfect flooring for the kitchens, halls, corridors and basements of old houses where it seems to settle down happily and come into its own.

Stones come in many different varieties, including granite, limestone, sandstone and York stone, and these too vary in texture and colour. For best effect, stone should be treated in a simple manner and it is usual to cut it into square or oblong shapes of varying dimensions. Sometimes a small diamond of a differently coloured stone or slate is inserted at the junction of the squares to add variety and create interest in large areas, and many other embellishments are possible.

TERRAZZO

Terrazzo is usually made from marble chippings and dust set into cement, and it takes its colour from whichever marble has been used. It can also be made from marble chippings set into a resin and this produces a slightly more flexible material which is softer to walk on than the cement-based variety.

Terrazzo is a very smooth and rather elegant surface, often used for hotel lobbies and reception areas. It also looks well in hallways, kitchens and bathrooms and, as it is so strong, the slabs can be very thin and laid onto most smooth surfaces without much difficulty; resin-based terrazzos can even be laid onto suspended floors providing they are strong enough. In appearance terrazzo looks mottled, rather than veined like real marble, and is available in quite a large range of colours. Upkeep is easy, just a sweep and a mop over with a damp cloth.

Cork makes an ideal flooring in Rupert's room, which has been decorated in gay primary colours

SEMI-HARD FLOORS

Hard floors have many advantages – ease of cleaning, durability and attractive appearance – but they can be too cool for some people, they are rather noisy and unyielding, and they can be tiring to the feet. If these disadvantages outweigh the advantages of hard flooring, it is worth considering the range of softer alternatives.

CORK

Cork is an extremely versatile and surprisingly hard-wearing flooring. It is warm, comfortable, quiet underfoot and has good insulating properties. It is made from natural cork, mixed with binders, and then baked. Its natural colourings range from light honey to a dark brown but it is possible to buy coloured corks now and also a pastel white shade

which can look very effective in the right setting. When using cork as a flooring it is important to choose the correct grade (not wall tiles). Some flooring grades have been finished with an impervious vinyl surface and so are ideal for areas where spills may be expected such as the kitchen and the bathroom.

Cork is usually slip-resistant, even when wet, and has good resistance to abrasiveness and friction. It is easy to lay, even by amateurs, and once it has been sealed is simple to maintain.

LINOLEUM

Linoleum has come a long way from the rather nasty, brittle and shiny flooring of the 1940s and is now something to be taken seriously. The word linoleum comes from the Roman words *linum* meaning flax, and *oleum* meaning oil, and even

ABOVE: *Here vinyl imitates wooden strips which have been given a paint wash. The effect is continued up the staircase*

ABOVE RIGHT: *Vinyl again, used here to great effect on a conservatory floor*

RIGHT: *The same design as that shown in the photograph above left, this time incorporating a marquetry border*

FAR RIGHT: *This mosaic inset marble floor is actually vinyl*

today, natural materials and oil are used in its composition. The usual ingredients include wood flour, cork, linseed oil and various resins which are baked together slowly at a high temperature and then rolled under heat before being pressured onto a strong backing such as canvas, hessian or jute. This 'recipe' produces a very strong and flexible flooring which is immensely hard-wearing and fairly quiet underfoot, and which also has a nice bounce to it.

Linoleum is available in sheet or tile form, and is increasingly being used to create individual floor designs. Borders, motifs and patterns can be cut and shaped fairly easily and put together in the most interesting way. However, unless you are a designer – and have a strong wrist for cutting – this treatment is best left to the professional.

Two points to bear in mind with linoleum: it is very slippery when wet; and if heavy furniture is to be placed on it, protective cups should be used under the legs to prevent ugly indentations forming. Maintenance is easy; a sweep and a wash with weak detergent will suffice, but a light coat of polish can produce a pleasing sheen.

VINYL

Vinyl flooring is one of the most versatile floorings on the market, available in a huge range of colours, thicknesses, textures and patterns. Gone are the days when it used to be rather brittle and cracked easily: now it is possible to buy cushioned varieties which are comfortable and warm to walk upon and have a nice spring to them.

Vinyl is available in sheet or tile form and can be laid over almost any surface without a problem. It is waterproof and resistant to oil and most domestic cleaning compounds, but it will mark and burn if something hot, such as an oven rack or saucepan, is placed on it. It is not too keen on stiletto heels, either! Very sophisticated vinyls can now be bought which mimic wood, quarry tiles and marble, and it is often difficult to tell the difference – just look at the photographs opposite.

Although most vinyl is easy to cut, it does help if you allow it to settle and acclimatise to the room temperature before cutting it; and most professionals would cut it slightly larger than the surface area and then trim it to fit, as it does shrink slightly when laid down. This amenable flooring is easy to maintain by sweeping and then mopping with a weak detergent solution, and should give good service for several years.

RUBBER

Rubber is not perhaps a material that immediately springs to mind when considering a floor surface, but it is becoming increasingly popular for domestic use and both natural and synthetic rubber are available.

Both these rubbers can be hardened by a vulcanising treatment and provide very tough, resilient floorings which have a warm feel. Rubber stands a good deal of abrasive wear, even stilettos, and it is non-slip. It is available in a good variety of single colours, or with a marbled effect, and can be pressed into various relief patterns which look extremely smart and high-tech.

Rubber needs to be laid on a smooth screed or subfloor which ideally should have a built-in vapour barrier, as condensation can cause deterioration. For a really smooth finish, rubber seams can be welded together, best done by a professional.

Again, maintenance is easy; wash with warm water and mild detergent and make sure that dirt does not build up around relief patterns.

WOODEN FLOORS

Some of the materials used to create smooth and even subfloors can themselves provide perfectly good and attractive floorings, and may be the answer in many situations.

HARDBOARD

This is made from a compressed softwood pulp; it is shiny on one side, rough on the other and can only

Create a 'rug' by cutting vinyl into decorative patterns which can then be stuck down and edged with a plain border.

109

Polished floorboards set off a beautiful piece of furniture in this unusual setting

be found in shades of brown. It is not particularly durable but it can be a short-term answer, being easy to lay and giving a smooth surface. Once in place, with the shiny side uppermost, hardboard can be stained or painted before being sealed and this could be a wonderful opportunity to try out some paint techniques such as marbling, sponging and stencilling – they can always be covered with a rug if not a success.

Hardboard hates water, so never use too much when cleaning it, and dry immediately – any stain will be permanent.

CHIPBOARD

Chipboard is thicker than hardboard. It is made from wood chips and resins bonded under pressure, and this gives it an appearance very similar to cork.

It is more durable than hardboard, is warm and resilient, and has good insulation properties, so is often used instead of conventional floorboards in new houses.

Available in both sheet and tongue-and-grooved form, it can provide a most attractive flooring but is even more prone to staining than hardboard, so should be treated with a seal before even starting the task of laying it. If allowed to get wet it will be considerably weakened and should not then be used.

Like hardboard, chipboard can be either stained or painted to fit in with the overall scheme, but it looks particularly attractive if given several coats of tung oil which will slightly darken it and give a warm finish with a slight gleam. Maintenance is easy and the flooring should last some considerable time.

PLYWOOD

In proportion to its size and weight, plywood has considerable strength and this is why it is often used in certain situations instead of solid wood. It also has a very stable composition which means that it is not affected – as solid wood can be – by changes in heat or moisture.

Plywood is made by bonding several layers together and is usually available in 3, 5 or 7 ply. Sometimes special 'cores' are included in the layers to meet specific requirements such as fire or insulation regulations. For domestic use a plywood with a foam rubber core can be extremely useful as a method of deadening sound and is particularly suitable in flats, semi-detached houses and rooms where noise could cause problems.

As with all manufactured wood finishes, it needs to be sealed properly after treating with a stain or paint, and then it can be maintained in exactly the same way as hardboard and chipboard.

FLOORBOARDS

Nothing looks nicer than smooth, softly gleaming floorboards, and they can provide a wonderful background to beautiful rugs and furniture. They are suitable everywhere – from kitchen to sitting-room – and are almost indestructible. Wood is a living thing and more than repays any attention it receives.

With new wood the choice is vast, ranging from soft golden pine to sturdy oak, and a good timber yard will be able to advise which is the best for a particular location. The boards come in many widths and it is also possible to buy short strips, 'tiles' and hardwood parquet to create all kinds of patterns. One way to create a feeling of space in a room is to lay floorboards diagonally instead of vertically, and this unexpected treatment of a conventional material can add great interest to a room.

Wood is a very durable and resilient material which seems to improve with age; however, central heating can cause the boards to shrink and twist, so some humidity should be maintained. Nor do floorboards like water, so spills should be mopped up immediately.

Floorboards are usually fixed directly onto the joists – do make sure that water pipes and electric cables are properly located – but wood block, wood strip and parquet flooring should be laid on a level timber base such as ply, chipboard or hardboard.

Although expensive, new floorboards are pretty straightforward to fit. But what about old floorboards? It is easy to get carried away with the possibilities of stripping and sanding but the boards must be in a decent condition to start with, and it may take a great deal of hard and messy manual work, as well as a great many hours, to get even near a decent finish. Old floorboards may also have gaps between them which will cause draughts from the ground floor, and although it is possible to fill these with a special material, this often does not take a stain or seal to the same degree as the wood, and can look very strange. A professional would meticulously fill the gaps with old or damaged floorboards – a time-consuming job, but worthwhile if the boards are good. If you decide to go ahead with sanding, it is important to remember that the sander should always be used along the length of the boards, never across; and when finished, use a tack rag to clean up all traces of dust before giving the boards a final wipe over with white spirit.

The boards are now ready for bleaching, staining or painting, and to take other creative effects. For instance, they could be washed over with a weak solution of emulsion or flat paint to produce a 'limed' effect; or painted in chequer-board design by careful masking and using two colours. Carpets, rugs and borders can be created with stencils or, using the boards as guidelines, a striped effect can be achieved. Perhaps a natural finish is preferred; repeated polishing with an old-fashioned mixture of linseed oil and beeswax, or with several coats of tung oil, can look very rich. A wax applied on top of a painted finish will give an impression of age which will mellow with the years.

Floorboards are maintained by sweeping or vacuuming, followed by a light wash or deep polish.

SOFT FLOORS

This is the generic term for all forms of carpeting and rugs.

COIR AND SISAL

RIGHT: *A chunky-weave, heavyweight sisal flooring, ideal in a simple setting*

BELOW RIGHT: *A selection of sisal and coir floorings, demonstrating the possibilities*

Coir is the rather thick and rough fibre which protects the inner 'nut' of the coconut from the outside casing, and it has been used for years as a cheap floor covering. Although still relatively cheap, extremely tough and hard-wearing, it has now taken on a more sophisticated appearance, sometimes being combined with sisal or other natural materials which may have been dyed in interesting shades which contrast well with the golden colour of the coir. One problem with the old coir matting was that dust would penetrate the fibres and it was difficult to keep clean. Nowadays, however, coir is often backed with latex or vinyl, which makes cleaning more easy and adds durability. Many attractive designs are available, and some of these are shown in the photographs.

Although it has a rather attractive, rustic appearance which suits many houses, it is undoubtedly rather uncomfortable to bare feet; it needs to be fitted tightly, too, or it may produce 'waves' which not only look untidy but can also be dangerous. It is produced in rolls, and lengths can be stitched together to form a wall-to-wall covering.

The best method of cleaning it is to use a vacuum, and any marks can be scrubbed away with a detergent, but do not make it too wet.

MAIZE, RUSH AND SEAGRASS

All these are natural materials which produce wonderful floor coverings, not as robust as sisal but more comfortable and very attractive to look at. Maize is the finest fibre and is a lovely creamy colour. It is often woven into circles and squares and then stitched together into mats and carpets.

Rush and seagrass are much tougher, but still smoother to the touch than coir, and they are woven into complex plaits and herringbones which

the denseness of the pile, and its resilience by pressing your hand onto the surface to see how quickly it springs back into shape – the faster it does this, the better it is. Shag piles and long, looped piles may look thick and bulky, but for durability, a carpet with a short, dense pile is better. A reputable carpet manufacturer will always label his products with their fibre content, how many stitches per inch they contain, and what kind of backing material has been used. He will also list the available widths, the type of traffic it is intended for, and how it should be laid to give best results. Carpets are made in light, medium and heavy weights – for long wear, an 80/20 mixture of wool and a synthetic fibre is probably the best. Carpets made from totally synthetic fibres used to look terrible, but things have improved dramatically in recent years and some are now very acceptable substitutes for the real thing. One of the problems used to be the build-up of static, but these synthetics can now be made with static-repellent fibres. Another point in their favour is that there is a continuity of colour which can sometimes be difficult to achieve with large areas of wool carpet.

There are also carpets with a special border to fit around the contours of a room and give it a tailor-made appearance – at one time only contractors or professional interior designers could order these; though now anyone can buy this sort of service, and there are quite a few specialist carpet suppliers who will be happy to make up special designs to match a curtain fabric or a particular paint colour. A sample board of a special design is usually produced in about 6—8 weeks, which is really not that long to wait for something totally unique.

As with wallpapers, paint colours and curtain fabrics, it is worth buying just a metre of the carpet chosen to see how it looks in natural and artificial lighting, and also to judge how the light is reflected off the tufts, as this may affect how it is laid. Patterned carpets are undoubtedly easier to maintain, but in a small apartment a plain shade used throughout will increase the feeling of space.

Ideally, carpets should be laid by a professional who has served a proper apprenticeship; if doubts

LEFT: A fitted seagrass floor covering looks good in this kitchen

look marvellous, particularly in old buildings where they complement stone perfectly.

These natural fibres may suffer from being in too dry an atmosphere, and an occasional light misting of water sprayed on will restore and maintain their good looks.

CARPET

Carpets almost deserve a whole section to themselves. The choices and types are many, and the terms used are not always obvious to the layman. There is a feeling of comfort about a carpet, and it is not always necessary to use the most expensive to create the right setting for furniture and possessions. For instance, bedrooms do not have anywhere near the amount of traffic that a hallway has to contend with, so a non-wool fibre, or a fibre/wool mix could be used instead of 100 per cent wool.

A carpet's durability can be assessed by looking at

arise as to the fitter's ability it would be wise to get a reference before allowing him to touch any carpet. A professional fitter will be happy to give an itemised estimate, separating the costs of the carpet and the underfelt, and he will also discuss where the seams should fall so that they avoid the areas of heavy wear and do not appear too obvious. A good carpet fitter also knows that any woven carpet will stretch, and he will usually be happy to return, free of charge, to restretch it after about six weeks.

Unless the carpet is foam-backed, an underlay is essential – and never be tempted to lay a new carpet on an old underfelt or old carpet as the previous areas of wear will soon show through to the new surface. There are various underlays available: the kind made from animal fibre is very resilient and should be used with seamed carpets; whilst the latex and plastic foam underlays should be laid over a strong paper first to stop them sticking to the floor. Remember that a carpet is only as good as the floor beneath it.

With the exception of loop pile, all new carpets tend to 'fluff' because of the short fibres left in the pile when the yarn was cut, so for the first few weeks do not use a vacuum cleaner but brush lightly with a handbrush instead.

There is a wide range of carpet types available.

Axminster: The name derives from the loom on which it is woven, and one way to judge whether a carpet is an Axminster or a Wilton is to see how it can be rolled. An Axminster can be rolled lengthwise but not crosswise, as the loom on which it is made inserts the pile tufts into the weave from above and a shuttle does not run backwards and forwards. This method means that many colours can be used and Axminster carpets are therefore usually patterned. Axminster carpet is available in widths ranging from 27in to broadloom and has about forty-nine tufts per square inch. The fibres used to produce an Axminster carpet can be pure wool, a wool and fibre mix, or entirely synthetic, and in appearance the surface can be cut pile, shaggy or contoured so these combinations produce an enormously wide selection from which to choose.

Wilton: Like Axminster, Wilton derives its name from the loom on which it is woven, and because the loom weaves the yarn in a continuous strand, it means that only a limited number of colours can be used; Wilton carpets therefore tend to be one-coloured.

The pile is close-textured, with between seventy-seven and eighty-two tufts per square inch. This produces a smooth, velvety finish although Wilton too can be given a sculptured effect by using a combination of pile textures such as loops and twists. Yarn not used on the surface is woven into the backing, and a characteristic of a Wilton carpet is the chain warp visible as a straight line in the heavily ribbed backing.

Traditionally, Wilton was always made in 27in (68cm) or 36in (85cm) widths which were stitched together when fitting, but it is now possible to buy Wilton carpet in 6ft (1.8m) and 12ft (3.6m) widths. Like Axminster, Wilton carpet can be made in pure wool, a wool and fibre mix, or entirely synthetic fibres, and both types can have backings made from burlap or jute, sometimes strengthened by polypropylene.

Brussels: When the Wilton pile is left uncut it is called a Brussels carpet and it can be a very hard-wearing finish compared with a cut pile. However, although it is more durable, it does lack the velvety appearance and sheen of cut pile which many people prefer.

Tufted carpets: Axminster and Wilton carpets are produced by very labour-intensive processes and are consequently expensive. Tufted carpets are much quicker to produce – about 3 yards (2.7m) a minute – and this is where the volume market lies. These carpets are made by inserting tufts into a pre-woven backing, and they are anchored by a latex or polyvinyl compound which forms a coating on the reverse side. The yarns used are the same as for the more expensive carpets and the pile can be cut, looped or twisted.

Tufted carpets are available in widths varying from 3ft (0.9m) to about 16ft (4.8m) and there is an

This colour scheme has been based around the colours in the rug, which gives life to the plain background carpeting

extremely wide variety of colours and textures from which to choose.

Bonded carpets: Bonded carpets are made by an entirely different method from those previously described and can range from the super-cheap to the superlative. The carpet pile is held, rather like a sandwich, between two specially treated adhesive bases and is then sliced through the middle to create two carpets. This means that all the pile is on the surface; but it can nevertheless be extremely hard-wearing, depending upon the fibre chosen.

Cord carpet: This is a woven carpet made from a mixture of yarns containing some cow, calf or goat hair and it looks rather like corduroy. It is extremely hard-wearing, but can feel harsh. It is available in a very wide range of single colours and is a good, reasonably priced background covering for large areas which can be given life by the use of rugs.

These are the usual types of carpet which are readily available but, if money is no object, then Aubusson, Oriental, Savonneries, Persian and Turkish carpets can be seriously considered. They are an investment which will give pleasure for countless years and, in their very different ways, all are beautiful. One needs to take expert advice, however, before going ahead with such a purchase.

RUGS

At their most basic, rugs provide decoration for the floor, breaking up large areas of plain floorboards or carpets, providing focal points or defining particular areas in large rooms and generally creating a feeling of warmth and caring. The variety available is bewildering and they are an even more complicated subject to cover than carpets, so it is only possible here to give the briefest descriptions of some of the main types which are available today.

Afghan kelim: These are thickly woven in wool and are hard-wearing. Made in two distinct regions, Baluchistan and north-west Afghanistan, they are usually made in rust, brown, blue and ochre shades and have less pattern than a Kurdish kilim.

Berber: Not to be confused with Berber carpet which is now a general term for nubbly, flecked carpets, these rugs are woven by Berber tribes in the Atlas mountains of Morocco and are easily recognisable by their distinctive colours – blue, green, scarlet and yellow – which are made from vegetable dyes. They exude a great vitality, both in texture and pattern.

Chinese: These distinctive rugs are very rich and thick. The traditional Chinese designs are usually woven in very soft pastel shades of pink, peach, jade, apricot, yellow and blue, but are now being seen with dark blue and black backgrounds.

Dhurry: This is a traditional flatweave rug made entirely in cotton in India, which has recently become enormously popular. Mostly available in delicious and subtle pastel shades, they are relatively inexpensive but the colours can sometimes bleed so a cotton interlining is advisable when used on top of an expensive plain carpet.

Flokati: Made in Greece from goat hides, these shaggy-pile rugs are usually in white or cream and are available in many sizes. They are also reasonably priced and add texture to any otherwise plain room.

Kurdish kilim: These rugs are woven in wool by nomadic tribes and are softer than the Afghan kelims. The colours, too, are brighter and the pattern more intense, sometimes being further embellished by embroidery.

Numdah: These are mostly of Indian origin and are very pretty in a naive way. They are colourful and cheap but will not stand up to heavy wear.

Persian: These are very beautiful rugs made of silk or wool which has been knotted by hand on to a firmly woven base. Richly coloured in reds and blues with stylised motifs they are considered to be some of the finest examples of rug-making. The high density of knots per inch makes them unique, and antique examples are much sought after.

Turkish: Turkish rugs often have a pointed prayer arch at one end, flanked by the two pillars of wisdom, but each region has its own distinctive design and they make beautiful floor coverings.

USEFUL TIPS FOR FLOOR TREATMENTS

- For safety, do not polish under rugs.

- Instead of using a fully fitted carpet on a traditional staircase, use a carpet stair-runner instead and fix it in place with traditional brass stair-rods.

- Always buy an extra 12–15in (30–38cm) of stair carpet so that the length can be moved up and down periodically to give an equal amount of wear.

- Give carpet joins in doorways a more decorative finish by using attractive brass or wooden strips. It is now possible to buy strips of wood with an inlay design, and this attention to detail adds a great deal to the final appearance of the carpet.

- Stripped floorboards can be stained in various colours to co-ordinate with a colour scheme. Some of the new woodstains combine varnish and colour so the usual two stages can now be cut down to one.

This has been a long subject to cover and in many cases it has only been possible to scratch the surface of all the types of floor coverings which are available today. However, you should have learned a little about each type and will probably look at all flooring with a different eye in the future.

A rug can be secured to a hard floor with mesh backing or nylon bonding strips. These will prevent the rug from slipping and 'walking'.

PROJECT PAPERS

The wide variety of today's flooring is quite astonishing and it should be possible to find something suitable for every pocket and every setting from the large range available. Gloriously patterned carpets and rugs almost furnish a room by themselves, whereas plain floorings – whilst sometimes seeming to be rather bland in themselves – do provide a wonderful foil to special furniture or accessories.

The following two projects should not only heighten your awareness of just how many floor treatments are possible, but will also make attractive additions to your growing portfolio of work.

PROJECT 13

From manufacturers' leaflets and magazines, select photographs showing:

- An example of hard flooring
- An example of semi-hard flooring
- An example of wooden flooring
- An example of a carpet with a border
- An example of the use of rugs

Attach each to an A4 sheet of paper and beside them note why you feel they work well in their particular setting. Taking each setting as a base, suggest an alternative treatment.

PROJECT 14

Imagine a large room in a warehouse development which is basically rectangular in shape but has a raised platform at one end. Your brief is to incorporate sitting, sleeping, bathing, eating and simple cooking areas into this space. Make a simple sketch of your design and alongside it explain your reasoning for the design, paying particular attention to the floor treatments for each area.

It is rare to find a house totally decorated in a certain style, be it modern or period. Most people have quite a wide selection of furniture. Some may have been inherited, some probably dates from student days, some was probably bought when price was the deciding factor rather than a particular style, and some will no longer appeal because of changes in taste but will be too good to be thrown out. There are many ways of dealing with disparate pieces of furniture to create an impression of harmony and 'whole' and these will be discussed later. First, however, it may be useful to look at the way in which furniture has evolved, concentrating on the essential pieces such as tables and chairs, sideboards or dressers, chests of drawers, easy chairs and sofas.

FURNITURE STYLES

Terms like Jacobean, Early Victorian, Late Victorian, Edwardian and Regency are always being used when talking about furniture styles, but not everyone knows exactly when these periods were and which materials were mostly used. The following outline should help.

An Elizabethan Glastonbury chair

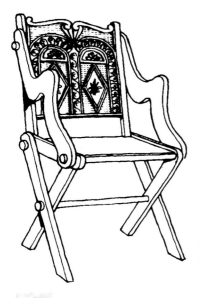

1500

English furniture styles are generally acknowledged to date from about this time: dressers were starting to appear and gate-leg tables were in general use; both would have been cared for with beeswax or linseed oil. In the living areas of wealthy houses benches were being replaced by joined chairs, and beds with a solid headboard and two pillars at the foot were in use. These designs were known as tester beds.

The material used for furniture was oak. In Britain in 1544 Henry VIII introduced an Act of Parliament limiting the number of oak trees to only twelve per acre to allow for growing space – this proved to be a wise precaution in view of the amount of oak needed for the building of galleons, particularly in the forthcoming battles with Spain.

1558–1603

This period was the Elizabethan age: refectory dining tables were introduced, dressers without backs became side tables for general use, and wooden handles were being replaced by metal ones as methods for making brass were introduced from Germany. Another development was the so-called Glastonbury chair which had a folding frame and was mostly used in churches (see illustration).

Farthingale chairs appeared, their wide seats designed for ladies wearing the fashionable farthingale dresses; they were probably the first chairs to be upholstered.

Court cupboards for storing and displaying drinking vessels were introduced, and splay-fronted cupboards were evolving. Chests of many kinds were being carved with the newly fashionable linenfold design.

1603–25

These years saw the reign of James I and were known as the Jacobean age. Oak would still have been the main source of material for furniture, but hinges, handles and locks, previously made by blacksmiths, became more refined as locksmithing became a trade in its own right. Intricately carved and inlaid designs were used on chairs known as 'wainscot' chairs. These were lighter versions of the early joined chair and the name is actually a Dutch one meaning quartered oak, from which the chairs were made.

The process known as 'japanning' was first recorded in England in 1610, and the first English glass factory was founded in Vauxhall in 1615.

1625–49

The reign of Charles I was known as the Carolean period. Walnut was being increasingly used for furniture, although oak was still the firm favourite. However, furniture development was pretty static during this period – perhaps one of the most interesting things to happen was that the London

Court of Aldermen ruled that only joiners could make tenon and dovetail joints, carve or make panelling; carpenters were henceforth only allowed to undertake boarded and nailed work.

1649–60

The Commonwealth or Cromwellian period in the mid-seventeenth century was a time of great austerity – the furniture was sturdy and very plain as the Puritans regarded anything excessively decorated as idolatrous in the extreme; the custom of painting furniture was replaced by simple polishing. However, during this period chests of drawers came into being, and chairs started to be made with recessed seats to take cushions.

1660–89

These years under Charles II and James II became known as the Restoration period, and there was a great explosion of highly decorated and carved furniture. New techniques were introduced and woods other than oak and walnut were used.

Grinling Gibbons was just becoming known as a most gifted wood-carver, and he had a great influence on the designs which fellow wood-carvers used.

Cane was being imported from Malaya and was often used to make the back and seat panels in richly carved armchairs; these nearly always had a royal emblem incorporated into the carving in celebration of the new reign.

New techniques included marquetry, veneering, inlay and varnishing; and pegged mortise and tenon joints were being abandoned as glue and gluing techniques improved.

During this richly creative period the first designs for wardrobes, day beds, dressing tables, settles, tallboys, bookcases and secretaires appeared; and another development was that the Duke of Buckingham was given the sole right to manufacture mirror glass. The first spoon-back chairs were seen; and upholstered armchairs made in walnut, as well as wing chairs became very fashionable – for the first time pieces like these were further embellished with fringes and braids.

1689–94

The William and Mary period was very short, but it was rich in innovation: the first castors, glass in cupboards and bookcases, small tables especially

LEFT TO RIGHT: *A Cromwellian chair, reflecting Puritan ideals of simplicity; a functional gate-leg table of the Commonwealth period; a heavily carved walnut chair of the Restoration period – note the royal crown*

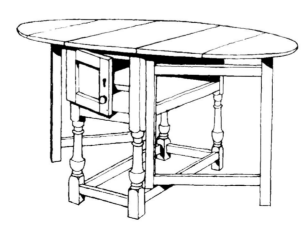

made for cards and gaming purposes, and settees designed to resemble chairs joined together, with a divided instead of a solid back.

1694–1702

During the reign of William III, decorative effects such as marquetry and japanning were increasingly fashionable. The first chairs with cabriole legs, often with hoof or pad feet, appeared; drop-in chair seats were introduced; and at about the same time, handles fitted with a solid backplate were first seen.

1702–14

The Queen Anne period saw the development of the first fiddleback chairs and kneehole writing tables. It was also notable for an extremely severe winter in 1709, which meant that walnut was in very short supply for exports.

The Baroque style was at its height, introduced to England first by the Dutch and then the French Huguenots, and famous craftsmen such as William Kent, Grinling Gibbons and Daniel Marot were much influenced by it. Its chief design characteristics were swags, festoons, cherubs, human masks, shells and musical instruments, and these appeared on many pieces of furniture and remained popular until about 1740.

During this time the first 'Knole' sofa from France arrived, and love seats, too, became popular. However, this whole period is perhaps best remembered for the one piece of furniture styling which everyone can recognise – Queen Anne cabriole legs.

1714–1812

This period spans the reigns of George I, George II and George III; furniture made up to 1727 is known as Early Georgian, that made from 1727 to 1760 is Georgian, and that from 1760 to 1812 is known as Late Georgian. The general term 'Georgian' therefore covers nearly a hundred years, and a lot happened to furniture styles during this time. Famous craftsmen such as Thomas Chippendale senior, Robert Adam, George Hepplewhite and Thomas Sheraton were very influential, and all left an indelible mark on the period.

The Early Georgian period saw the introduction of many new designs: folding and hinged card tables as an alternative to the previous design which had a swinging leg hinged at the back; 'loo' and console tables; and the first nests of tables. Chairs began to

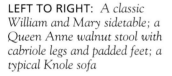

LEFT TO RIGHT: *A classic William and Mary sidetable; a Queen Anne walnut stool with cabriole legs and padded feet; a typical Knole sofa*

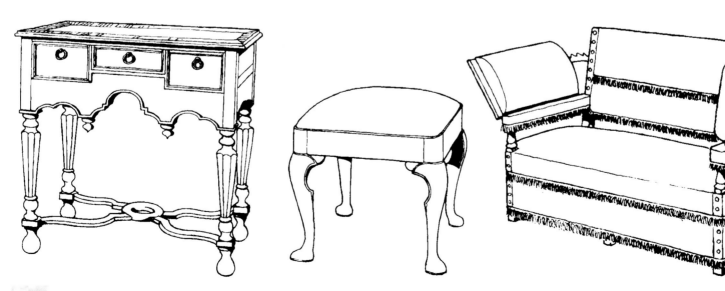

proliferate, and ladderback, library, reading, writing and Windsor chairs became fashionable. Cabriole legs were still very popular, and began to be decorated with acanthus leaves and with claw and ball, eagle's claw or lion's paw feet. Import duties on wood from the colonies were abolished, and this meant that American black walnut replaced the banned French imports, whilst mahogany was imported from Spain and Cuba. It was during this time, too, that American pine was imported and became an important source of timber.

The Georgian period was also rich in new ideas and styles: the very pretty Bergère chairs appeared from France, and corner chairs also became fashionable; bow backs were introduced on Windsor chairs and Gothic Windsor chairs were also popular. In fact so many new designs were introduced during this period that it is simply not possible to list them all here; however, chairs apart, some of the more noteworthy innovations were: card tables with square corners or triangular tops, architects' and artists' tables, tables decorated with piecrust tops, the first Pembroke tables, and the first drum, or rent, tables. Furniture such as commodes, sideboards with cupboards, breakfronted presses and bookcases and free-standing corner cupboards were all in use, and serpentine shapes in both cabinets and seating became very popular. Styles varied from French Rococo to Chippendale's Chinese and Gothic designs; and imported wood such as satinwood further increased the design possibilities. It was a very exciting and rich period indeed.

The late Georgian period saw the reintroduction of painted furniture, and it was to remain in vogue for many years. Sofa tables, pedestal tables, wine tables, chaises-longues, ottomans, chiffoniers, roll-top and cylinder bureaux, and bow-fronted chests of drawers were introduced, and the first buttoned upholstery was seen.

1812–30

The years 1812–20 were known as Regency, and 1820–30 as Late Regency; during this relatively short period the designs of the Georgian era were refined, and furniture became more delicate in appearance. The exhibition of the Elgin Marbles also increased interest in classical Greek ornamentation. Regency furniture was characterised by the use of such woods as amboyna, calamander, rosewood and zebra, many of which had exotic figurings and so were ideal for the

Chairs designed by the master craftsmen. **LEFT TO RIGHT:** *Chippendale; Sheraton; Hepplewhite*

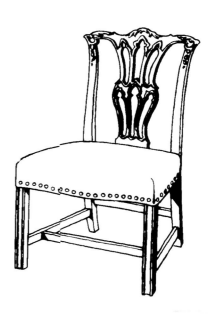

furniture with straight lines, unbroken surfaces and low height which the period demanded. Brass and other metal adornments such as lion masks, lyres and neo-classical motifs were used with these exotic woods, and the Battle of the Nile had made Egyptian motifs such as lotus patterns and sphinxes very modish. The sabre leg made its appearance; and it became much more desirable to use French polish with its high, durable gloss than to undertake the hard work involved in waxing furniture. Some very beautiful furniture was produced during this period. Finally, on a more mundane note, the first coiled upholstery springs were patented, both for general upholstery and mattresses.

1830–7

The William IV period was even shorter than the Regency period, and so furniture made during that time is rather rare and therefore much sought after by collectors. Stylistically the Regency period spread beyond 1837, so to find a genuine William IV is quite an achievement.

1837–1901

This was the reign of Queen Victoria; furniture made between 1837 and 1860 is known as Early Victorian, and that between 1860 and 1901 as Late Victorian. Woods such as mahogany, rosewood, walnut and oak were all popular, and whilst there did not seem to be much need for further furniture development the Victorians made a determined search through history to see what it had to offer. This resulted in some horrendous 'grafts' being made on to contemporary designs and much of the furniture shown at the Great Exhibition of 1851 actually had its roots in the Elizabethan or Gothic designs of the past. This was particularly true of one Exhibition exhibitor, known as the Warwick School of Carving – its version of Tudor-style carving was vulgarly over-ornate in the extreme. To the Victorians dark wood meant antiquity and they would smoke oak in ammonia to darken it artificially and achieve the effect they required.

A fashionable late Georgian Egyptian-style stool with an X frame

However, it would be wrong to think that every piece of Victorian furniture was dark and over-ornate; in fact, furniture made from papier maché was also first shown at the Great Exhibition, and this was very pretty, with a light-hearted appearance that still appeals today. Another successful exhibit was some elegant small chairs and rocking chairs made from bentwood. The process of saturating some woods with steam to make them pliable so that they could be bent into shape had been known for years, but it took a German called Michael Thonet to perfect the process and, after the chairs' success at the Exhibition, they were widely imitated and remain popular today.

The Victorians began to manufacture iron hallstands and garden furniture and soon moved on to produce a cast-iron bed; it was cheap and functional and ousted the wooden bed. As the years went by, the cast iron was replaced by brass which was twisted into intricately shaped bedsteads.

One of the most useful, and enduring, of all Victorian designs was the balloon-back chair. Its gentle curves were very comfortable, particularly for ladies in crinolines, and it became the standard drawing-room and dining-room chair for many years. Another popular introduction was the prie-dieu, which had its roots in the Restoration period, and which was used for family prayers, often being covered in needlepoint or Berlin woolwork, which was so popular during this period.

The men were not forgotten either; their study would probably have contained an enormous upholstered couch known as a chesterfield, named after the Earl of Chesterfield. In the drawing-room there would have been a round upholstered seat known as an ottoman, and later the box ottoman provided storage as well as seating.

Not all Victorian furniture was over-ornate, over-stuffed or intricately twisted, for this was the period of people like the great William Morris, Charles Rennie Mackintosh, Charles Voysey and many other notable designers. The first Art Nouveau designs had appeared in 1867 and the so-called 'art furniture' became quite the rage, with innovations such as plain oak being stained green, furniture being painted with scenes or ebonised and decorated with Japanese-style ornamentation. By 1888 the Art and Crafts Movement was formed and it has to be admitted that whilst some of the furniture was beautiful, it was not exactly cheap or especially useful. It must have been with a great sense of relief that people greeted the first catalogue produced by Ambrose Heal in 1898. This catalogue illustrated a selection of pleasingly simple, no-nonsense furniture designs which were both ageless and functional. Indeed, Ambrose Heal's influence persists today.

1901–10

This was the reign of Edward VII, although the multiple influences of the Victorian period spread into these years. By now the functional furniture introduced by Ambrose Heal had many supporters and imitators, and Edwardian furniture tended to be extremely well made, solid, practical and inexpensive. This type of furniture was welcomed by the majority of ordinary people, but the fashionable set preferred reproduction Georgian styles made in mahogany with satinwood inlays and stringing. Because of its superb quality, this furniture is much sought after today.

1910–45

After the exuberance of the Victorian period and the solid practicality of the Edwardian period, furniture design seemed to lose its way in the years after World War I; although there were certain crazes, such as Chinese-style décor, and some avant-garde, one-off pieces, most interiors were a mixture of the old and the chintzy with heavily flowered fabrics dominant. There was a plethora of gimmicky additions such as kitchen cabinets with masses of small drawers and shelves but very little space on which to work, and wardrobes incorporating drawers for stud boxes and handkerchiefs, or tie-racks and mirrors.

All was not gloom, however, as in Germany and Scandinavia young designers were using new materials and mechanised production to make furniture which was stripped down to the bare essentials: thus Art Deco was born. French designers produced some of the very best Art Deco furniture made from materials as varied as smoked glass, chrome, painted wood and, harking back to Thonet, bentwood. Some of the furniture was austere and geometric, some incorporated elements from ancient civilisations such as the Aztecs, and there seemed to be a fascination with curved forms and metal.

In less extreme form, Art Deco became familiar in everyday locations such as cinemas – think of the distinctive Odeon buildings – hotels and department stores; but somehow, although the general public bought radios and ornaments which were definitely influenced by Art Deco, they did not seem to see the furniture itself fitting into their homes. Good Art Deco pieces were well made but expensive, and they still fetch good prices today.

A designer called Marcel Breurer has probably had the most impact on metal furniture used in the ordinary living room: he designed a tubular steel

BELOW LEFT: *A late Victorian side table with squared, tapered legs and swan-neck broken pediment*
BELOW: *A typical Thonet-type bentwood rocking chair*

125

cantilevered chair which became known as the Cesca and which is still being sold today. He also designed a chair made from tubular steel and leather which was known as the Wassily armchair and is now regarded as a classic of its type.

Another Frenchman called Le Corbusier made extravagant use of tubular steel and leather and produced a very beautiful chaise-longue which can be adjusted to suit a variety of positions (see illustration opposite). He then reworked the traditional overstuffed club chair and produced the Grand Confort – five fat leather cushions sitting within a steel cradle. It is interesting that the output of both Breuer and Le Corbusier was limited to a very short period. Breuer produced all his outstanding tubular steel furniture in just three years, whilst Le Corbusier designed three chairs in only one year and then gave up.

1945 ONWARDS

During and after World War II the British authorities banned the production of all furniture except for one type, which was known as Utility. It was very plain, devoid of all ornament, functional, and the upholstered pieces were not particularly comfortable. It was generally disliked – it has been said, rather unfairly perhaps, that the furniture of the Art and Crafts Movement had returned and been given the official stamp of approval. Nevertheless, this Utility furniture certainly had a profound effect on post-war styles.

It would also be true to say that the streamlined furniture of the 1920s and 1930s, as well as the austerity of the Utility era, both have a profound effect on furniture design even today – just think of the styles to be seen in Habitat, for example. Of course there have been innovators such as Gian Carlo Piretti, Vico Magistretti, Mario Bellini, Fred Scott and Charles Eames who all produced wonderfully stylish furniture, particularly chairs; but in the main, furniture today still has its roots in the past. It is possible to buy reproduction furniture of almost any period. Some is acceptable and some truly terrible, but in essence, if you want to create anything from Strawberry Hill Gothic to Victorian plushness you should be able to find the furniture you need in auction rooms or from firms who specialise in recreating designs from the past.

BUYING FURNITURE

Your own furniture will undoubtedly owe its being to some of the designs just discussed. Even that hated television table may be a relic from the 1930s, and the sofa may be a reproduction of the one first introduced during the reign of Queen Anne. Now is the time to look at the furniture you have, to try and decide exactly what is needed in a particular room. You may be able to bring in pieces from another room which will blend with existing furniture or perhaps replace some of it. You may decide that some different pieces would add style, and these could be brand new ones or something found in the local auction room or antique shop. Whatever you decide, however, it is worth waiting until you find exactly the right piece, something you would happily live with for years, rather than buying something simply as a stop-gap which you will never like.

Unless you prefer something really high-tech or definitely brand new, it is worth studying the local newspapers to see what furniture is being offered for sale. The auction room is the obvious place, but there are often sales in private properties arising from people moving to a different size or style of house. Sometimes solicitors and executors are winding up an estate and items may be sold to raise money for taxes or bequests, or they may be surplus to the beneficiaries' needs. Keen collectors may be upgrading a present collection or changing to another period, and some people simply have too much furniture and want to sell some of it. Also, look out for 'good buys' when a local shop sells up; it will often contain nice old counters or other fittings which could have endless uses, and maybe some useful pieces of furniture.

If you do decide to go to an auction room, the following few tips may be helpful:

An interesting mixture of walnut, mahogany and oak furniture works well with the modern sofa in this panelled sitting room

1   Do not view on the actual day of the sale, as the room will be crowded and it will be difficult really to study a possible purchase

2   Do read the catalogue carefully to see if the item you like is the only one in the lot, or whether you would also be getting other things.

3   Note also how the item has been described. A favourite term is 'after the style of', which means that it is not actually of, say, the Regency period but could be a good reproduction.

4   If you find something you like, have a really good look at it. Check chair joints by pushing from the back, and table and chair legs to see if they have been repaired at the top or bottom; a favourite trick is to repair any breaks quickly using metal brackets. Line up sets of chairs to see if they are the same height and, indeed, if they are the same as each other. They may have a number underneath indicating how many there were in the original set.

5   If you are looking at a dining table and chairs, measure the clearance between the chair and the apron of the table to ensure that you can actually get your knees under it. Stretchers can also be a nuisance, making it impossible to sit comfortably, so it is worth checking that point, too.

6   Check for signs of woodworm, which could be hidden from view in the rails under upholstery.

7   Remember: mahogany furniture is the least expensive, then walnut – rosewood is the most expensive.

8   When buying chairs, remember that drop-in seats are easy to re-cover – although this does, of course, also make them more desirable.

9   Sets of dining chairs are dependent on quality, age and, above all, quantity. For instance it is possible to buy odd numbers of chairs – three or five – as cheaply as a pair. However, the more even numbers of chairs there are in a set – eg two, four, six, eight – the more valuable they are, and if carver chairs are included this will also affect the price.

10 With tables, ensure that the top and bottom belong together and that the top is not warped.

These are just a few general pointers to look for when attending an auction; though if you are at all interested in old furniture, you will soon become adept at looking at it critically – and reading some good guides about any favourite pieces of furniture will also help. It is also quite possible to buy some really worthwhile pieces of furniture in auction rooms which are of no great age or value, but which you can see will suit your purposes well. You may want a table which you intend to cover with a long cloth, so as long as the top is not warped, it really does not matter what it looks like, as it will never be seen. Some very plain, but sound, chests of drawers can be painted, and decorative treatments applied which will make them unique and will give pleasure for many years to come. As with every other aspect of interior decoration, a 'seeing eye' is probably the most valuable asset anyone can have.

PAINTED FURNITURE

The subject of furniture would not be complete without a few words about painted and other decorated furniture. Painted furniture was very popular towards the end of the eighteenth century, and was usually made from deal or pine which was cheap and plentiful. These basic pieces – usually

A contemporary painted chest of drawers, decorated in country style

chests of drawers, bookcases, chairs, side-, dressing and occasional tables and mirrors – would be decorated in all manner of ways, the most usual being in the form of simulated expensive woods. Because this type of furniture was cheap to produce it would often be used in rooms not on public view, such as bedrooms and dressing rooms. Painted furniture reached its height of popularity during the Regency period, with items being painted to simulate bronze, marble, stones, and various woods and would sometimes be further decorated with brass inlay. Some pieces of furniture would be painted in a base colour and then beautifully decorated with flowering garlands, urns and all manner of things before being given a crazed, or cracklure, finish. These are very desirable items and much sought after.

The Orientals took painted furniture to the ultimate with their lacquering technique. Many oriental cabinets with background colours of black, red, blue and green, and red and green, were imported into England during the seventeenth and eighteenth centuries and it was not long before the Europeans began to copy the technique. Everything that could be lacquered was, and this included screens, tables, desks, bookcases, chairs, whatnots and mirror frames. Lacquered furniture reached its height of popularity in Regency times but enjoyed a revival during the Edwardian period and is still much sought after. Furniture such as chairs, beds and mirror frames was also sometimes gilded, but as it was an expensive and lengthy process it was only used in the grandest of houses. There were two basic ways of applying gold leaf – oil gilding and water gilding, and the choice depended on whether or not the gilding was to be burnished. Water gilding can be burnished but oil gilding cannot, and both would have been applied on top of a fine, compact clay, usually coloured red, and known as 'bole'. As the gilding wears, this red colour shows through attractively.

One very popular finish in the 1920s and 1930s was known as 'liming'. This was a technique which involved stripping wood and then finishing it, sometimes with a thin wash of paint, to give it a very pale, even white, appearance. The woods generally used for this technique were pine or walnut, and chairs, tables, sideboards and bedroom suites would receive this treatment. There has been a recent revival of this type of finish and it does look very effective, particularly on simple shapes.

The techniques mentioned above were all used on English furniture, and France, Italy, Spain and Holland were also busy producing decorated furniture, some exuberant, some restrained, so that many pieces can still be found today.

ARRANGING FURNITURE

When it comes to arranging furniture in a room, remember that it is not simply a matter of displaying individual pieces, although of course they do have their place in establishing the character of an interior. Each piece should live happily with another and, if space is at a premium, it is essential not to try and cram too much into a room. The furniture layout can make or break a room and a few vital points must first be considered, such as whether there is a fireplace or not. If not, should a focal point be provided, to prevent the room looking like a waiting room? Is there to be a television set in the room? If so the placing of the TV point can be crucial to the whole layout.

The best way to decide how furniture should be arranged is to make a plan, and this is where the original room plan which you drew up in Chapter 2 will come in extremely useful. Having a definite plan of how to arrange your furniture will help make the most of the available space and will also ensure that everything you have, or plan to buy, will work both functionally and visually. For instance, a conventional three-piece suite may overwhelm a small sitting-room and it may make more sense to use only single chairs or to consider lining the sofa and chairs against two walls to form an L-shaped sitting area instead. However, pushing sofas or tables against the wall does not always work: it may be necessary to get around them to a door or cupboard, and chairs must have enough room to be pulled out from a dining table or a desk. As a general rule, approximately 36in (85cm) walking space around each piece of furniture should be allowed. The traffic flow around the room is also important – remember that the more furniture you include in a room, the more the ease of access will be limited.

Large rooms can be broken up into sitting and working areas by the clever use of furniture, bookshelves or a screen – a bookcase placed at right angles to the door can give an immediate impact and make the space beyond it seem inviting and exciting. If a room is very symmetrical it is often wiser to go along with that formality and arrange the furniture accordingly. For instance, in a classic Georgian room of medium size with the door opposite to the fireplace, two sofas or two easy chairs with tables placed on either side of the fireplace will always look balanced. Sometimes furniture can be used to disguise defects in a room – for example, if there is a door which is never used, think about placing bookshelves across it.

Once everything has been considered and noted down, take the original floor plan and set to work. Measure each piece of furniture, and draw up simple squares, circles and oblongs to represent the various items, remembering to use the same scale as the room plan, or buy a plastic template on which furniture will have been reduced to scale. Cut out the scaled-down furniture shapes and try out various configurations on the plan until the layout which seems to offer the best possible solution both in terms of appearance and ease of movement is found. It will very quickly become obvious whether your first thoughts on the layout are practical, or whether they need to be revised. Once you are happy with a layout, stick it down in place and stay with it.

To give an even better idea of how the proposed layout will look, you may decide to sketch in the elevations; this will also show the effect that the chosen curtain treatment will have on the room. Have a look at the plan overleaf to see what a difference this can make – it is the best way of focusing one's thoughts on the overall room design, and it is the professional approach.

Never try to 'restore' a gilded piece of furniture as it will immediately lose its value.

Final room plan with elevations

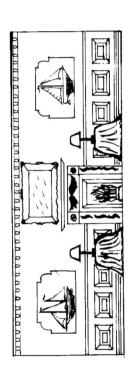

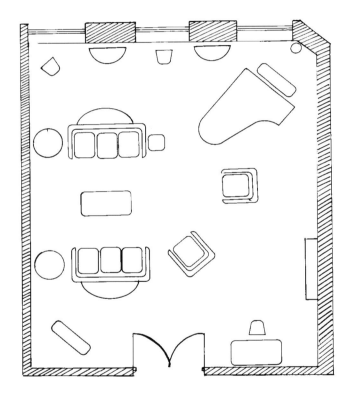

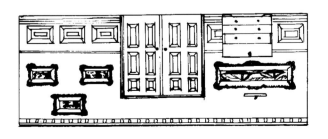

PROJECT PAPERS

The study of furniture can be a lifetime's obsession; there is so much to learn and the more one reads about and looks at it the deeper one becomes involved in and enthused by it.

For the purposes of this book it is even more important that you realise how critical it is to plan the furniture layout of a room. The following two projects will exercise your design skills, and your floor plan will add an important dimension to your portfolio.

PROJECT 15

Take a copy of your original floor plan and, with pieces of paper cut to scale, try out various furniture layouts until you are happy with the result. Remember to take into account such things as traffic flow, electrical points, radiators etc. Draw around the final arrangement so that a permanent record appears on the floor plan and then project the wall elevations showing how the various pieces would look when placed against these walls. Add a legend to the side of the plan, or on a separate piece of paper, explaining exactly what each piece is.

PROJECT 16

Select and cut from magazines six pieces of furniture which you particularly like. Beside each write a caption explaining the piece of furniture and suggesting a room, or rooms, in which it would look most suitable. Do not crowd the cuttings and display them well.

CHAPTER 9

SOFT FURNISHINGS

HOWEVER DISPARATE THE PIECES OF FURNITURE in a room seem to be, it is perfectly possible to pull them all together by using various soft furnishings to create the desired look. Whether your preference is for the cosy or the high-tech, soft furnishings can literally be tailored towards the style you want to achieve, and working out the furniture plan will provide an even better idea of what is needed. Soft furnishing is a generic term and does not necessarily mean that everything is soft and frilly; it can be tailored and elegant. For instance, wood-framed furniture could be given a new lease of life by painting the wood a matt black and covering the cushions with a plain fabric piped in black. What could look more tailored? Curtains and blinds are also 'soft furnishing' and can be severely tailored – Roman blinds look particularly smart in a modern setting. The beauty of soft furnishings is that they can be used to cover existing furniture to create the look you want; they can camouflage battered tables and chests, refurbish lampshades and provide pools of comfort, and the same fabric, or variations of it, plus some that is contrasting, can be used to harmonise all these disparate pieces and make the room appear 'designed' rather than thrown together. It does not necessarily have to be expensive; cheap fabric used generously can look wonderful, although it is best to use a firmly woven furnishing material for chairs and sofas.

Strictly speaking, upholstery is a form of soft furnishing too, because it uses fabric to create the finished look, but the fabric is permanently nailed or stapled in place and cannot be removed for cleaning. This means that when considering upholstery it is particularly important to choose the right material, for it must be resistant to wear and tear, and stains should be relatively easy to remove. Dralon velvet has long been popular, but it is not suitable for every room and a loose cover may well be a wiser choice. It is perfectly possible for the keen amateur to learn upholstery techniques and to carry out such work, but apart from something simple like a drop-in seat or a piano stool, most pieces of furniture are best left to a professional.

There are many ways in which the appearance of

a room can be changed by using a variety of fabrics, and whether a professional is employed or you make an attempt yourself, it is as well to know what is involved and the results that can be achieved. The exact sewing techniques will not be described here as there are many excellent books detailing these.

LOOSE COVERS

One of the fastest ways to revitalise a chair or sofa is to provide it with loose covers, although it is a waste of time and money to cover anything which has sagging springs or lumpy padding. Covers can be made to fit over most styles and, more important, they can be removed for cleaning. Take time to consider the effect you want to achieve – tailored with box pleats, or finished with a frill – and then take a careful look at the fabrics which are available and how they would work with the rest of the scheme you have in mind.

The fabric should be hard-wearing and able to withstand washing or dry-cleaning without shrinking. Firm, closely woven, stain-resistant fabrics are the most suitable, and these include linen union, furnishing weight cotton, cotton rep, heavy-duty needlecord, cotton damask and tapestry. Plain colours or small overall patterns are cheaper than large designs as these have to be cut to balance the pattern and so take more fabric. However, if you do prefer a design with a large motif, the motif should be centred on each cushion, and each arm, particularly the front, should mirror the other. Stripes should match across the inside and outside arm joins and run down the chair back, seat, front and skirt in continuous matching lines. Avoid any fabric which is very thick or heavy as it is extremely difficult to sew and, if piped seams are required, as many as eight layers of fabric may have to be fed through the machine. If self-piping is planned, then extra material for this must be allowed for.

As a rule, loose covers are made in sections which correspond to those of the original cover and the best way to measure up is to take each section of the chair in turn. Make allowances for tuck-ins and,

A rough rule of thumb for calculating the amount of material needed to cover a chair is that 5 times the height of the back of the chair to the bottom edge will be needed.

Remnants of the curtain fabric have been used to make piped and frilled cushions for this cane armchair, which has a carefully toned plain seat cushion

initially, assume that each piece will be cut in rectangles as these will later be laid over the chair, wrong side out, and then pinned into shape. Always double-check the amount of material needed before buying, as loose covers take a lot of fabric and overestimating can be expensive. It is also a good idea to allow extra fabric to make separate arm caps and chair backs so that areas which are likely to become heavily soiled can be protected; these can then be taken off and washed without having to remove the entire cover. Arm caps should preferably be made the same depth as the arm so that they can tuck down beside the seat cushion.

Piping the seams will not only give a cover a longer life but will also make it look more tailored. An added bonus is that piping will focus the eye and disguise any pattern mismatches and crooked seaming!

Once the basic cover has been fitted there are many different ways of finishing off the skirt – the simplest is a plain, tied-under base. This is suitable for some types of furniture, but a smarter finish is a straight skirt with inverted pleats at the corners. A box-pleated skirt also looks good, particularly in plain fabrics, and a gathered skirt will add an air of rustic charm. Bullion fringe gives an elegant finish but it is rather expensive, and is not ideal if there are young cats around – they love playing with it!

One tends to think only in terms of chairs and sofas when talking about loose covers, but there are many other types of furniture which will take on new life when covered in this way. For instance, a bedroom chair without arms can be dressed with a fitted cover to seat level and then a long, gathered skirt added which gives a very soft effect. Because the chair would not be constantly in use, lighter-weight fabrics could be used, and more elaborate trimmings such as bows and ribbons could be added. The long skirt is also a nice treatment for dining chairs and, in this case, something like a plain linen with contrasting piping could be used, perhaps with a monogram or some similar motif stencilled onto

135

the back, probably in the same shade as the piping. Footstools and pouffes can also benefit from a new loose cover – and this could be a good opportunity to introduce a contrasting fabric colour into the overall scheme, as these pieces are not too large or blatant, and a contrast here could be just enough to bring the whole scheme to life.

Not every cover has to be fitted; if the idea is to transform a piece of furniture instantly then the answer could be a throw-over cover. When covering a chair or sofa, be generous with the amount of material used – drape and arrange it attractively, perhaps fixing certain shapes with invisible stitches. Shawls with heavy fringes make wonderful throw-overs to cover a chair or sofa partially, and old patchwork quilts, car and knee rugs, crocheted bedspreads and old lace curtains can all be put to use in this way.

CUSHIONS

Cushions were perhaps the earliest form of 'furniture' used by man and initially would probably have been made from straw or dried leaves covered with a skin or fur. Since then, cushions in all shapes and sizes have adorned chairs, settees, settles and beds, and they are still used on the floor to sit on. Floor cushions made from structured blocks of foam and covered with fabric make substantial chairs which may convert into beds, and granular polystyrene will create the familiar bean-bag cushion which children love. Window seats are usually made with large cushions and can be covered in the same material as the curtains to create a feeling of a cosy nest; or a contrast note can be introduced by covering them in a plain fabric, perhaps piping this with the curtain material.

Cushions serve both a practical and a decorative purpose in a room as they can soften the angular lines of modern furniture, add colour and excitement to a neutral scheme or give an impression of ease and luxury. Even if a bed or sofa does not actually need cushions, a great pile of them is somehow comforting and satisfying.

A plain cushion cover can have a design painted or stencilled onto it, and this could be a motif taken from a patterned curtain or loose cover fabric which could be further emphasised by quilting around the design.

There is an enormous variety of cushion shapes – square, rectangular, round, heart-shaped, kite-shaped and bolster-shaped – and they can be made from almost every fabric imaginable. Floor cushions really need heavy-duty fabrics but the other shapes can be made with cotton, lace, satin, velvet, tapestry, gingham, patchwork or broderie anglaise; it all depends where the cushions are to be used and whether they are going to be purely decorative or receive a lot of wear. Remnant counters are a good source of material for cushions, and for a co-ordinated look fabric left over from curtains, bedcovers or upholstery can be used. If using a fabric with a bold pattern it is worth taking a little trouble to centre the design so that it is shown to best advantage, rather than having it sliding over the side of the cushion. This sort of care makes all the difference to the final appearance.

Cushion pads should always be used; the most luxurious are feather and down, but some of the synthetic fillings are perfectly adequate for the majority of situations; foam rubber works well for shaped kitchen chair cushions as it is simple to take a paper template of the seat shape, draw around it onto the foam and cut this shape out with kitchen scissors or a bread knife. The cushion pad is itself a template for cutting a cushion cover, and the pad can be measured across the width and length from seam to seam. An allowance of $1\frac{1}{2}$in (3cm) should be added to these measurements, but if a very plump cushion is wanted then this allowance need not be added. A round cushion cover should be a perfect circle, and the best way to achieve this is to make a paper pattern first: fold a square of paper, slightly larger than the cushion pad, into four; tie a piece of string round a pencil and cut it to half the length of the diameter of the cushion, plus $\frac{1}{2}$in (1·5cm) allowance. The string can then be pinned to the folded corner and with the string taut and the pencil upright a quarter-circle can be drawn on the paper, this producing a perfect circle from which to cut the fabric.

For a professional touch, cushions can be trimmed in a variety of ways – they can be piped with matching or contrasting fabric, or a gathered

These twelve patterned cushions illustrate how effectively a mass of different designs can work together, particularly when there is a common theme

single or double frill of matching fabric or lace; or with a ruched insert, small boxed pleats, knife pleats, zigzagged and scalloped edges, or furnishing cord slip-stitched around all the edges. Dainty cushions can have ribbons trailing from them with tiny bows sewn onto the surface; a kite-shaped cushion can have a tail made from fabric or braid with ribbons knotted into bows at regular intervals. Pieces of precious needlepoint or embroidery can be inserted into a frame of velvet before stitching the cover together, or appliqué shapes can be sewn onto a plain background. Bolster-shaped cushions can be made to look very important with piped and gathered ends finished with a covered button or an elaborate tassel; and shaped chair cushions, also known as squabs, can be tied onto chair backs with large matching bows.

A more mundane but important point to remember is that a cushion opening should be sufficiently wide to take the cushion pad – this will also make it easier to remove the cover for cleaning. Cushions can be fastened in many ways, the simplest being just to slip-stitch the edges together, but press fasteners, fastening tape, velcro touch-and-close spots and zip fasteners are all suitable. Sometimes a back vent opening is used and this is a quick, easy and inexpensive solution.

Cushions are all about attention to detail – this is what makes them unique, and how they will further emphasise the thought and care which has gone into your room design. The ways in which they can be adorned, finished and trimmed is endless, and the variety is only as limited as your own imagination.

TABLE LINEN

Old and perhaps outmoded tables can easily be camouflaged, and a table cloth is one way of achieving this. Rather like the 'throws' used on chairs and sofas, a cloth can instantly transform a table and add an extra touch of colour and interest to a room. Not only will a cloth protect a good table top, it can also hide a multitude of sins such as battered or ugly table legs, and a full-length cloth over an old dining table will not only disguise it but will give the room an instant intimacy.

As with every aspect of soft furnishing, the variety and permutations are endless, and the final choice depends on what you want to achieve. Do you want to disguise a table, pretty up a room or create a background for precious ornaments? Quilted fabrics make excellent table cloths; they not only protect the top but they will hang in stiff folds which make them ideal for floor-length round table cloths. For a feeling of extravagance, two or three cloths can be layered, and lace tops on plain fabrics or rectangular cloths on top of full-length round cloths can look very elegant.

Cloths are usually round, square, rectangular or oval and all these shapes can be trimmed in various ways to add extra interest. For instance, all could have appliquéd or scalloped edges, or a ruffle could be added to give a frothy, feminine effect. Embroidered table cloths look pretty, and old dressing-table sets can often be displayed to advantage on top of a long-skirted cloth. The

Keep a look-out for old shawls at flea-markets or jumble sales as they could make wonderful table cloths.

A small, round chipboard table and a basic lampshade have been given a new lease of life by covering them in the same fabric as the bedlinen

painted or stencilled design used on a cushion cover could be transferred to the table cloth as well, or a patterned cushion fabric could be repeated as a table cloth.

Although most table cloths are basically 'throws', they can also be fitted, and to achieve this effect the top is usually piped and then a gathered skirt is sewn on. Kidney-shaped dressing tables are often dressed in this way. Cloths can be trimmed with lace, ribbon, fringing or beads sewn on to the corners, and it is worth looking on market stalls or good haberdashery counters to see what could be used to add interest to a simple cloth.

Table mats and napkins can be made easily to add a personal touch. The napkins could match or contrast with the table cloth or mats, and all sorts of finishes, such as zigzagging the raw edges or applying a pretty cut-out motif to the corners, can make something really special from a piece of cheap material. Large motifs from patterned fabrics can often be cut out to make stunning table mats, so do consider this when looking for suitable table cloth materials.

LAMPSHADES

Although lampshades are essentially functional items they are very important in a furnishing scheme as they are also decorative, and the light they dispense could make a vital difference to a night-time setting. The style of a lamp should therefore blend with the other furnishings, so the choice of lamp base and the colour and texture of the lampshade are all important.

Parchment and silk have been used for many, many years for lampshades and they still look right in traditional settings. However, it is now possible to buy material which consists of a fabric bonded on to a thin card and this is ideal for coolie-style and pleated lampshades. Depending upon the style of lampshade, almost any fabric can be bonded on to buckram, and lightweight cottons and lace are suitable for many styles. The main thing to bear in mind is that the colour will affect the light shed. For

instance peach, pale pink and cream will produce a soft, warm glow – white may be too glaring, red too obviously cosy and blue too cold. Dark colours absorb the light, but the pools of colour they shed beneath the shade can look romantic, restful or dramatic. One way to test the effects that different materials and colours will produce is to hold different pieces of fabric over a lit but unshaded lamp base and observe how the light is radiated through the fabric. It is worth taking some time over this, as the whole scheme could be affected by the wrong choice of colour. If you are convinced, however, that for example a black lampshade would look perfect in a particular spot but you need it to shed light, then it is possible to make, or buy, a black shade lined with white which will reflect the light and get over this problem.

It is important to choose a lampshade which is in proportion to the base, and which will cover the mechanics such as the lampholder and switch. As a general rule the shade should be about the same height as the base and the diameter of the bottom of the shade should equal the height of the base.

The same basic rules apply to hanging lampshades, and the various shade styles can be used to create a particular look. Frame shapes are shown on p140.

HANDKERCHIEF LAMPSHADE

This is by far the simplest shade and is easy to make at home. It is basically a bound utility ring with a square of fabric draped over it. The edges of the fabric can be scalloped, fringed, beaded or finished with a frill to create a very soft and feminine effect. It is an ideal bedroom lampshade, though depending on the material used, it can look very smart as a low central light over a dining-room table.

TIFFANY LAMPSHADE

This is another lampshade which is easy to make, as it is simply a tube of material, slightly larger than the bottom circumference of a Tiffany base and

LAMPSHADE SHAPES

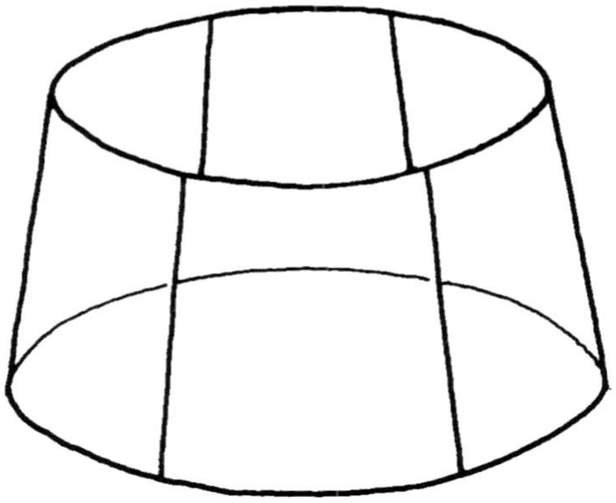

Tapered drum

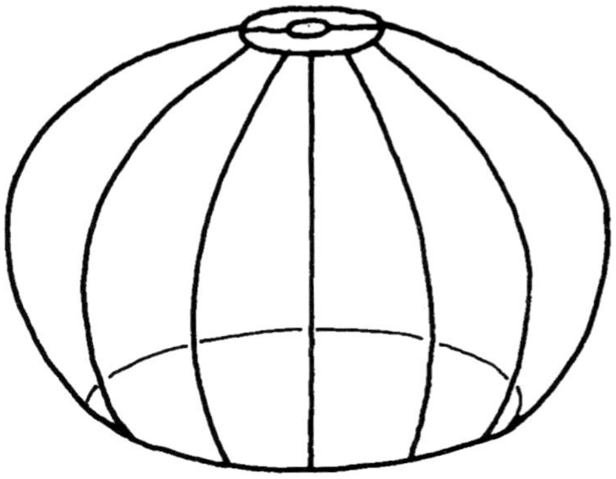

Tiffany with pendant fitting

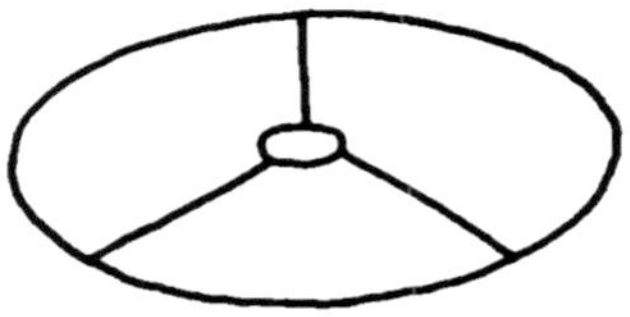

Utility ring

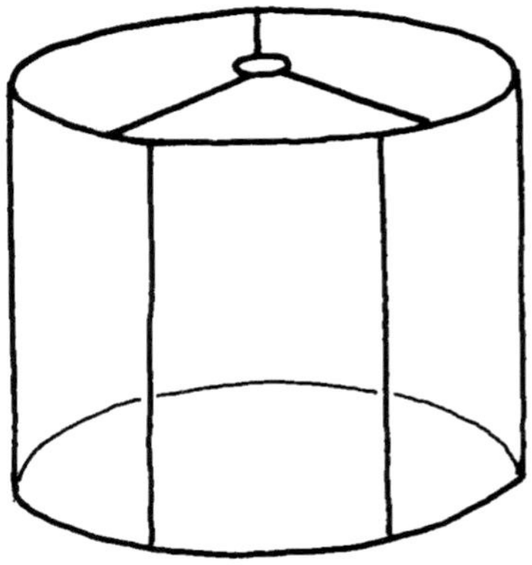

Straight-sided drum

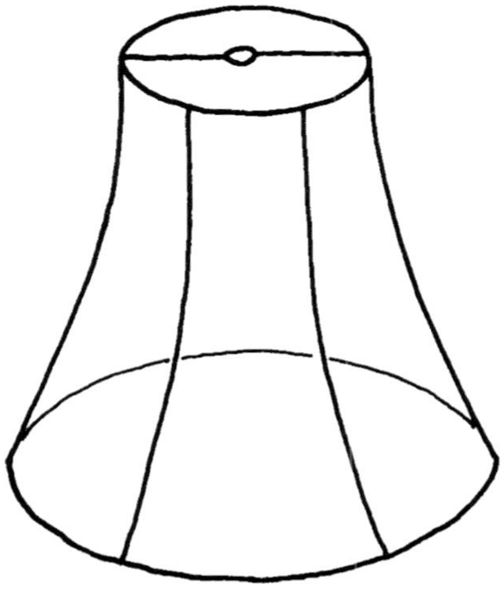

Classically shaped shade

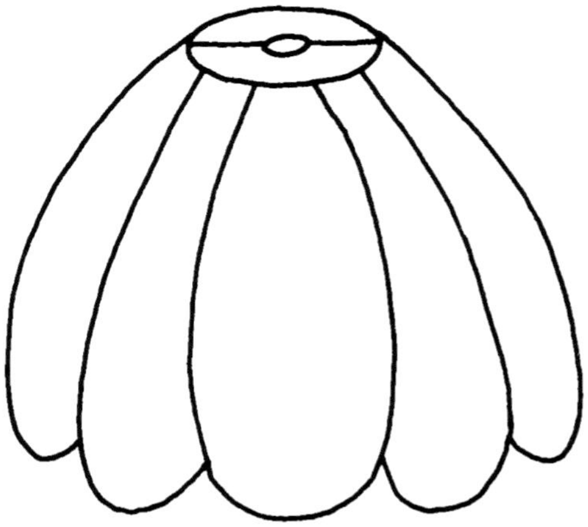

Curved Tiffany

about 3in (7·6cm) longer. This tube has elastic run along both edges, one being drawn up to fit the top ring while the other is drawn under the bottom ring and then usually finished with a ruffle or fringing. This lampshade looks very pretty in a girl's bedroom.

PLEATED LAMPSHADE – FABRIC

A straight-sided, or tapered, drum shape or a coolie shape are the best frames for pleated lampshades and the fabric used should be soft and lightweight such as georgette, silk chiffon, lawn or glazed cotton, as these will all pleat easily and look luxurious. It may be necessary to interline the very fine fabrics with a lightweight interfacing so that the struts do not show through. The amount of fabric needed is usually three times the circumference of the frame so that the pleats are generous and evenly folded. Pleating a coolie shade is slightly more difficult because of the size difference between the top and bottom rings but the thing to remember in this case is that the fabric should be cut one and a half times wider than the circumference of the bottom (bigger) ring. The edges on both styles are usually bound with a self bias-binding but the drum shapes are sometimes finished with a smart fringing. Pleated lampshades look well in both sitting-rooms and bedrooms and will suit most kinds of lamp base.

PLEATED LAMPSHADE – PAPER

Pleated paper lampshades look particularly smart on a coolie-shaped frame and they are easy to make. Fabric can either be bonded on to a paper or buckram backing, or elegant wrapping paper or wallpaper can be stuck to thin card and then pleated at regular intervals to produce a crisp concertina effect. Holes are punched into the top and bottom of each pleat and a cord is threaded through these so that the pleats fit the rings accurately before being stitched into place on the frame. No additional trimming is needed to finish off these shades.

BED LINEN

Of all the rooms in a house the bedroom is the one in which the character of a person is most revealed. It should be a private stronghold where one can retreat and be oneself, and soft furnishing offers endless possibilities to create a unique bedroom which expresses the way you like to live, and where it is possible to relax and be at peace.

The bedroom may be very basically furnished with just a bed and a chest of drawers, or it may be a repository for bits and pieces of furniture that do not fit in anywhere else and so clutter up the room. When thinking of a scheme for an individual bedroom the most obvious place to start is with the bed itself; this is where about a third of your life will be spent so it is important that it is welcoming and comfortable. There are countless varieties of bed linen available, although it could be more fun to create a totally individual look by choosing unusual fabrics and making your own. Pillowcases, sheets and duvet covers are all basically rectangles of cloth

This romantic four poster bed with handpainted supports must be every little girl's dream

and are easy to make, whilst an individual trimming can turn the plainest of shapes into something special.

There are three main styles of pillowcase: plain, sometimes known as housewife-style; self-bordered, sometimes known as Oxford-style; and frilled. All can be trimmed to add interest, and remember that a pillowcase does not necessarily have to match the sheets or duvet cover; often a completely contrasting set such as an emerald green duvet cover with daffodil yellow pillowcases will be sufficient to set the style of a bedroom. Old linen can often be given a new lease of life by adding lace or broderie anglaise ruffles, sewn onto the pillowcase with satin picot-edged ribbon.

For easy laundering, sheets and duvet covers should be made from cotton or a mixture of cotton and polyester, and it is increasingly possible to buy these fabrics in very wide widths so that no joins have to be made. Think about using a contrasting fabric for each side of a duvet cover; this will make it much more versatile and could, for instance, provide a light-coloured pattern for spring and summer and a darker one for autumn and winter.

Because valances are not washed as often as bed linen they can be made from a completely different fabric, and even a contrasting one if preferred. They will certainly give a neat finish to a bed, and have the added advantage of providing a screen for things which may have to be stored underneath. Valances can be frilled or tailored into box pleats, and it is a nice idea to match them to a covered bedhead so that although the bed linen may change frequently, the valance and bedhead give a constant identity to the overall colour scheme.

Of course, one of the quickest ways to change a colour scheme without having to go to the expense of new bed linen is to use a simple throw-over bedspread. If no valance is used this should touch the floor at both sides and at the foot of the bed; its edges could be finished with contrasting binding, deep fringing, frills or scallops. Bedspreads can be made from all kinds of material – soft wool, heavy linen, lace or cotton – and quite thin materials can be given substance by using them with a wadding

and a backing before quilting them into simple patterns and edging them with a contrasting binding. A more tailored appearance can be created by using a fitted bedspread, and this too could have a quilted top whilst leaving the sides plain.

The old-fashioned methods of covering a bed should not be forgotten either: patchwork quilts are charming and interesting in appearance, particularly in cottage-style bedrooms, and the old-style crochet or knitted bedspreads are worth looking out for, and are also worth making, as their pristine whiteness creates a wonderful feeling of simplicity.

If space is at a premium and the bedroom also has to be a sitting-room, a divan bed can be turned into a settee by pushing it against a wall and covering it with a tightly fitting cover, box-pleated or frilled at the bottom. Bolster-shaped cushions and pillows hidden in pillowcases made from the same fabric as the cover will also help the disguise.

CANOPIES

Canopies must be one of the most glamorous soft furnishing effects that a bedroom can have, and they can be made from the simplest muslin or the most elaborate brocade. A proper four-poster bed is not necessarily required to achieve a canopied look, as it is possible to create the impression of one by the clever use of fabric draped and held in various ways.

To create a feeling of the mysterious East, a veil of muslin or other semi-sheer fabric can be suspended centrally over the bed by attaching it to a ceiling hook with a tasselled cord or elegant knot and then draping it over the four corners of the bed. To hold the fabric further away from the bed a large circle of tape-bound wire can be inserted under the 'tent' and held in place with a few strategically placed stitches.

Another simple treatment is to fix a pole centrally over the bed, draping fabric evenly over it before catching it back at the sides with tie-backs or wall-mounted curtain holders. This treatment

A wonderful example of various aspects of soft furnishing. Note the frilled canopy edged with a contrasting fabric, which has also been used on the bed curtain. The matching bedspread has been quilted and the cushions expertly frilled and piped

works well with sheer or opaque fabrics, and a co-ordinated look can be carried through by using a contrasting lining with, say, a patterned cotton which is also used for the bed valance.

Coronet canopies produce a rather more elaborate effect than the one just described: a large, lined curtain is hung from a coronet or semicircular bracket fixed to the wall behind the bedhead, and caught back in swags at the sides. The hanging is fixed to the coronet with eye screws or on a curtain track which can be hidden by a gathered or pleated valance which may be trimmed with contrasting fabric or braid. This canopy gives a very luxurious feel to a bedroom and is a particularly useful way of furnishing a long wall in a high-ceilinged bedroom.

A simple but dramatic way of making a canopy which will create the impression of a four-poster bed is to fix curtain poles which are slightly wider than the bed across the ceiling at both the top and the bottom of the bed. Generous amounts of fabric can be fed over these poles so that it falls in folds at the back, forming a bedhead, and drapes over the length of the bed in a gentle swag before dropping

over the bottom pole where it could be caught up into a large, loose knot or gathered together with a large bow of the same or contrasting fabric.

Four-poster beds can be dressed in several ways, the most common being drapes which hang down the length of each post, valances which are suspended from the tops of the posts, and canopies which form a roof to the bed. Sometimes a combination of all these methods is used and some very elaborate effects can be achieved, one of the most spectacular being a 'sunburst' canopy which looks like a pleated, tented ceiling inside the four-poster hangings. However, not all four-posters need elaborate furnishings; beautifully turned posts look better unadorned by drapes, and a simple valance will be sufficient decoration. It is not even necessary to have a conventional frame to create a four-poster bed as a curtain rail can be fitted to the ceiling, echoing the shape of the bed, and from this filmy drapes can be suspended, creating a light and airy feeling.

BEDHEADS

If canopies and coronas, however simple, are not acceptable in a bedroom then a straightforward bedhead may be the answer. Many beds, of course, already have built-in bedheads, such as the old-fashioned brass bedsteads or beds with a wooden board at both the top and bottom. Some of these can be very beautiful in their own right, but a divan bed without a headboard can be given impact and interest by dressing the wall behind so that the bed space is defined and becomes a focal point in the room.

One of the simplest ways of dressing the wall is to hang a rug immediately above the bed. This could be something really special like an Afghan kelim, or a plainer dhurry, perhaps in soft shades which complement the rest of the furnishings. Both old embroidered and Indian bedspreads look dramatic when draped in folds behind a bed – and consider using lengths of figured brocade, woven tapestry or striped silk stretched flat to show off the beauty of

A modern version of the traditional four poster, which can be left unadorned or simply draped with lengths of fabric

the fabric. A screen also looks interesting, particularly if it is covered in a fabric which has been used elsewhere in the room.

If a padded bedhead is preferred, consider drawing up your own particular shape – this could be cut from chipboard or plywood before being padded and covered in a suitable fabric, and would certainly look more interesting than any of those which are normally seen. Look out for the tops of old sideboards; they sometimes had mirrors inside an elaborate frame, and the mirror space could be padded and covered to make a unique headboard.

Another padded treatment which looks effective is to suspend one or two cushions from a curtain pole which has been fixed to the wall at an appropriate and comfortable height. Foam cushions, perhaps covered in a fabric which matches the bedcover, give a firm, tailored shape, and they could be finished with a piping or a decorative frill.

DRESSING TABLES

If you have a beautiful or pleasing wooden dressing table then it will not need any further embellishment, apart from perhaps a dressing stool covered in a suitable fabric.

Kidney-shaped dressing tables dressed in frills and flounces look very feminine, and can be covered in spotted muslin edged in satin ribbon or perhaps in a fabric which complements the duvet or bedspread. A plain fabric overlaid with lace is another appropriate finish for this type of dressing table, whilst a crisp, striped chintz looks smart.

A dressing table is easy to create from an old table because fabric will cover a multitude of sins – no one need ever know that the dainty dressing table is, in fact, a battered kitchen table. For instance, an old side-table – perhaps covered in sticky varnish – can be transformed by fitting a padded and quilted top to which a full gathered skirt has been added. The skirt could probably be made in two layers so that the top layer can be swagged up and finished with bows; or it could be given weight by a padded

and quilted hem, about 6in deep, which would allow it to swing away from the legs and so add shape to the finished piece.

MISCELLANEOUS PIECES

This chapter has covered some of the most obvious candidates for a soft furnishing treatment, and wonders can be performed with just a little effort and quite a lot of fabric. The old side-table is a case in point, and it is worth taking a look at some of the other furniture you may have around to see if it, too, can be transformed with fabric.

Consider a new cover for a drop-in chair seat; it takes very little material, is easy to do and could give a new lease of life to an old chair. Squab cushions are good at disguising badly scarred chair seats, or can be used to make a kitchen stool more comfortable.

The life of old toy boxes and chests can be extended by padding the top with a thick foam cushion, fitted and gathered in the same way as a loose cover; and the square plastic tables which were seen everywhere a few years ago can be smartly updated by carefully sticking a suitable fabric directly on to the legs, top and sides.

Small boxes, photograph frames and coathangers can all be given a personal touch by padding them first and then covering them with material to blend with a bedroom scheme.

Wicker chairs can be made more comfortable by cutting out fabric shapes which follow the contours of the chair, and then using a wadding or quilting technique to make them into soft pads which are held onto the wicker with simple tapes or more elaborate bows. Small wicker baskets can also be lined and, these look pretty holding bread or sitting on a dressing table to take beads and other jewellery.

Have a look at the coloured photographs to see how some of the finishes, both elaborate and plain, can improve the appearance of a room, and consider if anything similar could be used in your own home.

145

This picture illustrates perfectly
how complementary fabrics can
pull a whole decorative scheme
together, and how the
unexpected splash of colour
from the bed cushions adds
spice to the gentle overall effect

PROJECT PAPERS

More than anything else, soft furnishings can transform an interior and their importance cannot be over-emphasised for they can pull a whole furnishing scheme together.

The possibilities are endless, from the simplistic to the elaborate, and the next two projects should start you thinking really constructively about them, not only as individual items but as a whole in your own room plan. Display your ideas attractively and really think why you have chosen them.

PROJECT 17

From your furniture plan in Chapter 8 decide how to use soft furnishing to unify the various pieces of furniture. Using sketches, illustrations or photocopies, make a note of each piece and say whether you intend to leave it or cover it in some way. Fabric samples would be helpful in illustrating why you have chosen a particular fabric, what its qualities are, and why you consider it is right for the room.

PROJECT 18

From your ever-growing library of samples, magazines and trade leaflets, select one example of each of the items listed below, attach it to an A4 sheet of paper and note beside it why it particularly appeals and in which setting you would like to see it displayed.

- A loose cover
- A cushion
- A table covering
- A fabric lampshade
- Bed linen
- A canopy
- An occasional chair
- A decorative accessory

A WELL-THOUGHT-OUT LIGHTING PLAN can be one of the most effective ways of bringing out the best in a room. It can highlight precious ornaments, disguise irregularities, create a warm, intimate atmosphere in a bedroom or a positive atmosphere in a working study. It can also be an economical way of changing the whole feel of a room, and with the right lighting, any room can be made to look more attractive and work more effectively.

Natural light is constantly changing according to whether it is sunny or dull, and it varies in intensity throughout the day. Without even looking at a watch it is often possible to know instinctively the approximate time of day by the quality of the light, and there is evidence to show that the way it fluctuates is important to concentration and comfort. An artificial lighting scheme should have these same qualities, and the most practical way of achieving this is to have good, general background lighting supplemented by lighting directed at particular parts of a room which can be brought into use as and when necessary. The background lighting will give most of the light needed, but the supplementary lighting will provide the highlights and shadows which will make the room look more interesting.

Just as with the other treatments, so considerable thought should be given as to how the room will be lit, not only to enhance the interior scheme but also to provide a good light source for the practical things that might occur in that room – everything from reading to cutting bread. Ideally the lighting should be considered when planning a room design so that sockets can be repositioned or added at an early stage; when drawing up a room plan it is sometimes possible to see straightaway that there will have to be changes made in the positioning of sockets and switches. Traditionally sockets are placed 18in (46cm) and switches 4ft 6in (1.3m) above the floor level, but for a variety of reasons, such as ease of use or appearance, it may be more convenient to have them at a different height; if this sort of change can be decided in the early planning, a great deal of trouble and work might be prevented at a later stage.

Comfort and safety must be the priorities when considering any form of light: bad lighting can lead to accidents, and both the very young and the elderly are vulnerable to trailing wires, badly placed sockets and unstable fittings. It is worth having as many power and lighting points as possible and the switches for background lighting should be located near the door so that it is easy to find them in the dark. A switch near the front door will illuminate the hall or staircase and if two-way switches are put in along the route from the hall to the bedroom they can be turned off on the way. Two-way switches are also useful when placed at the bottom and top of a staircase or when placed near the internal door to a kitchen and at the back door. Think carefully about the areas where it is important to be able actually to turn on the light; there is nothing more dangerous or frustrating than having to stumble across a dark room to find a switch.

It is not always easy to decide where to position lighting, and choosing the right type of lights can be even more daunting. The main things to take into account are the quality of light required in a specific area, and the type of fixture which will provide this and which will also look aesthetically pleasing in the room. Ultimately this will affect every aspect of the room, not only creating the desired atmosphere but also highlighting or minimising the entire decorative and furnishing choice. It is therefore worth spending some time finding out about the types of lighting which are available and which fittings you can afford. Specialist lighting shops are on the increase and have some beautiful lights, but there are also some very acceptable fittings in high-street department stores which may be just as suitable.

BULBS

To avoid confusion when talking to a professional electrician, note that what is commonly called a 'bulb' is in fact known as a 'lamp' in the trade; however, throughout this section 'bulb' will be used.

There are three main types – incandescent, halogen and fluorescent – and the type used can be just as important as the fitting itself.

The first commercially available incandescent bulb is credited to Thomas Edison, and this revolutionary light source was first introduced in 1879. These bulbs have since become known as GLS (general lighting service) bulbs. Incandescent bulbs produce light by heating a tungsten filament which both gives off warmth and sheds a warm light; this is ideal for domestic purposes, but compared to fluorescent bulbs, more are needed to produce the same level of light. Pearl bulbs give a more diffused light than clear ones, although clear bulbs can be tinted in various colours – ruby, amber, smoke, blue and green – to add a hint of colour to the light given out. Deeper colours such as red and orange are usually produced by applying a coating either to pearl or clear bulbs.

The best way to use an incandescent bulb is to buy one with the highest wattage possible for the fitting, and use a dimmer switch to control the intensity of the light shed. These bulbs cast light in all directions. The direction is usually controlled by the shade or fitting used, but glare can also be reduced by using opalescent or crown-silvered bulbs. The lower parts of these bulbs have a mirror finish which directs light back into the fitting and then reflects it back into the room in a more controlled beam.

Reflector bulbs contain internally silvered reflectors which direct light into a narrow beam, and they are mainly used in spotlights and downlighters. They are sometimes referred to as PAR (parabolic reflector) bulbs.

Incandescent bulbs are manufactured in many shapes – the standard household shape, teardrop, cone (often used in nightlights), bent candle, flame, globe, straight-sided and tubular – and most of them can be bought with either a bayonet or a screw-in fitting.

Halogen bulbs are in fact tungsten/halogen as they combine a tungsten filament with a halogen gas. They give an attractive bright, white light which is as much as 20 per cent more powerful than a standard tungsten bulb. Often halogen bulbs are very small, so light fittings can be much more compact, and although they are expensive they will last far longer than a conventional bulb. One important point to remember, however, is that they should be treated with great care; handling them without gloves may be enough to stop them working, because grease from the skin will cause a reaction in the bulb. For this same reason use only sealed halogen bulbs in kitchens where grease is likely to build up.

Halogen bulbs are available in two types – low-voltage and mains-voltage. Low-voltage bulbs have to be used with a transformer, which may be an integral part of the light fitting, or may be separate. Mains-voltage bulbs do not need a transformer but they give a particularly bright light, so the fitting must be designed to keep the bulb hidden. Mains-voltage halogen bulbs are increasingly available with both bayonet and screw-in fixings which means they can be used in ordinary lamp-holders.

Fluorescent bulbs produce light by passing an electric current through an inert gas such as neon, which sets off a discharge of light. This light is usually bluer and harsher to the eyes than that produced by tungsten bulbs, but it is possible to buy so-called 'warm white' bulbs which give a better quality of light. Fluorescent bulbs are cool to touch and cheap to run, being four times as efficient as tungsten lamps. However, they are rather more expensive to buy.

At one stage the fluorescent bulb was the poor relation of the lighting world, but now really compact bulbs which also shed a kinder light are available; these are often used in desk lights, where their low heat output is another point in their favour.

TASK LIGHTS

Task lighting is the term given to lights which are used in working situations to provide a strongly illuminated local area. This is very important for activities such as reading, drawing, doing

emphasise architectural features such as an interesting formation of roof beams or an elegant Venetian window on a stairway.

DIMMERS

Dimmer switches work by cutting the voltage passing through a bulb; this will not only cut down on the amount of electricity used, but also prolong the bulb's life. Dimmers change the colour of light and emphasise the golden-red end of the colour spectrum, so some very atmospheric room settings can be created by using careful adjustments of the dimmer switch. The switches are easy to install and it is possible to wire them to all kinds of fittings – from floor and table lights to ceiling and wall lights. Some task lamps also have dimmer switches attached, and this further increases their usefulness.

LIGHT FITTINGS

Light fittings should always be selected first for the quality of light they give and only then for their appearance; it is no use buying a beautiful desk lamp if it does not shed enough light to work by.

DESK LAMPS

These are the ultimate task lighting fixtures, providing concentrated areas of light, and they should be adjustable so that the fall of light can be altered. The classic Anglepoise lamp was designed to move like the human arm so as to give an easily adjustable and controlled source of light, and there are many variations on this theme now available. Another classic table lamp is shown opposite. The angle of its head can be adjusted, and it looks particularly well in period settings.

DOWNLIGHTERS

Downlighters constitute one of the most interesting ways of using light, and can carve out, expand and

A simple but effective brass picture light works well with the frame below it

Downlighters are useful in areas which have low ceilings and where light is needed, but where a normal pendant light would look out of place.

needlework, chopping food etc, all of which require a great deal of light and where working with inadequate lighting might lead to eye strain or even permanently damaged sight. It is also a fact that the older we get the more light we need. For instance, a sixty-year-old will need roughly twice as much light to carry out the same task as a thirty-year-old. Visually demanding tasks can be carried out by the window during the day, but at night the general background lighting should be supplemented by an adjustable light source brought to bear directly on the work surface. It should not cause glare or cast shadows as this will create further eye strain – and the type of task will dictate the amount of light needed, too, as a lamp suitable for needlework will not be suitable for, say, a woodworker, who would need the light spread over a larger area.

Task lighting need not be limited to working areas; it can also be used to highlight particular features in a room, such as a group of plants or a painting. Special picture lights are available, and spotlights are particularly effective highlighters as the narrow but intense beam can be concentrated on a particular object. These can also be used to punctuate space by attracting attention to particular surfaces rather than to the ceiling. They are usually recessed or semi-recessed into ceilings, and direct light downwards in a concentrated circle. The circle of light can be altered by the use of different bulbs and fittings; the light from a halogen bulb in a recessed fitting is more concentrated than that from a standard tungsten bulb in a surface fitting. The fittings are generally small, and are therefore often unnoticeable, which is ideal if a clean, unfussy look is preferred. A downlighter can be used directly over a dining table to create a pool of light whilst leaving the rest of the room dimly lit, or to give focus to a seating area so that it appears to be separate from the rest of the room. They can wash walls with light, making the colour more brilliant, and are useful for emphasising particular areas within a room.

FREE-STANDING LAMPS

Free-standing lamps provide an extremely flexible source of light and range from floor lamps to table lamps, both of which give localised areas of illumination. There is an enormously wide range available, and as they are likely to be prominent in a room, great care should be taken that the style of the lamp and its shade is suited to the style of the room. Not all free-standing lamps have conventional lampshades; they can be bought with shades made from frosted globes of glass which cast a diffused light, or from flexible tubing which looks fun in a teenager's room. On the whole, however, these lamps are mostly used to provide comfortable lighting in a conventional setting.

PENDANT LIGHTS

Light fittings which hang from the ceiling are called pendants and they can range from an ornate chandelier to a simple metal cone. They are the most common form of ceiling light, and the amount of light given out depends upon the height at which they are hung and the type of bulb and shade used. Some pendants can be raised and lowered, and this

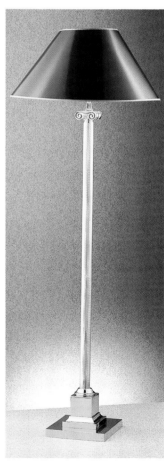

LEFT: *A classic desk lamp with adjustable head, which looks well in period settings*

BELOW LEFT: *An elegant table lamp*

BELOW: *A free-standing floor lamp to match the table lamp. Both smart black shades are lined with white*

153

An attractive multi-armed pendant fitting with silk shades

It is possible to buy spotlights which do not require a track mounting, however, and these can be fixed directly onto walls and ceilings or clipped onto shelves to accent particular areas or objects. Most types of spotlight fittings obscure the bulb from sight by a cowl, but some expose it, so be careful to select the correct bulb, not only for aesthetic reasons but also because different types of bulb cast different beams of light, and it is possible to achieve a very narrow beam or one which will cover a wide radius. Spotlights are ideal for task lighting and are an invaluable addition to the range of light fittings now available.

UPLIGHTERS

Uplighting directs light at the ceiling or wall, and this is then reflected back into the room to provide a very soft, general illumination with subtle plays of light and shadow. Uplights are sometimes referred to as 'wall-washers' because they do actually bathe the walls with soft illumination. Because of this they could highlight any imperfections in the wall so must be used with discretion and care. However, if the room has beautiful plasterwork with ornate cornices, then uplighters can only enhance them.

Uplighters can be attached directly to the wall, but increasingly they are being used to replace the standard lamp and are suitable for use in a variety of interior styles. Most standard uplighters are tall and elegant, and when used with downlighters can create very atmospheric rooms.

It is also possible to buy uplighters designed to be placed on the floor, and these look very effective when positioned behind plants, beneath glass shelves and in corners, as they produce accent lighting which can range from the romantic to the dramatic.

makes for greater flexibility, particularly over a dining table or working area; they are especially useful for people who cannot or should not climb to change a light bulb. Pendant lights are generally thought of as hanging from the centre of a ceiling, but they can be used creatively – fitted over a defined space, such as a breakfast bar, clustered to form a canopy of light, or hung in rows. A pendant should relate to the size and scale of the room, and a high-ceilinged room can accept a larger fixture than a low-ceilinged one.

SPOTLIGHTS AND TRACKS

Spotlights were originally devised for use in commercial premises such as art galleries and jewellers' shops to concentrate light onto particular display areas, and it was not until the 1960s that track-mounted spotlights began to be adapted for use in a domestic interior. The track system can work well, and is a flexible form of lighting to highlight furniture arrangements, pictures and collections, but it can also be intrusive, because the more spotlights you use, the more dominant the track will be. It is also necessary to ensure that the light fittings themselves are easily adjustable so that the angles of light can be changed without too much bother, and that the fittings are able to move along the track smoothly.

MAINTENANCE OF BULBS AND LIGHT FITTINGS

Apart from changing a bulb when it has burned out, most people pay very little attention to the upkeep

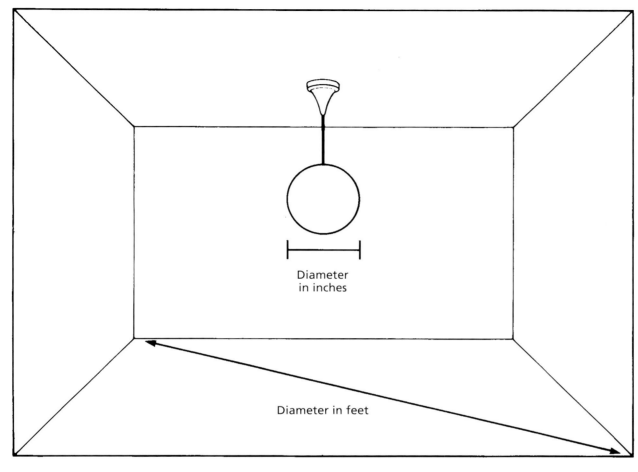

Diameter
in inches

Diameter in feet

A good rule of thumb when trying to determine the correct size for a pendant light is that it should measure across in inches what the diagonal of the room measures in feet

of their lighting systems; however, just a little care can prolong the life of a basically energy-inefficient form of light. For instance, most lamps produce heat, and this sets up convection currents in the air, which is normally full of dust motes. When these settle on a light bulb, especially one with a reflector, they can reduce the light output by at least 50 per cent. Moreover, what appear to be dirty marks around light fittings have also been caused by the dust being attracted to the light source.

Most bulbs can be cleaned by wiping with mild detergent and water, making sure that the socket end stays dry; reflector bulbs, however, need special care, because their reflective qualities can be ruined by fingerprints and smudges. For this reason a careful dusting with a lint-free cloth is the best method of keeping them clean.

Every light fitting is designed to take a particular bulb and it is important to use the correct one each time a bulb is replaced. It is a good idea to keep extra bulbs to suit each light fitting, and to write on the protective covering where each should be used.

LIGHTING FOR SPECIFIC AREAS AND ROOMS

It would be quite possible to write at length about lighting each area of an interior; however, there are many books which provide a more in-depth explanation of various lighting plans, so the following suggestions intend to do no more than help you decide what kind of lighting could be most usefully employed in various locations.

155

RIGHT: *A double wall lamp which would look elegant in a long corridor*

FAR RIGHT: *A reproduction lantern-type pendant, again suitable for hallways and corridors*

Use lighting to accent something such as a chest containing, perhaps, a pretty plant or flower arrangement, or use a covered striplight over a favourite picture to highlight and draw attention to it.

HALLS, CORRIDORS AND STAIRWAYS

The average hall is is very often simply an area through which one passes to reach a specific room; because of this, and the fact that so few activities take place there, its lighting is often an afterthought rather than a considered plan. This is a shame, because it is the area first seen by visitors and can give an immediate impression of both the house and its owners.

A hall should be a welcoming place where guests are immediately made to feel comfortable and at home – even if space is very limited it is possible to create a feeling of warmth and friendliness by skilful lighting.

At its most basic, the lighting should be adequate for safe passage from the main doorway to the rooms within; on the other hand, a uniformly bright hall can look just as bad as a poorly lit one, and the thing to aim for is contrast. If, say, the space beneath the stairs is not needed for storage, bring it to life with an interesting piece of furniture – perhaps a small

table holding a collection of pretty objects or figures – and accentuate it with a spotlight. Use shell-shaped or curved uplighters to wash the walls with light and throw interesting shadows, or put a lamp on the telephone table to create a pool of light and accent that area.

Lighting in corridors should also be considered carefully – nothing looks worse than a long corridor lit with just a line of pendant lights. Try instead to create pools of light by using downlighters or double wall-washers so that one feels drawn along it.

Stairways are often neglected, and people all too often rely on the light reflected from the hallway or other areas. Purely for safety reasons stairs should be adequately lit, but well-placed lighting can also emphasise an architecturally pleasing staircase and at the same time increase the feeling of space in a hallway.

At the very least the top and bottom of the stairs should be lit, but also consider half-landings, which could have a downward-directed light to emphasise the change in level and the possible danger of the next upward step. It is important to ensure that light does not shine directly into the eyes of someone going up or down stairs as this direct glare can be hazardous, and for this reason spotlights are not really suitable on stairways. Wall lights which follow the stair-treads work well and a time switch could be fitted to ensure that the staircase is automatically lit as daylight fades.

A dimmer switch is useful in halls, corridors and stairs as it can be turned to a very low setting at bedtime and provide a low-level and economical night light.

LIVING ROOMS

Perhaps of all the rooms in a house the lighting in a living room needs to be the most flexible. Most living rooms are multi-functional and many activities take place in them, so before deciding how to light them there are a number of questions which should be asked. For instance, is the room used primarily as a family room or for entertaining? Is it a formal room where precious paintings or objects are displayed, or an informal room where many activities take place, such as reading, watching television or sewing? Think about the room – where the activities are usually performed or where objects need to be highlighted – and then light it by concentrating on these specific areas.

Background lighting need not be limited to the traditional pendant light fitting: a general diffused light can be created by using one with a combination of down- and uplighting and dimmer switches. A special picture could be picked out by illuminating it individually, or a whole bank of pictures by using the wall-washing technique which will draw attention to that area of wall. If a writing desk is used in the room, then a desk lamp is ideal for providing a good local light, and for general reading ensure that there is a good table or floor lamp adjacent to an easy chair. For more detailed activities such as knitting or embroidery, a lamp which concentrates the beam of light directly onto the work is better, and a tilting shade will ensure that the strong light is directed where needed,

rather than creating an uncomfortable glare for others in the room.

Plants can be grouped together for greater effect, and if an uplighter is placed between them interesting effects can be achieved with very little effort – but make sure that the light is not pointing directly at sensitive leaves! Downlighters will emphasise an interesting piece of sculpture, and spotlights can be used to highlight decorative cornices.

Concealed lighting can also be very effective in a living room. For instance, cold fluorescent or cathode bulbs can be hidden under a pelmet to wash the curtains with light, or they can be placed on top of a pelmet board to bounce light off the ceiling and provide a soft ambience. Concealed lighting can also throw architectural features into subtle focus, and using it in recesses, niches and deep windows will add extra dimensional interest. Even without a roaring fire, fireplaces can be a focal point by using a light concealed by a pelmet or coving to illuminate objects placed on the mantelpiece or flowers placed in the hearth.

Two lamps which will create a general diffused light, the one with the bracketed arm being particularly adaptable

157

A modern solution to lighting a dining table

DINING ROOMS

Whether the dining area is part of the living room or separate, the main thing to achieve is a comfortable atmosphere in which to dine and relax. The lighting scheme should be designed to work equally well for relaxed family meals, elegant dinner parties and suppers *à deux*, so it should be carefully considered. Any table setting is flattered by a light suspended directly over the dining table, but the height at which it is hung is absolutely critical. The shade should not be so high that it produces an uncomfortable glare, nor should it be so low that it obscures the face of the person opposite. A rise-and-

fall fitting is probably the most flexible way of achieving this. The light bulb should not be visible from any chair, and a half-silvered one will further reduce any possibility of glare. If the table expands, then consider three lights, one over the centre and one at each end, possibly on different lighting circuits so that they can be used independently.

Although these suspended fittings are ideal for actually lighting and enhancing the table settings, they do tend to throw the people sitting at the table into the shadow; however, this effect can be countered in two ways. The first is to use a dimmer switch to create a less intense light which will bring the faces back into focus, though this does mean that the dramatic pool of light over the table is lost; the age-old remedy is to use candlelight. Placed along the centre of a table, candlelight provides a mellow, flattering light source which highlights both the faces of the diners and the sparkle of silver and crystal.

Most dining rooms have a serving and a carving area – either a simple side-table or a more formal sideboard – and ideally this area should be lit as well, not only to prevent accidents with knives but also to show off the tempting display of cheeses, puddings or fruit. A strategically placed downlighter works well in this situation, and gives a soft focus to the whole area.

Chandeliers are a traditional and beautiful source of light over a dining table, but care must be taken in choosing the right wattage of bulb. Low-wattage bulbs create atmosphere and sparkle but may not shed sufficient light by which to eat, whilst high-wattage lamps will produce too much glare. The answer to this problem is to use low-wattage bulbs to create the atmosphere but supplement them with strategically placed alternative sources of light, or with candles.

Light over the dining table is the main consideration in a dining room, but the atmosphere can be further enhanced by the use of perimeter lighting; this can be concealed lighting behind pelmets and controlled by a dimmer switch, or floor-sited uplighters, torchères and picture lights – all of which will provide a feeling of intimacy and comfort.

BEDROOMS

A bedroom can be a very private place and it is important to get the lighting right, for it usually needs to be both functional and intimate, and the two elements can be mixed by using the correct lighting.

A bedside light is essential to avoid having to stumble across to a wall switch during the night. Obviously this should be near at hand, and wall lights or mini-spots mounted onto the wall are ideal as they do not take up valuable space on a bedside

table. The light should also be flexible so that when reading, say, the possible glare from shiny pages can be avoided. If a bed is shared, it is useful to fix two spotlights over the centre of the bed so that the light from each can be focused outwards and away from the other person. On and off switches placed by the bed as well as by the door are both convenient and useful for controlling all the lighting in a room.

Make sure that there is a good light source near mirrors, not only for dressing but also for ladies making up, and for this a pair of lights placed about 3ft (0.9m) apart on either side of a mirror is ideal. For dressing, a narrow area of light placed at an angle of 45° above a full-length mirror should illuminate your whole figure in a most flattering way.

Wardrobes and cupboards are often forgotten areas, yet nothing is more frustrating than not being able to see clothes or shoes clearly. Both wardrobes and cupboards can easily be lit by a simple GLS lamp or fluorescent tube positioned just inside the door so that the light shines onto shelf areas as well as hanging clothing, and it can be activated by a small door switch or simple pull chain.

Not all bedroom lighting has to be practical; mood lighting can add interest to bedroom space, and again, uplighters, downlighters and spotlights can enhance various areas, architectural features or pictures, and create interesting effects.

BATHROOMS

Safety is of paramount importance here, and most countries have strict regulations covering electrical wiring in the bathroom area. Fittings which are likely to get wet should be enclosed to prevent shorting of the current and, even more importantly, electric shocks. In Britain only pull-cord switches are allowed inside the bathroom, and if a dimmer is used, it has to be wired outside the door. The high moisture level in most bathrooms means that fittings have to be approved for damp locations, which inevitably limits the choices available.

Most bathrooms have a mirror placed directly

Remember that light will be reflected from a coloured table cloth onto the faces above it: a bright green one can make people look quite unwell, whereas a pink one will give them a glow of health.

should not be possible to touch *any* piece when using the bath or shower.

KITCHENS

Kitchens should be enjoyable work places, and more thought should perhaps be given to the lighting system chosen for a kitchen than for any other room in the house. Its main function is to facilitate the preparation of food, and light needs to be directed exactly where it is needed, be it over a work surface or over a cooker. There are three main work areas in a kitchen – the preparation surfaces, the cooker and the sink – and all can be lit by a variety of task lighting.

The most commonly used lighting for a work surface is a long, fluorescent tube concealed beneath a cabinet or shelf, as it will provide a high volume of light and soft shadows. However, kitchen surfaces are often more reflective than those elsewhere in the house so this kind of lighting should be planned to minimise glare. It is therefore usually placed towards the front of the cabinet or shelf so that it does not shine directly on the working area.

Fittings should provide a wide coverage of soft-edged light and there are numerous ways of achieving this. Ceiling-mounted lights should be placed somewhere above the *edge* of any horizontal surface so that cabinets, shelves and the cook do not cast shadows onto the work surfaces. Recessed, pendant or surface-mounted fittings can all be used, and the final choice is usually dictated by the kitchen design. Track lighting means that spotlights can be directed onto the cooker and work surfaces or into cupboards, and eyeball downlights can be rotated to direct light exactly where it is needed.

Although the task lighting is of primary importance in a kitchen, it is also possible to use other lighting to create a relaxed atmosphere, especially if the room is used for eating in. A low light placed over the eating area will create a relaxing pool of light, and the task lights can be turned off or dimmed to hide the clutter of food preparation.

An absolutely streamlined bathroom with the only touch of colour coming from a simple fish bowl placed on a column. Note the concealed lighting, which fits perfectly into the feel of the scheme. The shower has been cleverly fitted into an alcove

over the washbasin, or certainly near to it, and lighting this area is very important. It is usually the first place you see yourself each morning and the last place you see yourself at night, and for your self-respect it is important to have lighting which is kind and soft, yet revealing enough to carry out the routine tasks of washing, shaving or making up. The traditional theatrical make-up light which surrounds three sides of a mirror is probably still the best source of illumination, and it can consist of long incandescent tubes or lots of small low-wattage pearl bulbs.

For general lighting in a bathroom, ceiling-mounted downlights with internal reflectors give good illumination, and these could be supplemented by spotlights strategically placed to illuminate various areas or by weatherproof surface-mounted fittings used, perhaps, to light a shower or bath area. The main thing to remember when fixing any electrical equipment in a bathroom is that it

PROJECT PAPERS

Most interior design schemes look attractive in natural light, but the whole effect can be ruined at night if the lighting is chosen without due attention to the function and general mood of a particular room. Not only should background lighting be subtle, but any special task lighting – whilst continuing to do its job – should not be too intrusive to the other people using the room.

There is such a large range of lamps and fittings available that almost any effect can be achieved. When working through the next two projects think hard about the possibilities and try to be imaginative in the final scheme.

PROJECT 19

Using the original room plan and the electrical symbols given in Chapter 2, show how you would light this particular room. Add brief notes explaining why you have chosen this particular lighting scheme and which bulbs and light fittings will be used to create it. Examples of these could be pasted onto a separate A4 sheet.

PROJECT 20

Imagine that there is a hall approximately 8ft (2·4m) square with a staircase leading from it, as well as a 20ft (6m) passage running to the back of the house. The whole area has until now only been lit by a pendant light in the centre of the hall. Think about this, and then show by sketches and illustrations how lighting could be used to bring the whole area to life, and what considerations will have to be borne in mind.

Imagine that there are doorways leading off the hall and passage and indicate their position on the sketch. Be as imaginative as you like – the effort put in will result in an increasingly varied and interesting portfolio.

CHAPTER 11

BATHROOMS

The Romans, Greeks and Egyptians placed great importance on the pleasures to be derived from bathing, and there is still evidence to suggest that their bathing areas were lavishly decorated and beautifully equipped to provide every comfort and ease for this pleasurable pastime. Sadly the importance that these early civilisations placed on such pleasures was gradually lost, and until relatively recently, personal ablutions were mostly performed in spartan rooms deprived of both comfort and warmth. Over the last few years, however, things have thankfully altered, and it is no longer thought sybaritic to indulge in a comforting hot bath and in soft, warm towels; the bathroom, in fact, has become a haven of privacy and warmth.

A well-planned bathroom can add considerably to the value of a house, but it can also be one of the most difficult rooms to organise and decorate successfully. In post-war houses bathroom space tends to be minimal, whilst in period properties where other rooms have been converted into bathrooms the space often appears to be cavernous. Whichever category a bathroom falls into, the first thing to consider is its functional aspect, for until that is sorted out it is difficult to consider a decorating scheme which is not only attractive but suitable for particular needs.

Whether the plan is to alter a present bathroom, create a new one from existing space, or start from scratch, first check through a few questions so you have a better idea of what you are trying to achieve.

1   How many lavatories, washbasins, showers or baths are really needed?
2   Could extra space be created if washbasins were put into suitable bedrooms?
3   How much hot water is needed and is the present system adequate?
4   Could the lavatory be in a separate room?
5   Is the present bathroom in the right location?
6   Are the present fixtures suitable or should new ones be considered?
7   Will the plumbing need to be altered?
8   Is showering preferred to bathing, or are both needed?

9   Does the bathroom have central heating or does it need a separate heater?
10   Is the lighting adequate and safe?
11   Is a shaver socket necessary?
12   Will the wall and floor surfaces stand up to a steamy atmosphere?
13   What sort of storage is required?
14   Is there an airing cupboard in the room?
15   Will small children or elderly people be using the bathroom?
16   What sort of taps would be suitable?
17   What colour suite is preferred?
18   If the present suite has to be retained, can a suitable colour scheme be worked around it?

These are just some of the questions to be asked. Perhaps there are others which are more pertinent to a particular bathroom, but hopefully this list will help concentrate the requirements and sort out the priorities. Here, in more detail, are some of the main points to be considered.

LOCATION

The location of a bathroom can be crucial to the smooth running of a household. It should be easily accessible from the bedrooms and, ideally, the lavatory should be in a separate room. Even a small two- or three-person household would benefit if room could be found for a separate shower or a washbasin in a bedroom, and a lavatory located downstairs is most useful. If there is room, a bathroom *en suite* is a very civilised addition to any household – but remember that if it is contained within an open bedroom then it cannot include a lavatory, as building regulations insist that a lavatory must be separated from any living area by a door.

All the possibilities, however, will hinge on the location of the main soil stack which services the house. In old properties it is likely to be a cast-iron pipe at least $4\frac{1}{2}$in (11cm) across and fixed to an outside wall; in newer properties it will be a boxed-in duct located somewhere inside the house. If,

When planning a bathroom for an old house it is worth checking with the local authority to see if it is possible to get a home improvement grant to help towards the cost.

In this narrow bathroom the only logical place for the bath was beneath the window and the pipework has been kept to a minimum by keeping the bath taps, the toilet and the washbasin lined up on the same wall

however, a lavatory is needed in a place where a connection to the soil stack cannot be made easily then a recent innovation, a macerator-style lavatory, may solve the problem.

PLUMBING

A basic bathroom consists of only three major items – a washbasin, a bath and a toilet – and it is important not only to site these as near as possible to the soil stack but also to remember that the pipework connecting these three items has to lead to the nearest possible link with a main public drain. These factors will determine the optimum position for any bathroom and, if every penny counts, then the shorter the distance the pipework has to run the better; in any event pipework is never pretty, so the shorter the pipe-runs the less there

will be to box in or disguise. It goes without saying that *if* existing plumbing can be used it will save a good deal of money; this may originally have been badly planned, however, so a visit from a really professional plumber will be very worthwhile.

In Britain it is actually illegal to alter or add to existing plumbing or drainage without reference to the local building department. It is not that they particularly want to be bureaucratic; their interest is mainly confined to falls, traps and vents, because it is their duty to prevent the possibility of nasty illnesses caused by the drains not working properly. The building department will probably also insist on a minimum number of air changes per hour in a bathroom; these can be achieved either by a window of a specific size or by a fan vented to the outside wall.

A good plumber who is familiar with the local building and water regulations will be invaluable

Note how in this bathroom the washbasin, bidet and toilet are lined up against the same wall to cut down on pipework, which would run beneath the floorboards to reach the bath

A corner bath has been used to good effect in this prettily decorated and irregularly shaped room

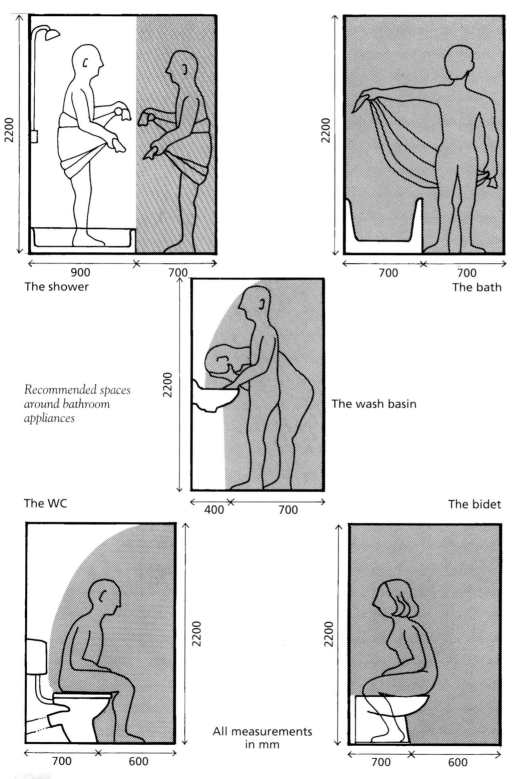

2200

900   700
The shower

2200

700   700
The bath

Recommended spaces around bathroom appliances

2200

400   700

The wash basin

The WC

The bidet

2200

All measurements in mm

700   600

2200

700   600

when alterations are planned, as he will take into account things that otherwise might not even be considered. For instance, he will check that the water flow is adequate to cope with the proposed changes; he will check to see if washbasins, baths and showers drain quickly; he will look for signs of leaking in existing pipework; he will turn the taps on to see if there is a banging noise and turn them off again to see if they drip; he should check the hot-water system to see if the boiler is adequate for the alterations intended, also that the overflow pipes from tanks and their outlets are not dripping onto walls and causing damp patches. Finally he will want to locate the stop cock to ensure that it is both accessible and working.

PLANNING A BATHROOM

Once it has been established – at least from the plumbing point of view – where it is sensible to place the necessary fixtures, spend some time planning what sort of bathroom can be fitted into the available space. In particular, try to plan it so that the toilet is not the first thing to be seen when entering the room.

Whether the bathroom is small or large, it is important to plan it so that the space is effectively used, for once the fittings have been plumbed in they are permanent; it is vital therefore to plan the layout before setting off to buy any new fittings. Remember that every activity carried out in a bathroom, be it simply opening the door or stepping out of the bath, requires a certain amount of room, and the best way to organise the space available is to draw up a scale plan. Consider whether the same space could serve two purposes; for example, could it be the area where you step out of both the bath and the shower, or could it be used to step out of the bath and to stand at the washbasin? Even this last activity takes up maybe more room than anticipated, because people usually bend when cleaning their teeth or washing and an allowance should be made for this. (see diagrams).

A scale plan may indicate that perhaps the bath

Ingenious use of space has provided a novel way of storing clean towels

should be located beneath the window – but this could be draughty, and could also make it difficult to open or clean the window when necessary; in this case a corner bath or shower might be the answer. Work out, too, where light fittings, shavers and hair dryers might be located, as well as dry towels, household linen, spare soaps and shampoos. If space is very tight then a basin could be fitted into a vanity unit, which could house toiletries and spare toilet rolls as well as concealing pipework. Other space-saving ideas might be a shower head over the bath, or to turn the bathroom door into a sliding one, or to fit roller blinds instead of conventional doors to conceal storage space.

Nothing is worse than a chilly bathroom, and some form of heating is essential. Try at the very least to install a heated towel rail and remember that most hot-water systems allow the bathroom radiator to be constantly warm. This has the added advantage of reducing the effects of condensation which, incidentally, can also be solved by fitting an extractor fan.

If it is really out of the question to fit a radiator then it is possible to buy specially designed bathroom heaters which can be mounted onto a wall, directing the heat downwards. As with all electrical fittings, this type of heater will be operated by a pull-switch.

Bathrooms are private places, and this is an important aspect to consider at the planning stage. To preserve privacy, many bathroom windows are fitted with obscured glass but this is not always the most attractive answer. If it is too expensive to replace this glass, consider covering it with a lace or muslin curtain which will conceal it but still allow in the light. Shutters to cover the bottom half of the window, and which can be pulled across when the bathroom is in use, offer one alternative; fitting the bottom half with mirror glass is another. A row of green plants on the window sill will also provide

To give an illusion of even greater space in a small bathroom it is a good idea to fit sheet glass or mirror tiles onto one or even two walls, as this will immediately double the perceived area.

daytime privacy, perhaps supplemented by a roller blind at night.

A bathroom must be easy to keep clean and it must work efficiently, but it should also be a place to relax and feel at ease. Some people prefer a bathroom to be absolutely streamlined with nothing to distract from the sheer pleasure of lying in a warm bath; others prefer a more intimate, even luxurious, room with tempting bottles of aromatic oils within reach, magazines close at hand, green plants to soften hard tiles and draped curtains to enclose them. Even in town a person may prefer a country-style bathroom with the bath standing free, perhaps simply painted on the outside, towels heaped in wicker baskets, naive animal paintings on the wall and old huckaback fabric trimmed with crochet fringing at the window.

Today there are so many bathroom fittings available that whatever the style desired, there is certain to be a fitting which will fit the bill. One enterprising company has even designed fittings which will turn the bathroom into a gymnasium, with a sunbed placed on top of the bath and various pieces of exercise equipment sited nearby. Look at the photographs throughout this chapter to get some ideas for planning and decorating your own bathroom.

Obviously a large bathroom offers far more scope for planning. For instance, consider making a sunken bath by building a series of platform steps up to the rim and covering them with the same carpet or tiles that are used on the floor; allow a free-standing bath to take pride of place, but add a few stylish accessories such as a large yucca plant or a floor-standing candelabra; put a small table holding books and magazines beside a comfortable chair or sofa for relaxing after a bath; or turn the room into a private gym.

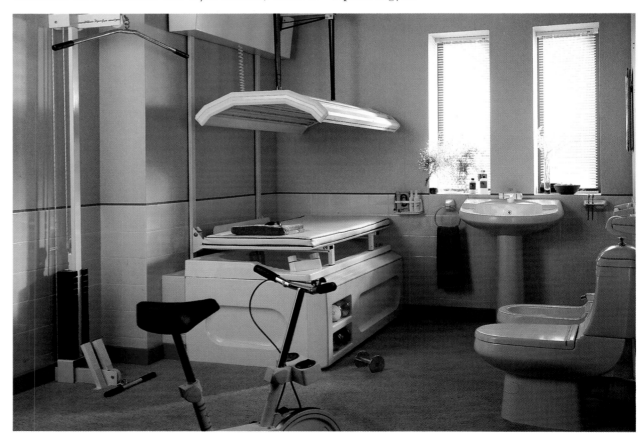

An Aquagym with a sunbed fitted over the bath, which is also a jacuzzi. Neat Venetian blinds add to the feeling of efficiency

Who would not feel at ease in this prettily decorated bathroom? The 'period' fixtures and fittings and large floor space re-create a feel of Victorian luxury

THE BATHROOM FITTINGS AND FIXTURES

There is such a wide range of coloured bathroom suites available today that it should not be difficult to find one to suit individual preference. Like everything else, some colours become fashionable and then disappear and I suspect many of us still have to live with the ubiquitous avocado shade which was so popular a few years ago. If a bathroom

suite is too good to change, the only answer is to 'go with it' and minimise its impact by repeating its shades in the other furnishings – the eye is taken by the feeling of the whole rather than the actual colour of the fittings. Look at the photograph on p165 to see what was done with a bathroom which had a melon yellow suite, which originally stood in stark contrast to a heavily patterned wallpaper of pale blue roses on a navy background! The new owners immensely disliked the melon colour, but

171

the suite was brand new and they could not afford to change it, so they decided instead to dissemble the shade by stencilling slightly darker arched window shapes onto the walls and filling them with lilies, all in various tones of the melon colour. And these colours were carried through to stencilled muslin curtains, so that the actual suite no longer dominated the room.

Very deep, strong colours seem to be the vogue at the moment, but really the only shade which will allow unlimited design possibilities is white. Remember that once the fixtures are in place they will probably be permanent – the attractions of a deep brown or ruby red bath might not last very long, and any decorating scheme would have to suit these colours. A white suite, however, would allow a change from, say, a smart navy and white scheme one year to a more romantic pink and floral one the next.

BATHS

Baths were traditionally made from cast iron which would then be finished with vitreous enamel to ensure long life. These, and pressed steel models, are still being made and old ones are much sought after. However, they are quite expensive to buy and many people settle for cheaper baths made from acrylic plastic. There is an enormous variety of styles and colours available in these plastic baths and they have two main advantages over the cast-iron or steel models: they are warm to the touch and they do not chip. However, they do have to be cleaned with care as it is easy to scratch them with cleaning abrasives, and they can become dull with use. Between the solid cast-iron baths and the flexible acrylic models is a range made from glass-reinforced polyester. This is a strong, rigid material and it is available in a wide range of finishes including luminous pearl and smart metal.

The standard British bath is usually 1,700mm long and 711mm wide (5ft 6in x 2ft 4in), but baths can be made to fit almost any shape or space – if space is at a premium a sit-up bath might be considered which is only about 1,070mm (3ft 7in)

long. And corner baths, although they appear quite large, actually take up less floor space than standard rectangular ones, so these could be considered, too – just make sure that it will be possible to get them up the stairwell and through the bathroom door.

The so-called spa baths are becoming increasingly available and popular. The first one was invented by a Signor Jacuzzi for his arthritic son, and today they come in many guises. Most, however, have strategically placed underwater jets which create invigorating, powerful bubbles to pummel and massage the body in a way which is increasingly recognised as being beneficial for stress. Steam baths and saunas are also increasing in popularity; they do not take up much room, and again, they promote a feeling of well-being and health.

SHOWERS

Nowadays many people prefer to use a shower rather than taking a bath. Showers are faster, and are very economical on hot water as they only use about one-fifth of the amount needed for a bath. Even more appealing is the fact that the water for showers can be supplied by a wall heater which takes water direct from the mains and heats it only when the tap is turned on; it thus provides an appreciable saving over water heated in the conventional way.

Showers also take up less room than baths, so they are ideal where space is limited. Although a drying area is needed outside the shower, an enclosed shower will fit into an area as small as 3ft (0·9m) square. The important thing to remember is that conventional showers need a minimum head of water 3ft above the shower head to produce adequate water pressure. Showers fitted with a wall heater are not restricted in this way.

Shower stalls can be bought as self-contained units or they can be built into the structure of the house. Airing cupboards or alcoves can be converted into showers by completely waterproofing the area with tiling, all over the walls, floor and ceiling. If a shower stall is chosen it

This photograph shows clearly the space-saving qualities of a corner bath

is wise to buy the largest tray possible, as nothing is worse than trying to manoeuvre in a very tight space; and a tray which is deep enough can be used for bathing small children. Corner quadrant trays are also available, and if space is very limited they may be the answer to getting a quart into a pint pot.

If it is intended to fix a shower head over the bath, try to choose a wide, flat-bottomed bath with a non-slip surface and ensure that the surrounding walls are adequately waterproofed by tiling, or by fixing rigid clear sheets of plastic over wallpaper. A fitted glass or plastic screen, or a shower curtain fixed to the side of the bath will protect the rest of the bathroom from splashes.

The electric shower giving instant hot water from a rising main has already been mentioned. The other two most common types are the mixer shower and the thermostatic mixer shower. The mixer shower draws on water from both the hot and cold storage tanks and the temperature is controlled by a lever built into the on/off knob. A thermostatic mixer shower has a built-in safety device to prevent water overheating if, for instance, a cold tap is turned on in another room, and is perhaps the best conventional shower to use.

A fairly recent and welcome addition to the bathroom scene has been the power shower, and according to the professionals, this is the fastest growing sector of the bathroom industry. Basically a power shower has its water pressure boosted by means of a pump, and this results in powerful, invigorating jets of water rather than the pathetic dribbles normally associated with British showers. Some companies are now providing power shower kits but, like all plumbing and electrical fittings, it is best to call on the services of a professional to advise on the type needed for a particular system, and also to fit it properly. Conventional showers need at least a 3ft (0.9m) head of water to function properly, but power showers offer anything from 25ft (6.5m) to 102ft (31m) heads of water – so there is a vast difference between the two types of water pressure. But what do these figures actually mean? It is quite simple really – a 30ft (9.1m) head gives the same effect as lifting the water tank an extra 30ft (9.1m) into the air.

The shower in this modern bathroom has been positioned neatly in one corner, while narrow Venetian blinds are used to obscure two large windows

If a shower curtain is needed but is not available in colours or design to match the rest of the colour scheme, buy co-ordinating fabric and line it with waterproof plastic.

Pumps can be positive or negative. A positive pump is used when the shower head is at least 9in (22.8cm) below the water level in the storage tank, and a negative pump is used in situations where the shower head is *above* the water storage tank. A plumber will also mention other factors to be taken into account such as 'valve value', 'flow control', 'water volume' and 'pump power', all terms which very few of us really understand – so it is essential to take some sound advice if considering a power shower.

One shower company has introduced a combination steam and shower unit in which the temperature can be kept at a constant level between 20°C and 30°C. Apparently this system will help those who indulge in it to relax, to breathe more easily and to become 'deep-down clean'. It is even fitted with a moulded seat large enough for two

people, and only takes up a square metre of space.

WASHBASINS

There are three main types of washbasin – wall-hung, pedestal and inset – and each has its own particular advantages. A wall-hung washbasin needs a strong, firm wall to support it, but it does leave the floor space below free and uncluttered. A pedestal washbasin is useful for unsound walls because, although bracketed onto the wall, most of its weight is taken by the pedestal fitting, which will also hide ugly pipework. A washbasin set into a vanity unit, an old washstand or a tiled surface with cupboards beneath looks neat and will not only hide the pipework but will also provide extra storage space.

In a bathroom it is best to choose as large a basin

FAR LEFT: *A fitted white vanitory unit with a feeling of period charm. The wide rim is a useful addition*

LEFT: *This prettily shaped white suite which looks good in its cottage setting*

as possible so that washing and shampooing can be more easily accomplished. Also, whilst a washbasin may look attractive, its surrounding rim may not be wide enough to hold soaps, toothpaste, toothbrushes and shampoos without these sliding into the basin itself; so make sure that the rim is sufficient for these necessary items.

Like baths, washbasins are available in all manner of materials, colours and shapes, ranging in size from the smaller space-saving basin to the extravagant double basins, and in style from the sleek Italian to the patterned Victorian. There is something to suit all tastes and spaces!

TOILETS

In old houses, toilets may be part of the bathroom, but in new houses the building regulations stipulate that they should be in a separate room, and this can certainly save congestion in the morning rush to get ready for work or school.

Toilet bowls are usually made from glazed vitreous china and are flushed either by means of a washdown or a syphonic system. A washdown system, although noisy, is the most common and the least expensive, simply releasing water from the cistern which is then flushed around the rim of the bowl and down an outlet pipe. A syphonic system is very quiet, using water to create a vacuum in the bowl and atmospheric pressure to force the contents into the outlet.

The bowls can be pedestal-mounted or wall-hung, and the water tanks can sit immediately above them, be concealed behind a false wall (remember to leave access) or made into quite a feature. Look at the photograph opposite to see how attractive the bracket-mounted tank looks with its brass accessories. Toilet seats should be comfortable and secure, and they are now available in warm-to-the-touch plastics which match the bowl and are easy to clean. Old-style wooden seats are enjoying a revival, too, and one firm even offers to paint the family coat of arms on the lid!

BIDETS

Although bidets have been common on the Continent for years, they have only recently found favour elsewhere. They cannot take the place of other bathroom fittings, but if space is available then they do complement the other washing facilities, and are particularly useful for disabled or

A shower over the bath has
been given the same grand
fabric treatment as the window,
but this time using waterproof
material to line the curtains

elderly people who cannot climb into a bath. They can be filled by conventional taps or by water entering from under the rim. Do remember to leave sufficient room at the back for knees and at the sides for legs.

Special regulations require bidets to have separate hot and cold water supplies and a vented soil pipe, so it is worth checking these requirements before installing one.

TAPS AND MIXER UNITS

After finally deciding on the colour and style of bathroom suite, it is equally important to select suitable taps. They should complement the chosen fittings and work into the decorative scheme. For instance, chrome taps would look totally wrong in a traditional bathroom where brass fittings would be much more appropriate, and equally, old-style brass fittings would not be appropriate for a modern streamlined bathroom where austere, simple fittings would look better.

Taps and mixers do not necessarily have to be fitted to the bath or washbasin; they can be fixed directly onto the wall, and this makes for easier cleaning all round. Some mixer units have a shower attachment which can be very useful, both for hair-washing purposes and for rinsing out the bowl or bath afterwards. Some taps and mixers use a lever movement instead of the more common turning operation, but whichever is chosen, check that it is easy to handle and that the water is directed straight down into the bowl or bath and does not spray out in a wide arc.

FITTINGS AND FIXTURES FOR ELDERLY AND DISABLED PEOPLE

Safety is of prime concern. Someone must be able to get into a bathroom to give assistance if necessary, and it is a good idea to fit the door with a special lock which incorporates a safety device so that it can be opened from the outside.

There should be plenty of handrails, especially around the bath and lavatory, and in some cases a wall-mounted adjustable sink frame may be immensely useful. This device is worked by lifting or pushing a contact lever at the side of the basin, which adjusts its height and locks it in place by means of an electric motor.

The floor should be covered in a non-slip vinyl or carpet so that there is no danger of slipping, and non-slip mats should be used in both the bath and the shower basin. If space is tight, then a shower with a fold-down seat is particularly useful, and a shower head position which can be adjusted by means of a slide bar control.

Finally, a dimmer switch fitted to the main hall or landing light will ensure that the route to the bathroom is visible at night, and extra safety is ensured by fitting a dimmer switch to the bathroom light, too, so that it can remain on all night at very little extra cost.

PRACTICAL DETAILS

A bathroom takes constant wear and tear, and it has to cope with extremes of temperature and with moisture and steam; particular attention should therefore be paid to the surface decoration, which includes walls, floors and windows. Suitable bathroom lighting was discussed in Chapter 10, but it is worth repeating that safety is of the essence. Now some of the other practicalities of bathroom decoration should be considered.

WALLS

Although it makes sense to tile certain areas of a bathroom – immediately above the washbasin, around the bath and certainly in a shower formed from a space in the bathroom – a fully tiled bathroom can appear chilly and rather uninviting. Use tiles by all means, but perhaps complement them with well-chosen eggshell or silk-finish paints, or with washable or spongeable wallpapers. This could be an opportunity to try out some of the special paint finishes such as marbling or sponging, and these could be carried through onto radiators or cupboard fronts; the durable oil-based glazes used in these techniques make them particularly suitable in a steamy atmosphere. The bathroom walls also offer the perfect chance to try your skills as a muralist or a stenciller. Any mistakes can be quickly erased with another coat of paint, but if the results are pleasing, a particular motif may be carried through onto something else in the bathroom.

Dark wallpapers and matching curtains could throw white bathroom suites into relief and create a feeling of luxury; whilst on plain walls, a ³/₄in fabric braid outlining the shape of the room and running up and around the door could complement a smart Roman blind and create a feeling of sophistication.

Marble is a traditional, luxurious bathroom surface for both walls and floors, but it is expensive, and its cool surface may not be ideal where condensation is a problem. However, there is a washable wallpaper available, and also vinyl tiles which imitate it; or try a marbled paint finish.

Tongue-and-groove panelling is a good choice for a country-style bathroom, and it could be used up to dado height so that the pipework and the lavatory cistern could be concealed behind it and a useful shelf formed along the top. A sharp, modern look could be achieved by using sheet mirror glass or mirror tiles, perhaps steam-sensitive so that condensation does not form on the glass, and lightly tinted to give a flattering glow of health.

FLOORS

A bathroom floor needs to be easy to clean and water-resistant. The size and age of the family may well dictate whether you choose easy-care vinyl sheeting, sealed cork tiles, ceramic tiles, sealed wooden floorboards or foam-backed carpet. The first four options are certainly water-resistant and easy to look after, but ceramic tiles can be cold to bare feet and both they and wooden floorboards can be rather noisy. Manufacturers are constantly improving their range of carpets suitable for the bathroom, and one of the latest has a smart twist-loop pile mounted onto a waterproof bitumen backing which is both moisture- and stain-resistant.

It is best not to fix wall-to-wall carpet permanently as it may need to be lifted in order to get to underfloor bathroom pipework, or to be dried if the bath accidentally overflows.

WINDOWS

The dressing of bathroom windows calls for particular thought – unless, of course, they are not overlooked. Most bathroom windows do need some form of screening, however, though preferably without taking too much light away – obscured glass has already been mentioned, with some of the ways to make it more attractive, and there are many other practical ways of treating a bathroom window. A full-blown curtain treatment is not the best or most obvious solution, unless there is plenty of room.

Consider instead using blinds: vertical louvred blinds, horizontal pinoleum and Venetian blinds, bamboo or roller blinds – the variety is immense. If a slightly softer look is preferred, then think about pleated Roman blinds, gauzy festoon blinds or perhaps even terry towelling with appliquéd shell motifs or bordered with a contrasting colour. Café curtains hung from a pole halfway down the window, or a lace panel stretched over the entire window area, are other attractive solutions.

If the view from the bathroom window is very dull, think about fitting a sheet of caning inside the window frame. This can be held in place with a narrow beading, and the cane theme could be carried through onto cupboard fronts or, perhaps, with a cane chair and cane shelves. Adhesive vinyl with a stained-glass pattern can also be effectively used in this way and is particularly useful for creating a period look.

Think, too, about fixing glass shelves at intervals over the entire window. These could be filled with a variety of delicate green ferns or with coloured glass bottles which would reflect their colours prettily into the room. Delicate china pieces which echo the colour of the fittings can look very effective; and all can be lit by a concealed striplight or downlighter at night.

Wooden Venetian blinds have been painted a rich, reddish brown to offset the white, cream and pale pink colour scheme. The cool, tiled floor completes the picture

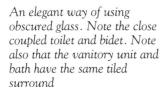

An elegant way of using obscured glass. Note the close coupled toilet and bidet. Note also that the vanitory unit and bath have the same tiled surround

STORAGE AND ACCESSORIES

Although the bathroom is often one of the smallest rooms in a house, all the equipment for washing and grooming the occupants needs to be near at hand and organised in such a way as not to appear too cluttered and messy.

The days have long gone when the only storage space to be seen in a bathroom was the traditional mirrored cupboard placed over the washbasin; at the very least space will be needed for towels, shampoo, toothpaste, toilet rolls, soaps, deodorants and medicines, not to mention such things as cleaning materials, a laundry basket and a waste receptacle.

Whilst it is preferable to hide – or even to lock – some of these away, a few things, such as a pile of fluffy towels, and pretty soaps and toiletries, can be

left on view; they actually add to the feeling and style of the bathroom, so consider an area of open shelving, perhaps at one end of the bath, to take these. The apparent size of a small bathroom can be increased by a series of mirrored cupboards on the washbasin wall; these will also hold and hide many necessities, and may incorporate such additions as a shaver point and fluorescent lighting, or even heated units which will help prevent the mirrors from misting over.

If it is intended to box in exposed plumbing, think about building a proper cupboard around it instead. It need not be very wide but the extra hidden space could solve many storage problems; and instead of completely boxing in the side of a bath, doors could be incorporated at either end to take all the cleaning equipment. And if the sunken bath idea appeals, why not arrange for extra space to be built into the framework? It could take the form of deep drawers or hinged-lid storage.

If built-in cupboards are fitted, consider fixing a waste-bin and a laundry bin to the insides of the doors; this will save on floor space and hide the detritus of everyday living. Also consider a range of cupboards fitted immediately over the toilet, particularly if the cistern has already been hidden by a false wall. For some reason this area is very rarely considered as possible storage space, but with thought, it can be put to good use.

Moreover, the accessories themselves can provide additional storage space. For instance, in a high-ceilinged bathroom a traditional clothes airer could be used to keep or dry towels, or to hold a mixture of clean towels and green plants. An old-style wooden towel rail is attractive and useful, and so are towel rings; and a range of hooks on the back of the bathroom door will hold bathrobes, towels or a laundry bag. A toothbrush holder can incorporate a space for a glass and a tube of toothpaste which leaves the washbasin free of everything except a bar of soap; and bathroom stools often have built-in storage space which can be used to hide dirty laundry or to hold clean towels.

Finally, try to be creative with bathroom space. Obviously basic storage is needed, but the other accessories will depend on the style you want to create. It may be absolutely clean and streamlined, or you may prefer green plants, wicker baskets, collections of shells and pictures on the walls. Only you can decide this, and it will be great fun putting all these ideas into practice.

USEFUL TIPS
WHEN DESIGNING A BATHROOM

- The outsides of rusty old baths can be given new life by cleaning them with a wire brush attached to a power drill and then painting with a rust-inhibitor and a primer before giving them a final coat of gloss paint.

- Instead of discarding a chipped cast-iron bath,

consider having it re-enamelled by a professional resurfacing company. It could save a lot of expense and mess.

- Classic-shaped, old but chipped basins can be repaired with a waterproof filler and then painted with an appropriate design using artists' oils before sealing with a polyurethane varnish.

- Corner baths use less space than rectangular ones.

- Savings can be made by fitting a timer onto heated towel rails so that they heat up, say, an hour before bathtime and switch off an hour afterwards when the towels are dry.

- Plain wall tiles can be given new life by stencilling them with acrylic or signwriters' paints and sealing them with polyurethane varnish.

- To prevent shadows when shaving or making up, direct the light source towards the face rather than directly at the mirror.

- A low box will hide children's bathroom toys and can be used as a step to help them climb in and out of the bath.

- Bathroom drawers can be fitted with sectional trays to hold small items which can easily be mislaid if left free in the drawer.

- If the bathroom is tall and narrow, consider bringing the ceiling colour part way down the walls, or make an eye-catching window valance.

- If there is no space to fit a mirror over the washbasin, fix up a concertina mirror instead. It takes up very little space and can be pulled into position when needed.

- Instead of a conventional towel rail, think about fitting a towel radiator which will not only heat the room but has horizontal bars which will hold several towels.

The sunken bath, richly painted walls, tiled floor and imaginative window screening give this bathroom a Moorish feeling

PROJECT PAPERS

So much has to be considered when planning a bathroom: the safety aspect is crucial and the range of fittings and accessories seems almost limitless. The projects below will be immensely useful additions to your design portfolio, and will show that your design skills are not limited to just living areas.

For both schemes, show as much detail as possible so that a prospective client will understand how the various problems have been overcome and the rooms improved.

PROJECT 21

Measure up your own bathroom and plot it onto graph paper with a scale of 1:20. Mark the position of plumbing points, windows and doors and, as with the furniture plan, cut out bath, washbasin, toilet, shower or bidet shapes and place them on the graph paper until a scheme is found which you feel will work best for you, remembering to leave enough activity space around each fitting as shown in the diagram on p168. When happy with the scheme, glue the shapes into place or draw around them directly onto the plan. Colour in or project the scheme however you like, but in any event complete a key and briefly make notes explaining the difficulties which have had to be overcome and why you feel this scheme is the best solution.

PROJECT 22

Imagine that you have been asked to suggest a scheme for a bathroom which is 7ft (2m) wide and 15ft (4.5m) long. It has a window in the centre of one of the 7ft (2m) walls and a door at the end of one of the 15ft (4.5m) walls. The bath, washbasin and toilet are in good condition and have to be retained, but are in the now unfashionable avocado green shade. They can be located wherever you wish in the room. Show by sketches and colour-boards how you would go about making the avocado shade 'disappear', and bring the whole room up to date.

CHAPTER 12

BEDROOM PLANNING

OF ALL THE ROOMS in a house the bedroom is perhaps the one which can be made the most personal. No-one else's preferences need be considered – unless there is a partner – and the room can be made into anything you want. This may be monastic simplicity with just a bed and a chair, or total indulgence in all your most romantic fantasies with lots of lace, frills and fresh flowers which the rest of the family would consider to be 'over the top' in the general living areas. It is the room where a person can most truly be himself, and should be filled with the things which give the most pleasure. For some this could be a good radio, a good light and a mass of books and magazines; for some it could be a small TV to watch the programmes *they* want to see; and for others it could simply be a place where they can relax and do nothing more than daydream. A bedroom is concerned with moods, and it should be somewhere to fall asleep easily and wake up ready to enjoy a new day. Whatever theme is chosen, whoever occupies that room must be really happy with it and want to spend time in it.

Obviously the bedroom's primary function is to provide a private area in which to sleep, and if this is all that is required of it, then planning is easy. But if it has to serve other purposes, then much more thought will have to be given to its design. As always, find some paper and a pen, as there is really only one way to get everything right and that is to plot it onto graph paper. This will not only make you aware of the available space but will pinpoint where the power sockets are, as well as wall-space gobblers such as large radiators or awkward alcoves. A plan will also show up any odd features which will have to be taken into account – for example, the room narrowing at one end, or windows of unequal height on the same wall.

A bedroom check-list could read something like this:

1   Is the room to be shared or for sole occupancy?
2   Has it to serve purposes other than merely sleeping?
3   How much storage space is needed?
4   Is fitted or free-standing storage space preferred?
5   How near is it to the bathroom or toilet facilities?
6   Would it be possible to create an en suite bathing area?
7   Is there room to create a separate dressing area?
8   Does the room get the morning or evening sun, or none at all?
9   Is the room soundproof?
10 Are there enough power sockets by the bed for lighting, radio etc?
11 Are power sockets available on other walls for a TV, a trouser press or supplementary lighting?
12 Is there a switch by the bed to control all the lighting?
13 Are the windows overlooked?
14 Is there a fireplace?
15 Should a telephone be installed?
16 What kind of flooring is preferred?
17 Is the room to be used by an elderly person?
18 Will special facilities be needed?
19 Is there enough space around the bed for changing sheets, cleaning etc?
20 Is the route between the door and the bed clear or are there obstacles in the way?

Before any decision is made as to how to decorate a bedroom, it is important first to take a look at some of the basic necessities.

THE BED

About one third of a person's life is spent lying in bed so it is worth investing in the very best mattress and bed base that you can afford. Some people may feel that the money spent should represent a lifetime's investment, but even the best bedding companies suggest that a mattress or bed base should be changed at least every fifteen years. And if the amount spent is divided by the number of nights one might expect to spend in the bed over a fifteen-year period, then this will actually soon be appreciated as a very small investment for the comfort received in return.

Old beds can become lumpy or uneven, perhaps

This light and airy bedroom carries the stencilled theme through onto chair cushions and bedspread for a perfectly co-ordinated look

sinking into the middle if one partner is heavier than the other, but whether the bed is soft or hard, it should always give adequate support. People who suffer from backache may prefer a harder bed than normal, but even then the main thing to remember is that when lying down, the body should make an impression on the mattress, but the mattress should not mould itself to the body's shape. Couples who have different levels of comfort may find that two connecting mattresses offer the most versatile way of achieving this but the only true way of finding out what really suits the individual is to spend some time lying on beds in a showroom. Good salesmen are quite prepared for this, and there is no need to feel embarrassed, particularly if the normal sleeping position is assumed. The salesman may suggest that you should first lie flat on your back and see if you can get your hand into the small of your back. If this is easy to do then the bed may be too hard; but if you have to struggle to slide your hand in, then it may be too soft. If you then try to turn onto your side but find it difficult to do so, this also means that the mattress is too soft for you. The mattress needs to be at least 6in (15cm) longer than the tallest person who will be using it, and wide enough to put your hands behind your head without your elbows hanging over the edge. There is nothing worse than sleeping in a bed where your heels rub on the edge of the mattress or where you feel that you will roll out every time you turn over, so it is worth going up a size to get the ultimate in comfort.

At this stage do not worry about how to dress up the basic shape, just concentrate on buying the most suitable mattress and base for your needs and think about the styles you can create later. If you cannot afford to buy a mattress and a base at the same time, then buy the mattress first and use the floor as the base, perhaps building a platform to make it look more interesting or imposing. There are four main types of mattress:

OPEN-SPRUNG

To date this has been the most commonly used system. It is basically a row of springs joined together at the top and bottom by a continuous small spiral spring and enclosed within a wire mesh framework. The springs can be upholstered with hair or layers of padding and move as one unit, allowing the pressure to be spread evenly throughout the mattress. The gauge of the wire used to make the spring will govern its resilience – the higher the gauge the thinner, and therefore more giving, the spring will be. Do not buy a spring mattress if the label does not state how many springs it contains; a top-quality double will contain at least 1,000 and you should not go lower than 500 at the cheapest end.

POCKET-SPRUNG

This is the most expensive form of sprung mattress, with as many as three times more springs than in an open-sprung mattress. Under tension, each spring is hand-sewn into its own calico pocket and moves independently, so that it only 'gives' where weight is actually applied. This means that if two are sharing a bed the heavier partner will not cause the mattress to dip, and if one is restless the other person's part of the mattress remains relatively undisturbed. These are points well worth considering when making the final choice.

CONTINUOUS SPRINGING

This is a continuous length of wire which is knitted together to produce an interwoven springy web rather like the old iron-frame beds. The web is held in place by a wire framework within the mattress, which wears and moves in a way very similar to an open-sprung type.

FOAM

Love them or loathe them, foam mattresses are here to stay and they are undoubtedly the best choice for people who suffer from dust-induced allergies, whilst those made from 100 per cent foam are recommended by many osteopaths. Best-quality foam can be as expensive as a sprung mattress. Indeed, some foam mattresses have open-coil springs inserted into them, but perhaps the best combination is a mixture of polyurethane and latex foam used in layers. The top layer is usually made from latex as this will mould to the contours of the body, and if a honeycomb formulation is used the degree of firmness or softness can be varied. Foam mattresses are light to lift and move, but they can be hot to lie on in the summer.

MATTRESS UPHOLSTERY

Whatever the choice of mattress, they will all be covered in some form of upholstery: however, never be swayed into buying an unsuitable one just because you prefer the colour or design – after all, it will very rarely be seen in that state again.

Sprung mattresses will have layers of padding directly under the top cover – sometimes known as ticking – and these may consist of hair, felt, coir or wool. Apart from covering the springs, their main purpose is to provide comfort and warmth. A good-quality ticking is usually made from a natural fibre such as cotton, which will allow the mattress to 'breathe' more efficiently than a cheaper synthetic fibre – these may also be slippery in use. The ticking and layers are held in place by some form of stitching or tufting, the tufting being done by hand and found in good-quality mattresses. If a mattress has a completely smooth top, be wary, for it means that the cover has simply been pulled tightly over it and the layers have not been stitched into place.

BED BASES

The traditional bed base was an iron frame with a webbed wire stretched over the springs, and although these can still be found they are very heavy and collect a great deal of dust. The modern equivalent is the so-called divan base which is the same size as its mattress, and they are usually sold

From cot to first bed is an exciting move for a child, and this small bed designed in a ship's cabin bunk style cannot fail to win approval. The integral drawers are extremely practical, too

together as a pair. This base is available in several versions:

Firm edge: This type of base confines the springing within a wooden frame and is therefore a good choice if the bed is also to be used as a seating unit in a teenager's room, for example. Firm-edge bases sometimes have built-in storage drawers, so they are to be recommended if storage space is critical.

Sprung edge: This is the most expensive and luxurious base, giving even support to a mattress, thus prolonging its life. The springs are supported on a wooden base and go right up to the edges; this means that the whole of the mattress can be used, and that it will not dip in the middle.

Solid top: This base has no springing at all, being just a wooden platform, sometimes upholstered with foam for added comfort. It is a perfectly acceptable alternative to a sprung base as, providing the mattress is of good quality, it will provide all the necessary support. Check that it has ventilation holes as these will help the mattress breathe.

Other bases include:

The slatted wooden base: This base has no springs, but is often made from pre-sprung timber. The slats are held on two side support rails and are either screwed into place or stapled onto lengths of strong webbing, but a double bed should also have a central support of some kind to prevent the slats from sagging.

This type of base is often found on space-saving beds such as children's bunks, pull-out trundle beds where a second bed can be stored beneath a single bed, and wooden-framed beds, and it is always well worth checking that there are sufficient slats to prevent the mattress protruding down through them.

The pallet base: For people who have to live and sleep in the same room, the Japanese-style *futon* is gaining in popularity as it will double as a seating area and is simple to unroll at night. The pallet base is designed to be used with a futon and can be a very simple solid wooden structure or made with wooden slats.

189

A plain but thickly padded headboard in the same colour tones as the canopy, whose material is also used for the decorative bows over the mirrors and the edging of the throw-over quilt

BEDHEADS

The main purpose of a headboard is to protect the wall behind from getting grubby and to provide a comfortable support against which to rest. A padded headboard will suit this purpose well, but do try to be imaginative in the choice of shape and fabric, as nothing looks worse than a shallow, meanly padded board covered in a shiny, synthetic 'velvet'. If necessary, get a local carpenter to cut an interesting shape and then have it professionally upholstered, perhaps in the same fabric as the window treatment or bed-hangings.

In Chapter 9 it was explained how to make a headboard by suspending foam or feather pillows covered in a suitable fabric from a curtain pole; this is an easily achieved alternative to a fully padded headboard.

Some headboards are purely decorative, and these include elaborate brass or metal designs as well as those in open bamboo and cane. They can

look stunning and a chosen bedroom style may demand this type of treatment; though make sure there are plenty of plump pillows available, as these bedheads are not comfortable when sitting up in bed.

Do not confine your thinking only to conventional bedheads, either; a screen or a beautiful rug can add emphasis to the head of the bed, and in the right setting can be much more effective.

MAKING THE BED

In recent years the traditionally made-up bed of underblanket, a pair of sheets, two or three top blankets and a bedcover of some kind has gradually given way to the continental quilt or duvet. Each has its devotees and each has its own particular advantage. A bed made with sheets and blankets undoubtedly not only looks good but tidy too; whereas a duvet eases the chore of bedmaking but can look bulky and untidy. Some people prefer the weight of blankets to the lightness of a duvet and the final choice is very much an individual one. It may be useful to know the meaning of one or two of the terms relating to duvets:

Tog rating: In Britain, the British Standards Institute, in conjunction with manufacturers, has come up with a scale to explain the expected warmth of a duvet. Body heat is given off by the sleeper and the amount of warmth retained in the duvet is called a tog. In steps of 1.5, the scale ranges from 4.5 to 13.5 togs – if 4.5 togs is the equivalent of a single wool blanket, then it should be easy to assess the warmth one might expect from, say, a 10.5 duvet. It is generally reckoned that duvets with tog ratings up to 7.5 are ideal for summer use, and 10.5 is the norm for winter use. But for people who live in a particularly cold area, and for those who feel the cold badly, a duvet with a tog rating of 12 or 13.5 would give the necessary extra warmth.

A recent addition to the duvet range has been the double-decker. This is made from two duvets, one with a summer tog rating and one with an autumn one. For winter use they can be fastened together by means of velcro tape, and in theory the result is three quilts for the price of one. It has to be said, however, that the two together can be quite weighty and it might be a better idea to have a summer and a winter duvet and leave it at that.

Duvet fillings can be natural or synthetic, the most luxurious being made from duck down which is exceptionally light and warm. However, good-quality synthetic fibre fillings are now being created which have a softer feel than the original synthetics and they will mould themselves to the body in the same way as a down or feather duvet. They are a good choice for people who suffer from asthma or are allergic to natural fillings, and because they wash easily, they are ideal for children.

Loft: Loft is a rather technical word used to describe bulk in relation to weight. The more air in a filling the better its insulation; that is why eiderdown is so prized for its light fluffiness and warmth.

Size: A duvet labelled 'double' has been designed for the average double bed, but if a bed is not a standard size it is best to measure the mattress and then buy an appropriately sized duvet. The thing to remember is that it should be at least 18in (45·5cm) wider than the bed. If one partner is particularly bulky or tall this should also be taken into account with, perhaps, two single duvets working better than one large one.

PILLOWS

Like duvets, pillows can be filled with feathers or down, a combination of both, or polyester fibres. Foam pillows were very popular at one stage, particularly for allergy sufferers, but they seem now to have been overtaken by the various synthetic fibres. Fillings are usually described as medium or firm, and whichever is chosen the standard sized pillow measures approximately 18 x 30in (45 x 75cm) and will fit most pillowcases on sale.

BED LINEN

There is such an enormous range of bed linen available that when planning a new colour scheme it should be no problem to find exactly what is needed in both the material and the colour or design. Traditional linen sheets are wonderful to sleep between but are difficult to launder; cotton is soft and comfortable; flannelette is comforting in the winter; and only a masochist would sleep in nylon! There is also the cotton/polyester mixture which combines the feeling of cotton with the bonus of a minimum-iron finish.

If the bed linen turns out to be the wrong colour but too good to discard, think about hiding it beneath a bedspread or comforter which complements the overall scheme. Thin Indian quilts are not very expensive and come in some stunning designs and colours; old white cotton bedspreads can still be found in flea markets, and so too can crocheted ones; and an extra length of curtain fabric could make an attractive throw which will help tie the whole scheme together.

In summary, when considering beds and bedding it is important to know what to look for and what to expect for the money invested in this large item. With such a confusing mass of products around it is vital to know what you are looking at, as a slick salesman could easily talk the unaware into something which is not at all suitable for their particular needs.

STORAGE

The next most important thing in a bedroom is storage space, for unless there is a separate dressing room, the bedroom has to cope not only with storing winter and summer clothes, hats and shoes but perhaps suitcases and other baggage too. And if the bedroom has a dual purpose then it is even more important to find a home for everything, and every space should be utilised to the full.

Storage drawers in the bed base have already been mentioned, but if you do not have these, consider using other forms of underbed storage such as shallow boxes on wheels or strong plastic rectangles with rigid sides and a zipped top; both these will hold spare bedding or clothing which can easily be reached.

Custom-built bedroom units are now much more attractive than they used to be, and together with a good bedroom designer will undoubtedly make the best possible use of all the available space, incorporating hanging and shelf units as well as dressing tables, bedside cabinets, book shelving and light fittings. The fronts of these units can echo existing architectural mouldings and features or they can follow through a decorating theme, perhaps being covered in fabric or given a special paint finish which will make them 'disappear' almost completely. Needless to say, such units can be expensive, and in the event of a move will have to be left behind; but they could well add value to the property, which would be one way to recoup the investment.

There are many ready-made fitted units available which may be perfectly adequate – though by their very nature it is unlikely that they will exactly fit a particular space, and infill panels may have to be used. If sliding doors are used then check that the floor is absolutely level; they will never work properly if it is not, so folding doors may be a better alternative where opening space is tight.

Unless they are really well built and in keeping with the architectural features of the room, fitted units may not always look right, particularly in a period property, and free-standing wardrobes, drawers and dressing tables may be a better option. There is a large range of modern styles available and auction rooms are good hunting grounds for traditional designs. Free-standing furniture is obviously more versatile than fitted furniture as it can be moved from room to room and also from house to house, so for those who are likely to move fairly often it could be a more sensible buy.

Do not forget, either, that blanket boxes and ottoman chests offer good storage space and can double as tables or seating where necessary.

HEATING

Although the temperature in the bedroom is usually lower than in other rooms, some form of warmth is vital at bedtime and when getting up in the morning. With luck the bedroom will already be connected to a main central heating system, in which case there will be no problems, although 'inherited' night storage heaters may be worth keeping even if they *are* incompatible with a new design scheme: instead of going to the expense of removing them in order to fit something more aesthetically pleasing, they can always be hidden by a fabric screen.

If there is no form of heating at all, but gas is used in other parts of the house, then it is possible to fit a wall-mounted gas convector heater which is fairly unobtrusive and will warm the room quite quickly. An electric blow-heater will also give instant warmth, and this could be a short-term solution, particularly if the room is carpeted. And do not forget the most comforting thing of all – an electric

Instead of bedside tables, use chests of drawers to provide more storage space.

An ugly radiator has been concealed behind a fabric 'balustrade' with urns of flowers placed on top, so turning an eyesore into an attractive feature

blanket. An electric underblanket is cheap to buy and costs little to run, though remember that the underblanket should be turned off when you get into bed. An electric overblanket, however, can be tucked in and left on all night – utter bliss for those who feel the cold.

EN SUITE BATHROOMS

The luxury and glorious privacy of an *en suite* bathroom is beyond price, being able to use it exactly when and for as long as you wish without feeling guilty about other people's needs; and when guests come to stay, no quick dashes in and out and no more queuing!

The drawings on p194 may help in planning, and if the bedroom leads off a landing or a corridor extra space can be stolen by blocking off a part of it and opening up the internal bedroom wall to give access to it. Even with limited space it may be possible to

fit in a fold-away shower, or at the very least, a washbasin built into a unit which will also provide extra storage space.

When planning extra washing facilities, remember to choose a wall which will allow the waste pipe to be connected to the main drainage system by the shortest possible route, and think about screening the fittings in some way so that they are not too obvious, and appear to be as one with the rest of the decorating scheme. For instance, a shower cubicle could be disguised by fitting a sheet of mirror glass against one or two of its sides; this will act as an excellent looking glass whilst adding space and light to the room. A range of cupboards could also screen the bathroom from the rest of the room; or consider building a half-wall which will hide the fittings but still give a feeling of space. And a tall decorative screen is another option, not only adding interest but also concealing the washing facilities.

Of course there is no need to separate the bathing

area from the bedroom physically at all. An elegant bath can be the basis for a whole decorating scheme, with carpet linking the two areas and individual pieces of furniture such as a bentwood rocking chair, an antique washstand, a pretty table or a chest of drawers adding to the whole atmosphere of the room.

THE GUEST ROOM

Few people can afford the luxury of having a room which is used solely by guests; it usually has to be put to other uses and may double as a study or a sewing room, so extra thought must be given as to how it is furnished and decorated. Whatever its day-to-day function, a guest room should feel warm and welcoming – though whilst it is important to create pleasant surroundings, it is not necessary to spend a great deal of money on furnishing and decorating it. It is also important to remember that the 'spare' room should not be a dumping ground for the assorted bits and pieces which have no place elsewhere.

Basically, a guest needs a comfortable bed, some hanging space and a good light by which to read; if a washbasin, tea-making facilities and a radio or TV can be added, then so much the better as they will make life easier for everyone in the household. Two single beds are much more versatile than one

Buy extra curtain fabric to make bed valances and to create a co-ordinated look.

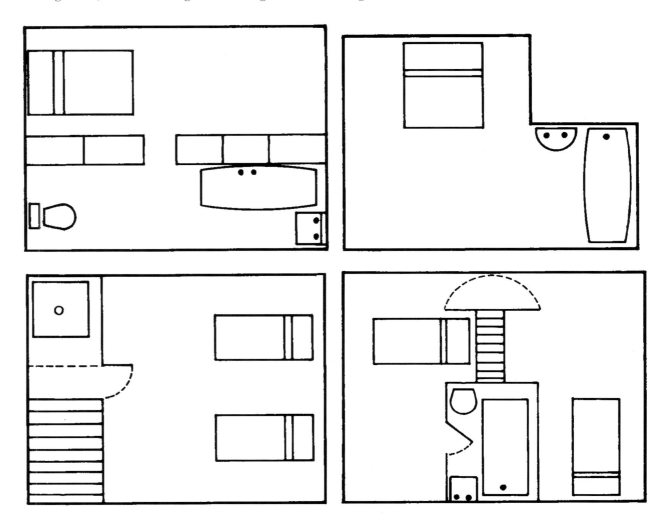

Bedroom/bathroom combinations:
TOP LEFT: *A large bedroom divided by fitted cupboards to provide an* en suite *bathroom*
TOP RIGHT: *An L-shaped bedroom provided with a bath and washbasin, shielded by a screen*
BOTTOM LEFT: *A shower room created from the end of a corridor, enclosed by a sliding door*
BOTTOM RIGHT: *A tightly fitted bathroom created over a stairwell*

A young girl's bedroom. The nursery combination wardrobe and small table have been updated by covering them with an attractive paper, from which the rest of the room takes its theme

double bed, and if space is tight, it may be possible to place them at right angles, with a lamp table where they meet, rather than placing them side by side. When the room is not being used as a guest room, this arrangement can be made to look like a luxurious sofa, with the addition of lots of cushions, particularly if fitted divan covers are used. Underbed storage drawers are useful so that duvets or other bedding can be tidied away when not in use.

Sofa beds are no longer uncomfortable horrors, and some elegant designs are now readily available; moreover, in a modern setting, a Japanese *futon* looks stylish and takes up relatively little room. A blanket box will hold the bedding and double up as a bedside table, and a screen covered in the same material as the curtains will hide a simple hanging rail which will take the visitor's clothes.

A thoughtful host will make sure that not only does a guest room have a few welcoming flowers, but that a bottle of mineral water and glasses are provided, also some tissues, a clock, a wastebin, guest towels and soap, perhaps a new spare toothbrush and toothpaste, some writing paper and a pen, a small repair kit and some magazines or books. All these items will help the guest feel at home and independent.

CHILDREN'S ROOMS

When a baby is expected, particularly when it is the first, the temptation is to decorate its bedroom with miniature furniture and nursery wallpaper. But a child grows fast, and as time goes on there may not be either the time or the money to redecorate the room very often. It makes sense therefore to start with furniture which can be adapted as the child grows, and to choose a relatively simple decoration scheme, perhaps in a basic primary colour stencilled with an animal frieze or with a small-print wallpaper which will not date.

Cots are now available which can be converted into beds as the child grows, and a wardrobe with adjustable hanging rails will serve for many years. The top of a wooden chest of drawers or low cupboard could initially be used as a changing area, with clean nappies stored beneath; then later the chest could provide storage space for clothing. A low comfortable chair will always be useful, for feeding the baby or for those sleepless nights when a cuddle is the only answer; later on the child may

Single small chairs found at an auction can be painted with lead-free colours and then painted with the child's name, to make unusual christening gifts.

A delightful nursery, featuring an unusual canopied cot and child-size painted furniture. Notice how the blue edging on the soft furnishings matches the paper frieze perfectly

This four-poster bed, with its feminine fabric, adds importance to a simple period room

want to fill it with teddies or other soft toys. Bunk beds with built-in storage and desk space will be useful as the child gets older, as they take up relatively little room; however, it is important that they are substantially made because they will be jumped on and generally abused.

Children are messy creatures, so a warm but easily cleaned flooring such as cork tiles or cushioned vinyl, perhaps supplemented by a washable rug, is the answer and should last for years. On the safety side, all sockets should be fitted with safety covers, windows should have safety catches so that they do not open too far, furniture should only be painted with lead-free and non-toxic paint, and rounded corners are kinder to small heads.

A room should be able to grow with the child, and he or she will undoubtedly soon have very strong views on how the room should look – so get the basics right in the first place, and schemes can

evolve and develop as the years go by.

DECORATING A BEDROOM

Many of the ideas and suggestions already discussed concerning lighting, wall finishes, types of flooring, soft furnishings and window dressings are equally applicable to sitting-rooms and bedrooms. Perhaps when reading through them you already had a fair idea of the look you wanted to achieve, particularly in a sitting-room. In the bedroom the morning light is particularly important because it really can affect one's outlook to start each day. We all feel much more positive if we awake to sunshine – even when the sun is not shining or cannot reach the bedroom, it is possible to create an impression of warmth and sunlight by the colours chosen for the walls and ceiling, complemented by well-chosen fabrics.

An interesting treatment for a single bed fitted into an alcove. The window curtains are duplicated around the alcove, and complementary wallpaper adds to the feeling of warm opulence

Warm yellows are a good choice; even on the dullest day they give instant sunshine which will raise the spirits, and this is true of the whole spectrum right down to soft terracotta which is a comforting, friendly colour. Soft pinks have long been a popular choice for the bedroom and can be enlivened with a dash of fuchsia or complemented by a sagey-green. Strangely, whilst blues and greens can look too cool, a pure white will reflect every ray of light and makes a perfect backdrop to dramatically patterned fabrics.

A bedroom is the one room where the ceiling is likely to be looked at almost as often as the walls, and instead of painting it in a bland colour, consider giving it a cloud effect or create a ceiling rose with cut-out wallpaper or with a stencil. If the ceiling is very high, paint it in a dramatic warm colour such as a honey-gold, bringing this right down to picture-

rail level, and then echo the shade with a design painted below the picture-rail or by using a matching braid to outline the doors and windows.

Tenting and walling could have been invented for the bedroom – they create a stylish and private cocoon, and can disguise insulating felt panels, uneven walls and very high ceilings.

The bed will almost certainly be the most dominant piece of furniture in the room, so enhance it with rich hangings or drapes combining textures and colours in an interesting way. Toning stripes and paisley patterns can look wonderful when used together and could turn a bed into a Bedouin tent; or indulge your most romantic fantasies by using lots of lace, muslin and silk to create a veritable boudoir.

If your taste is formal and elegant rather than romantic, then you will probably prefer to let the simplicity of traditional furniture set the mood instead. Nothing else looks quite so sumptuous yet so simple as a beautiful sleigh-shaped Empire bed or a Biedermeier-style wardrobe made from the very finest woods. To set off lovely furniture, walls should be subtly textured with dragging or sponging, and trompe l'oeil panels would look very distinguished. Striped wallpaper would also enhance this classical look, and windows need to be given a long, narrow treatment in proportion to the furnishings. Polished wooden floorboards strewn with Persian rugs or a fitted carpet with a subtle pattern work well with this style of furnishing; accessories should follow through the elegant theme.

For those who are devotees of modern furniture with its plain simple lines and bold shapes, there is no reason why it should not look just as stylish in a period house as in a contemporary one. Clean, modern furniture makes rooms appear larger, and if you are a tidy person you may find this style far more appealing and calming in a bedroom than the rather fussy romantic look which relies heavily on more of everything, be it frills, cushions or ornaments. The modern look is expressed in cupboards, drawers and tables made from matt-finished woods such as beech and ash, sometimes stained, or decorative veneers like burr walnut or bird's eye maple. Clear and smoked glass side-tables, plain mirrors, chrome and fabrics made from natural fibres will all add textural interest, and discreet modern light fittings will help to create a relaxing atmosphere. In any room furnished in the modern style, accessories are much more obvious and they should add important colour accents. Simple shapes in strong colours work well for lamp bases, vases or ornaments, and green plants with stiff, sculptured leaves are a better choice than, say, fussy maidenhair ferns.

The main point to bear in mind when decorating a bedroom is that it is not necessary to adhere slavishly to any particular theme. It is your personal space, and it is important to surround yourself with furnishings and accessories which you like and which will add to the overall ambience of well-being, comfort and relaxation – because that, after all, is what the bedroom is supposed to provide.

USEFUL TIPS WHEN DESIGNING A BEDROOM

- Tall candlestick-style lamps on either side of a dressing-table mirror cast even light across the face when making up, and look elegant, too.

- A small ugly table can be given new life by padding the top and then covering it with a suitable fabric, stapled into place. A full-length skirt can then be gathered into fullness and stitched onto the top, making a perfectly acceptable dressing table.

- Give a battered stool the same treatment as above and create a matching dressing stool.

- Wide curtain net can be used lavishly to create an attractive, airy, and reasonably priced canopy over a bed.

- If plans include a built-in wardrobe, make sure its depth is sufficient to take a coat-hanger straight on.

- Wire baskets hung from runners are useful for storing small items in a fitted cupboard.

- A small wall safe disguised as a power socket is a useful place to hide jewellery.

- A pale colour scheme gives an illusion of space in a small bedroom.

- Two-drawer metal filing cabinets painted in bright enamels make sturdy storage in a child's room.

- A range of fitted wardrobes can be made to look less prominent by covering them with the same wallpaper as used in the rest of the room.

- An old patchwork quilt suspended from a curtain pole makes an unusual bedhead and adds interest to a plainly furnished room.

A perfect example of how straightforward materials such as muslin and pretty flowered cotton can be used to create a stunning bedroom. An old dining chair has been given a new lease of life, the hatboxes have been covered in matching material and the cushions piped in blue – simple details, but carrying the mark of someone who cares for the overall 'design' of the room

PROJECT PAPERS

Planning a bedroom is becoming an increasingly important part of interior design. For many people their bedroom is their refuge and can be decorated accordingly. However, with more and more people working from home and needing office space, or for families having to adapt a room to create a comfortable self-contained area for an elderly relative who likes to retain some measure of independence, a bedroom may have to serve several purposes.

These two projects are based on typical situations often faced by an interior designer. They should make you think long and hard about the best possible use of space, and will add worthwhile material to your portfolio.

PROJECT 23

Imagine a bedroom approximately 12ft (3·6m) square which has a central window, facing west, on one wall and a centrally placed fireplace on another wall. Next to the bedroom is a small room 5ft (1·5m) wide and 8ft (2·4m) long. Taking these basics and using graph paper, first draw the rooms to a scale of 1:20 placing the doors wherever you wish. Decide how you would adapt the accommodation to make a bed-sitting-room with an *en suite* bathroom for an elderly relative. When happy with the adaptations, ink them in and mark on the plan where various fittings and pieces of furniture would be placed. Make notes of what had to be done, what had to be taken into account, and what kind of colour scheme you feel would be appropriate. Enlarge upon these ideas as you wish.

PROJECT 24

A bedroom is a very personal place and anyone entering it can immediately get some idea of the kind of person using it. Either with sketches or pictures cut from magazines, illustrate what you consider to be an ideal bedroom, and on a separate A4 sheet list why you particularly like it, taking things like the layout, the furnishings, the accessories and the colour scheme into consideration. Also state whether you feel it could be easily adapted to fit into a different house style, and suggest an alternative colour scheme which would work equally as well.

CHAPTER 13

KITCHEN PLANNING

In MEDIEVAL TIMES the kitchen was literally the heart of the house, because it consisted only of an open fire in the middle of the one room which also served as a living-room and bedroom. As life became more sophisticated the fire was set into a wall with a wide chimney above it; but the kitchen area remained a gathering place for most of the household, providing warmth, food and company. By the eighteenth century, however, the kitchen area had mostly been reduced to a rather cramped and miserable work place; it is only comparatively recently that it has once more become a central part of family life.

When planning a new kitchen the first and most important step is to decide what sort of room is required. Some people prefer streamlined efficiency with every modern convenience, others prefer to create a friendly, warm feeling with unfitted furniture and a large table which will serve both as a work space and as a centre for family meals. If the kitchen is very small and there is also a dining room, it may be possible to make better use of both areas with some strategic wall demolition, resulting in a more useful kitchen/dining room where people can have the pleasure of seeing a meal prepared and where the cook can join in the conversation.

A professional kitchen designer once described planning a new kitchen as a veritable minefield, with so much to take into account and consider, so the absolute first priority is a check-list which will leave nothing to chance. Here, in no particular order, are some things to think about:

1 How much money is available?
2 Which style of kitchen is preferred?
3 What are the priorities?
4 How many people have to be catered for?
5 How long is the kitchen expected to last?
6 How will the kitchen be used and by whom?
7 Is there sufficient space available for all the proposed requirements?
8 If not, can more space be found from an adjacent area?
9 Will the kitchen be used for snacks only, or for all meals?
10 Will there be room for a fixed or fold-down table, or would a bar serve the purpose better?
11 Does there need to be a hatch into the dining room?
12 If there is a boiler in the kitchen, could it be moved to create more space, or is it useful for warmth?
13 What kind of fuel will be used – gas, electric, solid fuel or a combination?

OPPOSITE AND BELOW:
Kitchen units and appliances to a scale of 1:20

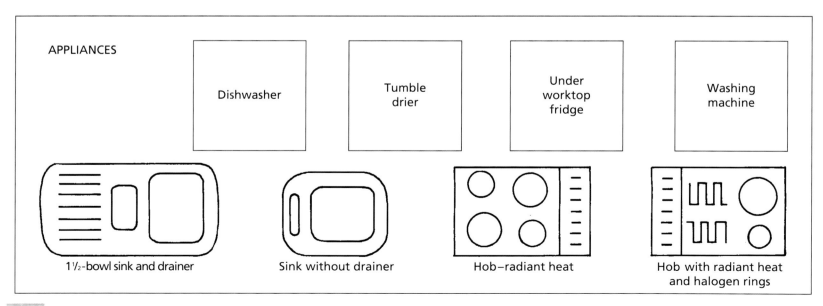

APPLIANCES

Dishwasher

Tumble drier

Under worktop fridge

Washing machine

1½-bowl sink and drainer

Sink without drainer

Hob–radiant heat

Hob with radiant heat and halogen rings

14 What cooking appliances are to be fitted – conventional electric or gas cooker, separate hob and oven, or an Aga-type oven?

15 Apart from the usual kitchen utensils and pots and pans, what else has to be stored in the kitchen – food, crockery, cutlery, glasses, cleaning materials, ironing facilities?

16 What appliances are to be incorporated – microwave, fridge, freezer, dishwasher, waste disposal unit, washing machine?

17 Could some of these be located elsewhere if necessary?

18 Is there adequate ventilation, or will provision have to be made for some?

19 Are there sufficient power points for all the appliances?

20 What combination of lighting will work best?

21 Can the existing plumbing be used, or will it have to be altered?

22 What form of heating would be the most effective?

These are some of the vital questions to be asked, and only when they have been resolved can kitchen planning really begin.

THE PLAN

In the first rough plan of a kitchen it is particularly important to mark the plumbing inlets and outlets, power points, gas points, light sockets, cooker points and ventilation, and the position of fixed items such as central heating boilers, separate timeclocks and various meters. Fitting a lot of equipment and storage space into most kitchens requires extremely accurate measuring, as a few millimetres' difference between the initial measurements and the delivered fitments can be vital. The golden rule is always to use a metal tape measure, and as all modern fitments are calculated in metric units, stick to a metric scale from the very outset: do not try to convert inches into metric later.

Start by measuring the walls and the positions of doors and windows, showing which way they open. Sill heights could also be an important factor, so measure these too and then add all the items mentioned above. If some equipment, such as a cooker or a refrigerator, has to remain, measure that too as you will need the dimensions if planning to move it or to work around it.

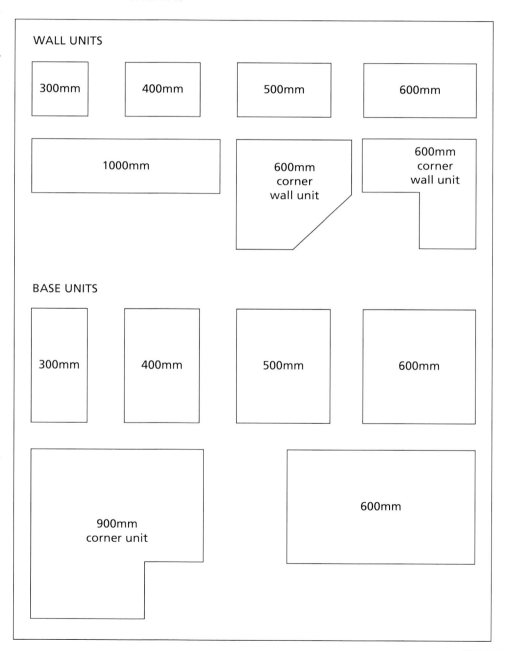

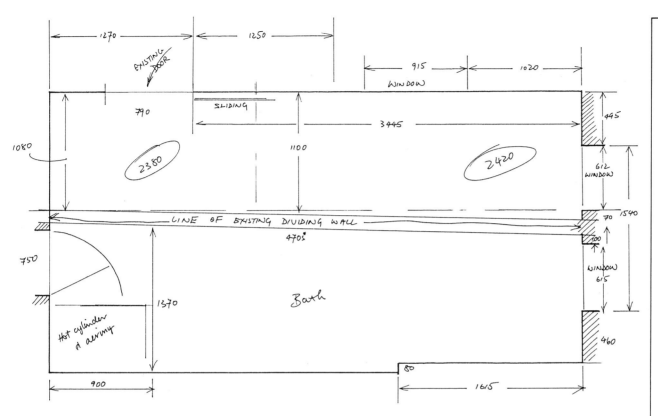

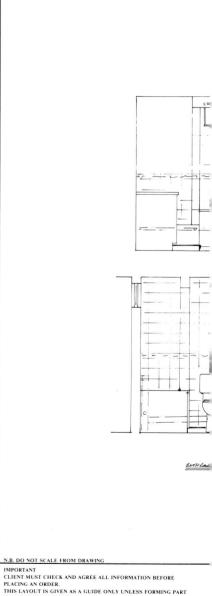

ABOVE: *Plan of existing kitchen*
RIGHT: *The finished plan*

All this information can now be transferred to a sheet of graph paper with a scale of 1:20, so that 25mm represents 500mm, the depth of many kitchen units. The scale models on p220 are to help plan your kitchen, so trace, enlarge and cut them out and play around with different layouts, incorporating as much storage space as possible and thinking about optimum cupboard space above work surfaces. Remember to leave room for doors to open and to plan it so that when, say, the dishwasher door is down, dirty plates can still be emptied into the waste bin.

Have a look at the two kitchen plans above and opposite which were drawn up by a professional kitchen planner. It can be seen clearly what the kitchen looked like on the first visit, and how a professional went about incorporating the practicalities of the client's requirements into the finished plan. Try to bring this degree of thought to your own finished plan.

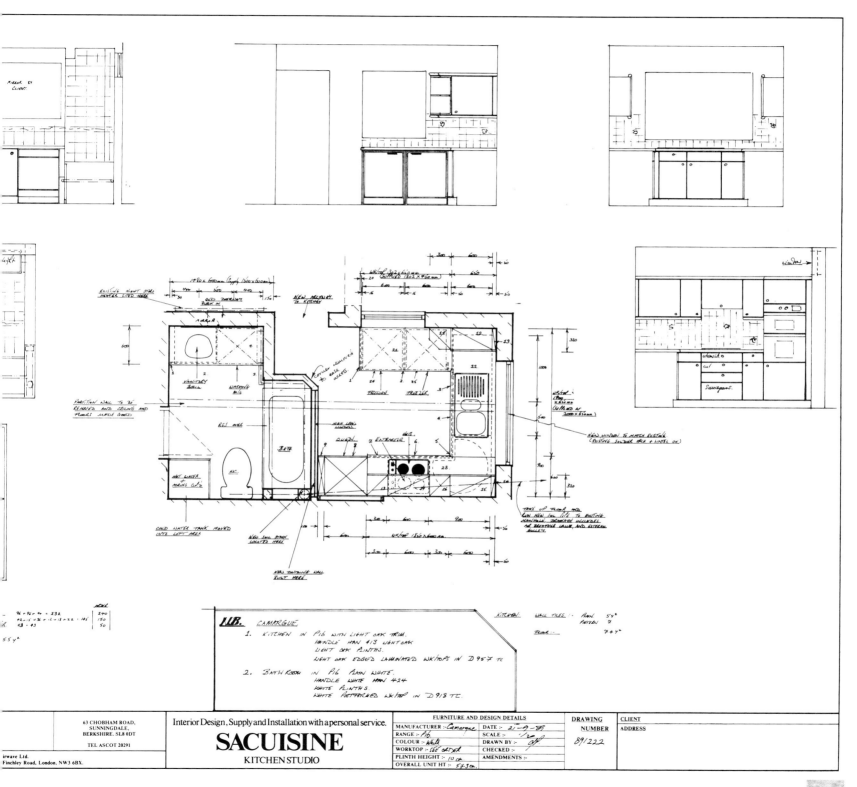

SACUISINE
KITCHEN STUDIO

Interior Design, Supply and Installation with a personal service.

63 CHOBHAM ROAD,
SUNNINGDALE,
BERKSHIRE. SL8 0DT

TEL ASCOT 20291

irwave Ltd.
Finchley Road, London, NW3 6BX.

FURNITURE AND DESIGN DETAILS		
MANUFACTURER :- Camargue	DATE :- 21-9-89	
RANGE :- P16	SCALE :- 1/20	
COLOUR :- White	DRAWN BY :-	
WORKTOP :- see order	CHECKED :-	
PLINTH HEIGHT :- 10 cm	AMENDMENTS :-	
OVERALL UNIT HT :- 57.3 cm		

DRAWING NUMBER	CLIENT
891222	ADDRESS

An ultra-modern galley kitchen, cleverly incorporating a breakfast bar

THE LAYOUT

In a small kitchen every inch of space can be used if a normal door is replaced by a sliding one.

There are three basic rules which should always be observed when planning a kitchen – the sink and the cooker should be linked by a work surface; the oven should never be placed next to a door; and the sink, cooker and fridge should be linked by a so-called 'work triangle'. To save a lot of walking, the sum of the three sides of this triangle should not add up to more than about 6–7m (20–23ft).

Kitchens come in many shapes and sizes, but basically there are only five practical layouts which will provide maximum working efficiency, and these are known as in-line, galley, U-shaped, L-shaped and island, as shown opposite.

An in-line kitchen, as the name suggests, consists of a single line of units and appliances arranged along one wall. It is a useful layout if space, or budget, is limited or if the room serves more than one purpose, as all the units and appliances are contained in one area. Plan an in-line kitchen so that the sink is in the centre with the cooker and fridge at either end with, ideally, the doors of each opening away from the sink so that access is easy. There should be worktop space between the sink and the appliances and the space beneath the draining board could be used for a dishwasher or washing machine which would also keep plumbing costs to the minimum.

A galley kitchen consists of two lines of units facing each other and makes the best possible use of every inch of available space. When planning either an in-line or a galley kitchen the thing to achieve is as much worktop and storage space as possible, and the choice of units is critical. It will be important to have enough room to open doors and move around easily, so consider narrow units instead of the standard sizes.

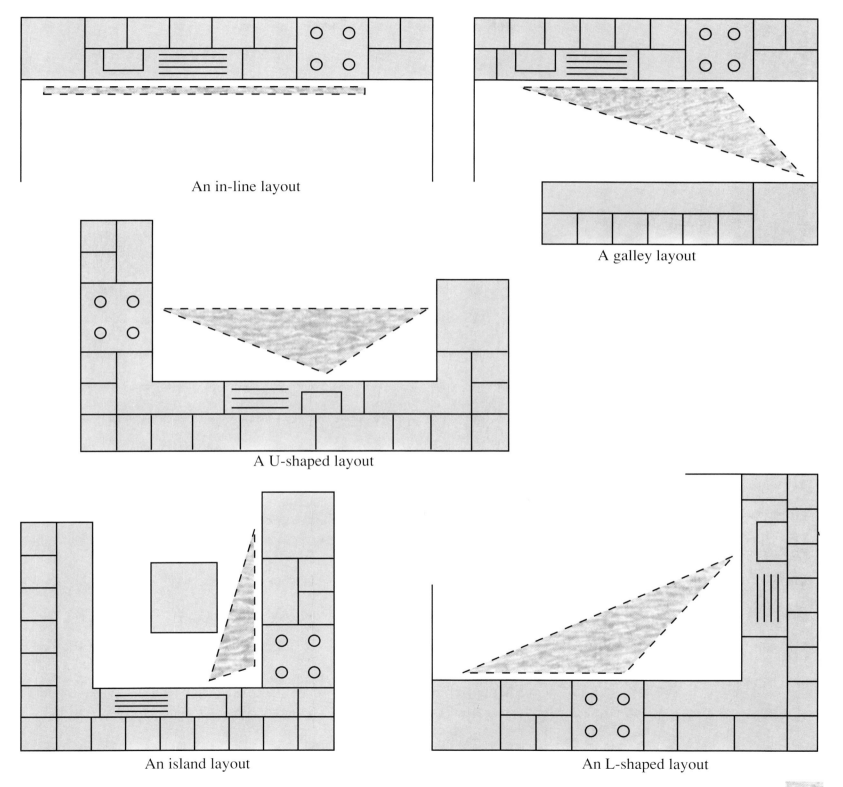

An in-line layout

A galley layout

A U-shaped layout

An island layout

An L-shaped layout

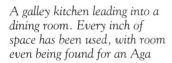

A galley kitchen leading into a dining room. Every inch of space has been used, with room even being found for an Aga

A U-shaped kitchen is probably the most flexible and efficient of all layouts, giving maximum worktop and storage space. Units and appliances are ranged along three walls with, ideally, no doors to break up the run of the work surfaces. The U-shape works extremely well in a small kitchen and gives a magnificent range of storage in a large one, but here it is important to keep to a restrained working triangle so that the cook does not have to travel too far between the three essential appliances. In a kitchen/dining room consider using one leg of the U as a device to separate the two areas. Instead of a solid wall of units some open shelving with pretty serving dishes or plants would look attractive. If a room is not large enough to have a separate dining area, a breakfast bar could form one leg of the U, probably incorporating a cutlery drawer and space for napkins.

The L-shaped kitchen is not only very practical, it is also very flexible, providing many possibilities for adaptations to suit particular needs or life-styles. It is basically an extension of an in-line arrangement, giving plenty of scope for creating a functional work triangle which is both compact and efficient, as it is not interrupted by a flow of traffic. It is a good choice for an oddly shaped room, perhaps where space is limited, and the run of work surfaces which it provides makes life easier for the cook. A typical L-shaped kitchen will incorporate the window wall so that every scrap of natural light can illuminate the working area, be it the kitchen sink or a surface doubling up as a breakfast bar.

Finally there is what is known as **the island layout**. This is usually an L-shaped or U-shaped kitchen with an island of units in the centre. Quite a lot of space is needed for this particular layout. A sophisticated island will contain the cooker, fridge and sink, making an ideal work triangle. However, all the necessary services such as gas, electricity and water have to be brought to the centre of the room, so such a combination can be very expensive to achieve. Of course an island does not have to be a unit at all, it could simply be a preparation area consisting of a butcher's block or a sturdy surface with cupboards below. Because of its relative isolation an island can be any height and depth to suit a particular purpose, but it is worth thinking about enhancing the area immediately above it to add definition and importance to this feature. This could be done simply by adding an interesting cluster of lights, or with a decorative rack for cooking utensils or dried flowers. If the island contains a hob then an attractive cooker hood in keeping with the style of the room may be the answer.

Whichever layout is most suitable, the essential components are work surfaces, storage space, a cooker and a sink. Even if space is tight, try to provide a food preparation area somewhere between the cooker and the sink. This surface will also be useful for serving up a meal, and as the cooker and sink are close to each other, vegetable pans can be drained easily and other saucepans can be placed in the sink ready for washing after the meal.

The storage for things such as cutlery, crockery and pans should be located near the sink so that they are close at hand both for the preparation of food and for ease and speed when putting them away after washing up. For these reasons, too, the dishwasher and waste disposal facilities should be close to the sink.

Here are some of these essential items in more detail.

WORK SURFACES

When planning a kitchen it is perhaps automatic to think that all the work surfaces should be the same height, but this is not necessarily so. The height of worktops usually varies between 34in and 36in (850mm and 900mm) and unless someone is very small or extra tall, these heights suit most people. However, some tasks are made easier by having a lower or higher surface. A lower surface is better for such operations as rolling out pastry or kneading bread, because is puts less strain on the arms and back. For someone who does a lot of decorative work such as icing cakes or intricate garnishes, then a higher than usual surface would be less back-breaking. For most everyday tasks a general rule of thumb is that the ideal worktop height is about 2–3in (50–65mm) below the level of one's bent elbow, but for tasks needing pressure then a worktop 10in (250mm) below the elbow level is better. Some units have adjustable legs which will alter the surface height, but usually the adjustments are made by reducing or increasing the depth of the base plinth, and this is quite simple to do at the fitting stage. The important thing is to think carefully about the tasks most likely to be performed at or on a work surface before blithely going ahead with a uniform height all around the kitchen. A little extra thought at this stage could prevent years of backache!

Most work surfaces have an average depth of 20–24in (500–600mm) but this can be altered, either by cutting the carcase down at the back to produce shallower cupboards and a narrower worktop, or by positioning the base units a little way in from the wall to produce deeper cupboards and wider worktops. If space permits, deeper work surfaces are to be preferred, as cooking and washing appliances can be pulled forward to fit flush with

Use any gaps in a run of units to hold trays, or maybe narrow shelves for cookery books, or fit a telescopic arm to hold tea and hand towels.

the units, leaving room behind them for wiring, plumbing and ventilation.

Ergonomically it is recommended that the worktop should project at least 19mm (³/₄in) in front of the base unit so that it is easy to wipe off waste matter. To stand comfortably close to the unit, toe space should be at least 75mm (3in) deep.

The materials used for work surfaces are many and varied, but perhaps laminates are the most widely used. They are the most economical way of covering large areas and are made by sticking laminated plastic onto blockboard, chipboard or plywood. Sometimes this wood is curved and the laminate follows the contour giving a very smooth appearance. If left flat, the edges may be finished with a wooden moulding. Many patterns are available, from imitation cork to imitation marble, with dozens of other designs in between, so it is usually possible to find something which will suit any particular taste and pocket. Laminated surfaces are easy to keep clean but can scratch, so chopping boards should always be used. Good quality laminates can withstand quite high temperatures, but even so it is wise to use a thick cork mat or something similar to hold a very hot pan, as a scorch or burn mark will permanently mar the overall appearance.

Closely grained hardwoods such as maple, teak or beech make good work surfaces and look particularly attractive in a country-style kitchen. The surfaces can be shaped as necessary and given a limed or stained finish if preferred, before sealing to produce a durable finish which is easy to keep clean.

Heat-resistant tiles make a very attractive worktop and wear well, provided that a strong sealant is used to prevent water penetrating their surface and leaving ugly stains. Obviously hot pans and dishes can be placed directly onto tiled surfaces but, like tiled flooring, they are noisy in use and crockery dropped on them tends to chip or break. Granite and marble look very stylish, too, but are expensive to fit and their disadvantages are the same as those of ceramic and quarry tiles. Marble also has a tendency to stain. Perhaps the very best way of using marble is to inset a block of it into a work surface so that it can be used for pastry-making and other tasks which demand a cool surface.

Corian is a tough man-made material which looks very like marble. It can be formed into various shapes, and scratches can be removed by gentle sanding, so although it is expensive, it is a very good alternative to marble. The manufacturers claim that the surface is non-porous and both stain- and heat-resistant, but it might still be advisable to place a mat under extremely hot pans. Other man-made materials include Asterite, Firon, Silacron and Resan, although these are not yet as well known.

For a high-tech look, surfaces made from stainless steel are hard to beat. Stainless steel, combined with solid wooden chopping boards, is the choice of professional cooks as it is very hard-wearing and easy to clean, making it an ideal surface where hygiene is of the utmost importance.

Hand-in-hand with good work surfaces go splashbacks. As the name implies, this is the area above the worktop which receives all the splashes and spills which cooking causes and which must, therefore, be easy to clean. Depending on the style of the kitchen it can be something as simple as water-resistant wallpaper or as sophisticated as marble. Ceramic tiles are a traditional splashback treatment and it is best to keep a balance by using, say, ornate or contrastingly coloured tiles with a plain work surface and vice versa. Try not to create conflict in the kitchen between a heavily decorated surface – whether on the wall or the worktop – and the kitchen utensils, as the end result will appear confusing, fussy and distracting to the eye.

STORAGE

The cool and spacious old-fashioned larder or pantry is still the ideal storage area for many people. Pre-dating the refrigerator, which has mostly taken its place, the larder was basically used for storing food, both unprepared and cooked. Bags of potatoes, fresh vegetables, eggs, preserves, pickles and home-made wine all kept perfectly in the fly-proof air-vented atmosphere, and nowadays, many a

Store little-used items at the top of wall cupboards and not on easy-to-get-at middle shelves.

A very sophisticated island kitchen with a hob and extractor fan built into the island, which is well lit from above

modern cook faced with a small modern kitchen must long for such flexible storage space.

Those without the luxury of a larder have to plan their kitchen storage space, whether fitted or not, very carefully. Cooking pans and utensils need to be near the food preparation area, detergents and cleaning materials are best stored beneath the sink, and crockery needs to be close to the sink or dishwasher. Different foods require different conditions: dry foods such as cereals, rice, pasta, sugar, biscuits and herbs need somewhere warm and dry, whereas perishables such as vegetables, fruit and cheeses need a well-ventilated, cool area. Tall storage units are now mostly used as larders, broom cupboards or as housing for split-level ovens. If possible, site them so that they do not break up a run of working surface.

Wall cupboards are usually half the depth of the base cupboards to prevent a bumped head when using the work surface below. And although sufficient space should be left beneath them to hold a food processor or similar appliances, do not site them too high on the wall, as it will be difficult to reach and use them. Extra storage space can be found between the base and wall units by fitting what the trade calls 'mid-range' cupboards. These are usually shallow shelves which are handy for holding spice racks, kitchen rolls or small items which tend to get lost in deeper cupboards.

Even an awkward corner space where two runs of units meet can be used by fitting an L-shaped cupboard which has either open shelves or a double-hinged door so that the entire contents of the shelves can be seen and are easily accessible. Some L-shaped base cupboards are fitted with swing-out shelves, and these make the best possible use of every scrap of space.

An ideal place to fit a waste bin is on the inside

of a door on a base unit beneath the sink, as food left over from meals or food preparation can be put straight into it – it is a much neater option than a free-standing bin which may take up valuable floor space.

One can never have too much storage space in a kitchen, so whether the decision is to go for a fully fitted look or separate pieces, do make good use of all the available space – perhaps a wine rack, or shelves to take cookery books, might be fitted into a narrow area which would otherwise be wasted. More than any other factor, the way in which storage needs are catered for – whether floor-standing, wall-mounted, fitted, or free-standing – will affect the style and appearance of the kitchen; so take time to look at and consider all the possibilities before buying anything.

COOKING APPLIANCES

Whatever the preferred method of cooking, the first consideration has to be the kind of fuel which is available. Even now, some areas are not piped for gas and although this can be overcome by the use of gas cylinders, they are not always the answer. Except in very remote areas, electricity and solid fuel are freely available, but perhaps the most flexible arrangement is to have both electricity and gas on hand and to use a mix of the two.

Apart from traditional kitchen ranges, the only choice for many years was a free-standing electric or gas cooker which incorporated an oven, a hob and a grill. These can still be bought but are difficult to fit neatly into a run of fitted units, and may spoil the look of a whole scheme. With sales of fitted kitchens increasing, the cooker manufacturers had to come up with an amended version. This is basically the same appliance cut off at hob level, which will slide between kitchen units to create a flush look. Some models have a fold-down hob cover which further improves the appearance and gives an extra work surface when the hob is not being used.

The latest trend has been for split-level cookers where an electric oven and a grill, perhaps at eye level, may be built into a unit, and a gas hob will be set into a worktop. This combination undoubtedly produces a very streamlined look, but it is quite expensive to buy and fit. Moreover once it is in place, it may not be feasible to take it when moving house so it does not have the flexibility of the slot-in cooker.

There are three different methods of cooking: natural convection; fan-assisted/ducted forced convection; and multi-function. With natural convection the top shelf is the hottest and the bottom the coolest and the oven has to be turned on some time before food is placed in it so that it reaches the required cooking temperature. A fan-assisted/ducted convection oven does not need pre-heating and operates by circulating heated air at an even temperature around the oven. The multi-function oven, as the name suggests, combines natural and fan-assisted convection, top or bottom heat only and sometimes automatic roasting and defrost facilities; it is therefore very flexible and worth considering.

Many gas and electric ovens are now self-cleaning and have ducted fume extractors, whilst hob units may incorporate extras such as charcoal grills and deep-frying pans. Some hobs have electric elements set into ceramic glass making cleaning easier, whilst others use tungsten halogen light filaments to allow heat levels to be changed instantly, thus giving the same flexibility as a gas jet. The range of options is vast and is only limited by the depth of one's pocket.

If the thought of these sophisticated appliances leaves you cold, then you are probably a devotee of an Aga or Rayburn-type cooker and anyone who has ever used one will undoubtedly never willingly be without it. They take up a lot of room, are difficult to regulate, and have no recognisable grill, but they cook like a dream, the two hobs will hold at least six saucepans, the two or four ovens give many options, and they make the best toast in the world! Even more appealing is the fact that they are a constant source of heat, and act like a magnet to most of the household. They traditionally used solid fuel but oil, gas and electric models are now available making life much easier for the cook. Apart from the traditional white and cream it is now possible to buy them in red, bottle green, dark blue and chocolate brown so it is possible to create really exciting decorating schemes based on these colours.

In recent years microwave cookers have become very popular. They have had some bad press but, by and large, they are a very useful addition to the conventional kitchen appliances, ideal for defrosting, reheating or cooking food quickly. They work by using a magnetron to produce waves which vibrate the water molecules in the food, causing the heat and friction which cooks it. Because the process is so fast, no warm-up period is needed and

A neat way of including a microwave oven has been used in this ultra-modern layout

the food retains vital minerals and vitamins. One of the problems with microwave ovens is that cooked food can look pale and bland but a combination microwave/convection oven has been developed to overcome this, and gives great flexibility in use.

SINKS

From the traditional deep ceramic sink to a small modern one meant only as a supplement to a dishwasher, the variety of sinks is enormous and the choice will largely depend on taste and space. Materials used range from everyday stainless steel or vitreous enamel, to custom-made teak with a host of alternatives in between and various combinations of bowls and half-bowls make the choice even wider. If space permits a double bowl is extremely useful, as it means that activities such as washing up and food preparation can take place at the same time, and a half-bowl is useful for straining vegetables and for a waste-disposal unit.

Whatever the choice, there are three basic types of sink unit: the lay-on sink and draining board which is designed to fit on top of a standard kitchen unit; the inset bowl and drainer which are designed to be set directly into the work surface; and the sink centre, which takes up less room as it does not include a draining board but instead uses a second bowl or half-bowl with a wire basket for rinsing and draining and has a wooden chopping board which will fit over the sink, making full use of the available space. It should be possible to work at a sink without having to bend to reach the bottom of the bowl; and if a traditional butler-style one is chosen, remember that it will be rather deeper than a modern one and may have to be raised in some way to prevent an aching back.

All sinks have taps either fitted into the horizontal surface or wall-mounted. Styles include the traditional cross head which is easy to turn on and off; the modern chunky, Perspex-encased head which may be awkward to turn; and the lever-operated head which gives good control over the flow of water and is a sensible choice for disabled or

It is useful to have a tall kitchen tap so that buckets of water can be filled easily at the sink.

elderly people. Mixer taps will control both the temperature and the water flow, and are therefore very useful; and both these and pillar taps are nowadays fitted with rotating stainless-steel balls or Teflon coated ceramic discs which do not drip and cut out the problem of replacing worn washers. Taps with swivel spouts are particularly useful over a sink, but if more than one bowl is used, be sure that the tap is long and high enough to reach both bowls. Now it is even possible to buy tap accessories: these include a flexible hose fitted with interchangeable heads such as a brush or a spatula, both of which are useful for scraping off food which adheres stubbornly to plates or saucepans. There is also a soap dispenser which can be fitted beneath the sink, and a hot-water dispenser – this looks exactly like a tap and is usually mounted alongside the normal taps, but in fact it is a quick and economical alternative to an electric kettle, providing instant boiling water for making coffee, tea or gravy, or for tackling really greasy spills.

In Britain, kitchen taps should conform to a British Standard (BS5412/3 parts 1 and 2, 1976), as this means that they have been tested to ensure that there is an adequate flow of water. They should also satisfy local water by-law requirements which safeguard against contamination and wastage. A good plumber will ensure that both these standards are met.

The style of the taps should be in keeping with the sink and the kitchen units, as nothing is more obvious than a badly chosen or unsuitable tap arrangement in an otherwise well-planned kitchen.

The subject of sinks is not complete without mentioning the waste disposal unit. The sheer volume of kitchen waste is incredible and anything that can reduce the level of smelly waste – fish skin, meat bones, left-over food etc, which is usually put into a normal domestic dustbin – has to be welcomed. Waste disposal units which can be fitted into the kitchen sink are a clean and wholesome way of disposing of waste food, as they grind it down into a fine soup-like mixture which is then washed away into the drains. Most disposers are fitted into a larger than usual sink outlet and are operated by an

This thoughtfully designed modern sink incorporates not only one-and-a-half washing up bowls but a drainer and cutting board too – a perfect food preparation area which is easy to maintain

electric motor which fits beneath the sink. There are two disposal methods, known as batch feed and continuous feed. Batch-fed waste is loaded into the disposal unit, covered with a lid and then switched on, and continuous-fed waste is fed straight into the already operating disposal unit. In both cases cold water is left running into the sink until all the waste has been disposed of.

The most recent method of getting rid of household waste other than food, is by using an electrically operated domestic compactor. This consists of a large removable container inside a drawer arrangement which, when full, is compressed to about a quarter of its original volume when the electric unit is turned on. At the same time it will pack the rubbish into a sack, making disposal easier.

OTHER APPLIANCES AND CONSIDERATIONS

The four essential components of work surfaces, storage space, cooking facilities and sink arrangement need a lot of thought, and not until these have been chosen and fitted in can other appliances be considered. A fridge and a freezer will undoubtedly be high on the list of priorities, and if there is no separate laundry room, a washing machine and dryer may have to be accommodated, too. The most obvious place for a dishwasher is next to or beneath the sink, but finding room for the other two items might be more difficult. However, don't forget that it may be possible to hide appliances behind décor panels so that they are not obvious in a carefully planned kitchen.

FRIDGE/FREEZER

The main consideration in choosing a fridge and a freezer is the size of the family and the amount of storage space these appliances will have to provide. Even if backed up by a larger freezer sited elsewhere, it is useful to have at least a small freezer in the kitchen, and matching freezers and refrigerators are usually made so that they can sit side by side under worktops or be stacked vertically. Some of the large free-standing combinations incorporate such extras as ice-making equipment and fruit-juice dispensers. Whichever fridge/freezer combination is chosen, make sure the doors not only open in the right direction but that they can be opened fully so that shelves and salad containers can be taken out and washed easily. Although most appliances are well insulated, if there is no option but to site the refrigerator next to the cooker then it may be wise to place a chipboard panel between the two.

For some time refrigerators have been fitted with an automatic defrosting device, and now frost-free freezers are also available. They are quite expensive but do cut out the twice-yearly ritual of finding somewhere to store the tail-ends of frozen food whilst defrosting the freezer.

LAUNDRY APPLIANCES

Without a separate laundry room space may also have to be found in the kitchen for both a washing machine and a dryer. To save on plumbing costs the washing machine should be placed on the same wall as the sink, and a tumble-dryer ideally against an outside wall so that hot damp air can be vented outside. A separate washer and dryer is a useful combination as it means that two operations can be carried out at the same time, but if space is tight, then a combined washer/dryer may be the answer. Twin-tub machines have largely been superseded by fully automatic front-loading machines. Generally, top-loading machines cannot be used under a work surface, but one is now available which tilts forwards and you can buy a very narrow top-loader for use where space is critical.

The choice of machines for both washing and drying is bewildering: ultimately these will be selected according to the capacity, programmes and spin speeds which are most suitable for the buyer's particular purposes. Some electricity boards and companies offer demonstrations of their products and it is worth asking if this would be possible before making a final choice.

DISHWASHERS

A dishwasher is one of the most labour-saving appliances one can buy – it has been estimated that it will save over an hour a day of precious time. And that is not the only saving, because a dishwasher uses less hot water than when the job is done by hand, and it can be run on a low-energy washing and drying cycle which further increases its efficiency. A whole day's dishes can be stacked away in the dishwasher, leaving the work surfaces and sink clear, and they will come out sparklingly clean and hygienically dried.

An average dishwasher will hold twelve place settings (each understood to be five pieces of crockery, a glass and a set of cutlery), but it is possible to buy larger machines which will hold up to fourteen place settings, or smaller, table-top models which will hold from four to six place settings. Until recently most machines were designed with front-loading doors, some being integrated into a run of kitchen units by the use of a décor panel, but now there is a more compact, top-loading machine which will fit neatly into a kitchen cupboard and slide out when needed. So whatever the space available there should be a dishwasher to suit.

HEATING AND VENTILATION

Cooking obviously keeps a kitchen warm, and even when the cooker is not on, appliances such as refrigerators and freezers also produce warmth; small kitchens therefore may not need an additional heating system. However, both for comfort when cooking during the winter and for drying tea towels, a slim radiator is a good investment. It can be fitted with a thermostat so that it can be set on low for most of the time, but will provide a good level of heat when needed. If a radiator would take up too much valuable wall space, then plinth heaters may be the answer. They are unobtrusive and can either be connected to the central heating system or be independently electrically operated. An Aga-type cooker will, of course, be a constant source of warmth and works particularly well in a family kitchen-cum-living room.

Condensation can be a problem in a kitchen, particularly with a gas stove, and although cooking

An attractive extractor fan, in sympathy with the overall scheme, is centred over the cooking hob in this light and airy kitchen

creates delicious smells, no one wants them to hang around for days afterwards. The answer to both problems is adequate ventilation, and this usually means fitting an extractor fan, a cooker hood or a hob ventilator. During cooking a kitchen needs about ten changes of air per hour so whichever system is chosen, ensure that it is robust enough to get rid of moist and stale air fast.

An extractor fan can be fitted into a window or installed in an outside wall or ceiling; however, a proposed purchase should be seen working in a showroom first, as some are incredibly noisy. Cooker hoods are positioned immediately over a cooker or hob, and remove steam and cooking smells either by recycling the air with an electric fan through a charcoal filter or by ducting the air

through a grease filter directly to the outside. Both are effective if the filters are kept clean, but whilst a grease filter can be periodically washed, a charcoal filter does have to be replaced regularly. Hob ventilators are usually fitted into the hob itself leaving only the grille exposed, and will efficiently expel vapour and fumes through a duct in the outside wall.

LIGHTING

Lighting suitable for the kitchen was discussed in Chapter 10, but it is worth repeating how important it is to have good task lighting over work surfaces, perhaps fitting it beneath wall units to concentrate it where really needed. Cooker hoods usually

A highly individual kitchen with strategically placed, flexible lighting over the main work and eating areas

incorporate a light which gives good illumination directly over the hob, and other preparation areas can be lit with spotlights or carefully positioned downlighters. These task lights should be supplemented by good overall illumination which does not cause dangerous glare or shadows; a good yardstick is to try to provide twenty-five watts of tungsten lighting for every square metre of kitchen. This should adequately cover all needs.

FLOORING

Kitchen flooring was discussed in Chapter 7. It will have to take a tremendous amount of wear, particularly in the work-triangle area, so the two main objectives must be to find a flooring which is extremely hardwearing and which will be easy to clean. It is also essential that a kitchen floor is free from damp, and is as smooth and level as possible. Damp is a problem which will be very difficult to treat once all the fitments and appliances are in place, and if the floor is not level most of the appliances, particularly the refrigerator, may not work as well as they might.

One possible kitchen flooring which has not been mentioned is a purpose-designed carpet: it has a warm feel to it, is stain-resistant and easy to clean, and although the colour and design range is limited it could be a useful option in a very cold house.

SAFETY

It is a fact that each year more accidents happen in the kitchen than anywhere else in the home, and that there are more accidents in the home than on the roads. What a frightening thought!

Obviously a kitchen holds many potential hazards, particularly if there are small children around, but given a little thought and attention the risks can be greatly reduced. The main danger area is the cooker, but a guard rail around the burners, burners placed at the back of the hob, and child-proof controls are all simple to organise, and the peace of mind they give will repay any extra expense. All wiring and plugs should be kept well

away from any water supply, and sockets should not be overloaded by plugging in an adaptor unit to run several appliances. They could also be fitted with safety shutters.

Safety is also maintained by keeping working surfaces uncluttered, and perhaps hanging sharp knives and kitchen tools on specially designed racks. Well-finished, rounded corners on cupboards and work surfaces will prevent bruises and splinters, and if possible position wall cupboards at a height where they can be reached without resorting to a stool, but not so low as to cause bumped heads.

It is useful to keep a portable fire extinguisher on one of the walls, or to buy a fire blanket specially designed to throw over a burning pan or hob to extinguish any flames before they can spread further. Both are simple precautions which could, at the very least, prevent a nasty accident.

STYLE AND COLOUR

When you know exactly how much space is available, and which appliances and storage units it will have to accommodate, then the really interesting part of kitchen design can be tackled: choosing the style and the colours.

The style of the kitchen will to a large extent be determined by the units and work surfaces chosen – whether it is fitted or unfitted, most of the storage space, apart from open shelving, will be hidden behind doors of some kind. These could be made from sleek stainless steel, mellow or prettily painted wood, or a strikingly coloured laminate, and it is the chosen finish of both the units and the work surfaces which will determine the look of the rest of the kitchen.

The choice is enormous, and there is no reason why a town flat shouldn't have a country-style kitchen if that is what is wanted. Equally, a house in the country could have a very high-tech flavour if its owners prefer clean, unfussy lines with the minimum of clutter. The main point to bear in mind is that a kitchen is an expensive room to equip and the fittings chosen may have to last for a good many years, so make sure that the design is right before even beginning!

The way the wall space is treated will also determine the style of the kitchen, and many materials can be used very imaginatively to create a finish which is unique. Don't just take the easy option of emulsioning or papering the walls; tiles could be laid in diamonds or diagonals, rough walls could be given an exciting colour wash, or tongue-and-groove wood strips could be arranged in various patterns.

Even though the colours chosen for the walls and accessories may well be determined by the units, do also consider the natural light which the kitchen receives. It may get the morning sun, the evening sun, sun most of the day, or none at all, and this should point the way to a sympathetic colour scheme. Yellow is always a cheerful colour, particularly on a grey day; shades of terracotta will warm a north-facing kitchen, and cool blues and greens will provide a feeling of cool calmness in a south- or south-west-facing kitchen.

Take time to study magazines, and have a look at kitchen room sets — many people find they are drawn towards a certain look and style which could be emulated or adapted for their own kitchen. Choose the accessories carefully, get the lighting right and, above all, create an atmosphere where cooking is a pleasure and not a chore.

USEFUL TIPS WHEN PLANNING A KITCHEN

- A plate rack positioned over the sink will provide both drying and storage space.

- It is useful to have a crockery cupboard immediately above a dishwasher so that clean plates etc can be unloaded straight from the washer into the cupboard.

- However tight the space, leave at least a 12in (30cm) surface either side of the cooker to hold hot saucepans or dishes from the oven.

- Eye-level, wall-mounted scales take up very little room and it is easy to see the dial.

- Put a narrow drinks tray beneath a slim toaster to catch the crumbs.

- Save space by using an iron tidy fixed to a wall or inside a cupboard to hold the iron immediately after use.

- Do not wash silver and stainless steel cutlery together in a dishwasher as when they come into contact it can produce an unwanted chemical reaction.

- A perforated plastic drainer which fits over the sink is invaluable for both draining and straining food.

- Glass doors and oven lights enable the food to be seen whilst cooking and prevent soggy soufflés.

- A partitioned tray will keep cutlery tidy and easy to find.

- Simple shelves provide useful and inexpensive storage space.

- A plain kitchen can be updated simply by changing the colour of door handles or knobs and introducing accessories in the same shade.

- If you grow tired of a plain wooden kitchen, consider using an emulsion or flat paint wash to 'lime' the wood and make it paler, or stencil the doors with an appropriate motif.

- An old-fashioned hanging rack will provide extra storage for pans, cooking utensils or baskets of dried flowers.

- A louvred window is useful for ventilating a kitchen as the opening can be varied easily to suit warm, sunny days as well as windy, cold ones, and all stages in between.

PROJECT PAPERS

For most people, the kitchen is the hard-working centre of the home, and a convenient layout, well chosen fitments and easy-to-clean surfaces are vital to the well-being, and temper, of the cook. Time spent planning any room is never wasted but this is particularly true of the kitchen, and the two projects below will be very useful exercises. The finished results should make for interesting discussions when suggesting ideas or deciding possible solutions with interested like-minded people.

PROJECT 25

Your own kitchen may be beautifully planned, have room for improvement, or be a complete shambles. Whatever the case may be, first draw up a rough floor plan and then plot it onto graph paper using a 1:20 scale.

Using the units on p220 as a guide draw up what you consider to be the best possible use of space for this particular kitchen and indicate what has been placed where. Take the positioning of sockets and lighting into consideration and add a key explaining what kind of units, work surfaces and appliances have been selected. Finally, suggest a suitable colour scheme by pasting appropriate samples onto a colour board.

PROJECT 26

Paste coloured illustrations onto A4 sheets showing what you consider to be:

- Your ideal kitchen
- An ideal family kitchen
- A well-designed large kitchen
- The best use of space in a small kitchen

Caption each illustration so that a 'reader' or possible client could get some idea of your preferred style and feelings about these kitchens.

CHAPTER 14

DEVELOPING AN INDIVIDUAL STYLE

THERE IS MUCH MORE to interior design than just flinging a few pieces of furniture, some fabric and a trendy paint finish together in a 'designerly' way and hoping for the best. Like everything else in life, it is important to build on firm foundations, and some knowledge of these marks the difference between those genuinely interested in interior design and those who merely like to say they are.

It has been the intention of this book so far to reveal the bare bones of interior design, how things have evolved, what a designer should be aware of, and the wide range of choices available. It has tried to give a fundamental knowledge of the basic processes so that, at the very least, its readers will be able to brief tradesmen, showing that they do know what they are talking about, and will not be bamboozled by cowboys who may try to profit from ignorance of the subject. A good tradesman will appreciate someone who can discuss the problems and solutions with him intelligently: it gives him a chance to display his own knowledge of the subject, and this co-operation should produce a finished result which is a credit both to your design and to his application skills.

Basic knowledge is very important, but the fun really starts when you begin to put all the various elements together to create your own individual style. But what *is* style? *The Shorter Oxford Dictionary* defines it as 'a person's characteristic manner, especially as conducing to beauty or appearance', and also as 'a way of presenting decorative methods proper to a person or school or period or subject … and the manner of exhibiting these characteristics'. Anyone interested in design will agree with both these statements. Most of us could, for example, instantly recognise a Zandra Rhodes dress, a Lowry painting or a David Hicks room; all have a distinctive style and bear the stamp of their creator.

For some people, a distinctive decorator look is what they want and are willing to pay for; others, however, may not find it so desirable, as it can erase their own personality and impose that of the designer instead. A professional interior designer must always be aware of this fine line, but when decorating your own house there are no such restrictions and the thing to achieve is a balance between style and function. For most people, the type of house or apartment they live in and the budget they can afford will be the two bases from which to start to create individual style and which, unless one is an absolute purist, will combine comfort with practicality.

Anyone interested in interior design will know that, as in fashion, styles and colours come and go. But do not feel pressurised into keeping up with the latest 'look' – this is merely the suppliers and manufacturers selling their products, however much they may like to dress it up in an aura of sophistication or culture. Of course some of it will appeal, and there is no reason why new furnishings and fittings should not be bought. However, the essence of developing personal style is to be selective and to choose things which particularly appeal to *you* whether or not they are fashionable. Very few people are born with an instant personal style – it usually happens over a long period as one gradually becomes aware of surroundings, develops interests and gains experience. Nor will style remain static: it will continue to evolve and change as the years go by and experience grows.

So the type of house may itself suggest a starting point for a scheme in a personal style, especially if it was built in a particular architectural period. For instance, the atmosphere of a thatched Devon longhouse or an elegant Georgian town house may inspire someone to fill it with aesthetically sympathetic contents, sending them off on a search for fabrics and furniture which not only do they feel will do justice to the house, but will also appeal for their own sake.

If period houses often succeed in suggesting a certain decorative scheme, modern houses offer a neutral background where anything can be created. To many people this may seem a daunting prospect, but in fact it is a wonderful challenge and an opportunity to develop and impose your own personality – rather like an artist revelling in a blank canvas. The individual budget will, of course, dictate how far a scheme is followed through – but

An expression of individual style, with a pretty games table placed in front of a voile-decorated window which filters strong light from a bright and airy conservatory

227

even when it is decided what 'feel' to create, it is by no means essential to have everything at once. In fact it is often better *not* to buy everything immediately, as a style can then seem contrived and too perfect; it is far better to let some things evolve gradually.

Surely collectors have a head start when it comes to developing a personal style. The mere fact that they have chosen to collect particular items, be it Art Deco china, pink glasswear or silver thimbles, gives some indication of their predilections and taste, and displaying them to their best advantage is often the start of a unique decorative scheme. Some of the best-known decorative styles have evolved simply because people liked a particular object or piece of furniture and went on collecting things which enhanced and reinforced that particular style.

VICTORIAN STYLE

Most of us have an immediate and often divergent picture of what constitutes Victorian style, but then the era did cover sixty-four years (1837–1901) and during that period many previous styles made a comeback. For instance there were Gothic, Elizabethan, Louis XVI, Louis XV, Renaissance, Graeco-Egyptian and Japonism revivals which all influenced the furnishings and decorative techniques during that long period. For most of us, however, Victorian style consists of solid furniture made from dark hardwoods, lots of pattern and textures, and rooms overflowing with an assortment of pictures, silver, ornaments and drapery.

The Victorian age was a time of enormous industrial development and the introduction of machines meant that factories were able to mass-produce many of the items which previously only the wealthy had been able to afford. Armed with pattern books, salesmen went from door to door and before long it was the taste of the masses which largely dictated design. Improved weaving and printing methods meant that fabrics and wallpapers could also be mass-produced and soon wooden floors were spread with Oriental-style carpets and rugs, and previously plainly painted walls were adorned with elaborately patterned papers. The British Empire was at its height during the Victorian era and this meant that all manner of Indian, Oriental, African and Middle Eastern artefacts and textiles found their way into quite ordinary households and, for the most part, settled in quite happily. What an extraordinary period this was.

Victorian style is still evident today, but the look, although cosy, is not as cluttered as the original and can be achieved quite easily. Patterned wallpaper could perhaps be the starting point and Liberty-style designs, medieval motifs such as stylised fleur-de-lys, trellis-work patterns or large floral patterns would all be in keeping. Sometimes a Lincrusta or Anaglypta paper would be used beneath a dado rail, and original designs are still readily available if this is the look you prefer. Both wallpaper and painted Lincrusta would have been in rich, strong colours, not necessarily on a dark background, and made dramatic backdrops for chairs and sofas covered in thick velvets.

Victorian furniture is generous and solid, and the shapes – balloon-back dining chairs and spoon- or button-back easy chairs – are pleasing and comfortable. Mahogany, walnut and satinwood were all popular choices. Chesterfields were covered with kelims and cushions, whilst side-tables tended to be round with tripod legs. However, these were usually concealed by a long cloth so today, any table with a round top can be covered with fabric and lace to emulate this style.

The Victorians also loved stained-glass windows; though sometimes the entire window area was covered with both floor-length lace panels (primarily to keep out dust and dirt) and heavy drapes which would have been held back with elaborate tassels. Curtains were often hung on heavy brass poles or decorated with elegant pelmets, sometimes hung in drapes, sometimes fitted to a shaped flat board which would extend some way down the sides of the curtains. This was called a lambrequin. Mantelpieces, too, often had their own curtains which would match the rest of the décor, and tassels and fringes would have been used on the

To make a lambrequin, draw out a template of the desired shape and ask a carpenter to cut it out in hardboard. Cover its surface by sticking fabric tightly onto it, and outlining the shape with braid or edging with a fringe.

bottoms of these small curtains as well as on upholstered furniture and table cloths to add weight and importance to the pieces. The restrained use of some of these decorative touches can still be effective today – indeed, round cloth-covered tables seem to be everywhere at the moment.

Patterned tiles would surround neat cast-iron fireplaces and would also be used to decorate porches, hallways, bathrooms and kitchens – the rule seemed to be the more patterned the tile, the richer the effect. Many houses still retain their original Victorian tiles and this could be a good starting point when putting a scheme together.

Victorians loved ornaments and major porcelain companies such as Minton and Copeland were kept busy producing figurines and dishes of all kinds. At this time, too, the British started to imitate the Chinese blue and white ware, but their designs tended to be far more ornate than the restrained Chinese taste. Colourful majolica and Staffordshire pottery figures were also very popular and the new electroplating process meant that silverware was much cheaper. 'Silver' candlesticks, dishes and ornaments were widely available to people who previously had not been able to afford such things, and they were proudly displayed. Walls would abound with pictures and religious tracts, and rooms were made cosy by the soft light shed by wall-mounted oil lamps or the latest gas lamps. The final touch to a Victorian house would be a proliferation of ferns – and, of course, a magnificent aspidistra!

Used with restraint the best elements of Victorian decoration can still be adapted today to create rooms or entire homes where a mixture of patterns, treasured collections and solid furniture blend to a comfortable but harmonious whole.

EDWARDIAN STYLE

It is almost impossible to define Edwardian style accurately because this relatively short period encompassed some very exciting movements which still exert an enormous influence on today's design. Edward VII acceded to the throne on 22 January 1901, but those interested in the decorative arts generally agree that the Edwardian era really began in 1890 and continued until the end of World War I. The reason for citing 1890 as its start is that not very much happened after 1900 for which momentum had not been built up during the 1890s; and designers and artists such as William Morris, Charles Annesley Voysey, Aubrey Beardsley, Arthur Mackmurdo, Arthur Silver and Charles Rennie Mackintosh had already started moving away from the traditional Victorian ideals, and were busy expressing new ideas which came to fruition during the reign of Edward VII.

William Morris hated mass-produced goods of any description and insisted that everything from furniture to ceramics was produced by hand so that the honesty of the materials and the integrity of their design shone through. Without doubt it was Morris who laid the foundations of the English Arts and Crafts Movement, where artists, craftsmen and designers of all kinds formed themselves into guilds based on those of the Middle Ages. The medieval influence was strong, and romantic knights and beautiful maidens featured in everything from stained-glass windows to paintings and ornaments. This decorative style became known as Art Nouveau and whilst the cabinet maker perfected his beautifully simple furniture, other artists and craftsmen created flowing, fluid shapes, and objects such as vases and lamps assumed the forms of flowers entangled with greenery. Sculptors too embraced the Art Nouveau style and the female forms they created are all instantly recognisable, with their gloriously free willowy bodies, and their flowing hair and robes entwined with stylised flowers, convolvulus and ivy.

During this period the ancient craft of stencilling was also revived and plain walls were sometimes decorated with hand-painted friezes, elements of which would also be stencilled onto unlined curtains. Charles Rennie Mackintosh perfected this look, and he had a marvellous ability to reduce shapes to the essentials without sacrificing sophistication. However, if Mackintosh was called upon to design a room he insisted on creating the

A bathroom given an
Edwardian feeling with dolphin
fittings and a high-level tank.
The wooden mahogany seat is
reflected in the side of the bath
and the wash basin unit, and all
blend beautifully with
the dark polished floorboards

total environment, and every detail – from the elegantly stencilled walls down to the teaspoons – would be given his complete attention.

Charles Voysey was a fashionable architect during this period; he was less extreme than Mackintosh, but he too turned his attention to every aspect of design and could move between metal, wood, textile and graphic design with seemingly effortless ease. His clean, unfussy wallpaper and fabric designs have stood the test of time and still look fresh today.

An Art Nouveau/Art and Crafts room would have been spacious and light, often painted white or a pale colour and the furniture spare and upright. To further emphasise and compliment the purity of line, the craftsmen again went back to the Middle Ages and produced articles made from pewter, silver, brass, copper and leather; and plain, natural fabrics would have been embellished with rich crewelwork and tapestry designs using vegetable-dyed wools. Many shapes were taken from nature, birds and flowers being very popular. Curtains would be hung on wooden poles, unadorned by the elaborate pelmets so beloved of the Victorians, and wooden floorboards or parquet floors were left plain or simply dressed with rugs or sisal matting.

Whilst everyone could achieve simple curtain treatments and sparsely furnished rooms, they could not all afford to have hand-made furniture, and this is where Ambrose Heal came into his own. It was Heal who pioneered the mass-production of simple furniture made in the lighter-coloured woods such as birch, oak and sycamore. He replaced fussy metal handles with plain wooden shapes or used hollow hand-holes, and although the lines of the furniture were simple, a great deal of it featured curved and rounded fronts which were sometimes highlighted with decorative carving.

Another person who had a great deal of influence on design during this period was Arthur Lasenby Liberty, the founder of the Liberty store in Regent Street, London. He was not a designer himself but was always associated with the artists and designers of this period. For some years he was a manager at Farmer & Rogers' Great Shawl and Cloak

Emporium in Regent Street. This establishment became the Mecca for artists of all kinds – they felt that young Mr Liberty took a very real interest in what was sold and had a 'seeing eye' for beautiful things, whether it was imported blue and white Chinese vases, oriental silks, folding screens or lacquer ware. His artist friends encouraged him to set up on his own in Regent Street, and by the early 1900s he was well known for promoting the aesthetic movement and as a pioneer of Art Nouveau.

This was a richly creative period, but here it is possible to give only the broad outlines of what constitutes a particular look. There is no doubt that the avant-garde style of Art Nouveau can be created in your own home quite easily, particularly if appropriate pieces of well-made furniture have been inherited or found. The curtain treatments could not be simpler, and needleworkers would enjoy recreating the richly coloured embroideries and rugs which were typical of this period. If the floorboards are not good enough to be left bare, then sisal and rush matting would be totally in keeping, and it is still possible to find copper-framed mirrors and picture frames and Tiffany-style lamps and shades which would further enhance this look.

It would be wrong to assume that the Art Nouveau look was totally embraced by all Edwardians. The move was certainly towards lighter furniture, simple lines and less clutter but they also loved the romantic look of delicate lace, and used it lavishly on everything from window panels to table cloths; and bedrooms, too, would be dressed with frothy dressing-tables, lace-edged bed linen, lacy bedspreads and clusters of lacy cushions. The romantic look would be further emphasised by the use of pretty wallpaper, perhaps with soft pink roses rambling over a pale background, flower-sprigged china, silver picture frames and tasselled scent bottles. Mellow brass was used for wall brackets, light fittings and door furniture and this added to the feeling of romantic opulence. Again, all these ideas can be adapted easily for today's home, and modern fabrics will make the upkeep much easier than in Edwardian times.

Flea markets and bric-à-brac shops are still a good hunting ground for Art Nouveau objects.

ART DECO

The style we recognise as Art Deco was first seen at the 1925 Paris Decorative and Industrial Arts Exhibition, and the luxurious woods, glass, chrome, lacquer and leather used to create furniture, and the brilliant colours such as lime greens, bright oranges and mauves, must have seemed outrageously daring. The colours had their origins in the sets and costumes designed by Diaghilev for the Ballets Russes, and the opening of Tutankhamun's tomb at that time produced a flood of Egyptian-inspired design. Other influences were Cubism, African Negro and Aztec art – the stepped *ziggurat* shape of Aztec temples was seen everywhere. Recurring motifs were sunrises, fans, deer, fronds, spirals and lightning flashes, whilst stylised, graceful female nudes were very popular.

During the 1920s people were obsessed with speed, and the increasingly streamlined cars, boats and trains influenced furniture design. Rounded corners are a feature of Art Deco furniture, with designs based on the circle or semicircle being particularly popular. Improved techniques for moulding plywood made it possible to create these shapes and for the first time coffee tables and cocktail cabinets were seen. Chrome and glass were used to make tables and trolleys of all sizes, whilst chrome and leather were combined to create very sophisticated chairs and loungers. Upholstered furniture was of generous, rounded proportions and the most favoured coverings were figured moquettes or soft leather.

Other geometric shapes such as triangles, octagons and cubes were also popular, and all these were used to decorate walls, floors, fabrics and pottery. Mirror glass was much liked and was often cut into these shapes, sometimes being used to echo the shapes of other fittings.

To set off Art Deco furniture the walls were pale, sometimes stippled or marbled in creams and beiges, and finished with a contemporary wallpaper or stencilled border which would extend part-way down the wall. Parquet flooring was fashionable and would be scattered with rugs which had bold

Mosaics and plain mirrored wall tiles are particularly useful for re-creating simple geometric shapes.

geometric patterns. Linoleum was increasingly used in homes everywhere. Curtains printed with animal-skin designs or with geometric shapes would be simply hung beneath a geometrically shaped wooden pelmet board sometimes outlined in braid to emphasise its shape. Venetian blinds made in metal or wood were used as an alternative to curtains as their clean, uncluttered lines were sympathetic to the whole Art Deco style.

Light fittings included marbled bowl pendant shades hung on chains, fan and shell-shaped wall lights in opaque glass and, most memorable of all, female figures supporting glass globes or lampshades. Glass ornaments and objects were popular too, the most outstanding examples being made by René Lalique.

Pottery and tableware designers such as Susie Cooper and Clarice Cliff produced some memorable pieces which are much sought after by today's collectors.

Tiled fireplaces, clocks, radios, ornaments of all kinds and even cocktail shakers echoed the shapes and motifs of furniture and fabric – and, fortunately, most items can still be found in junk shops and market stalls today.

The Art Deco look is not difficult to achieve; if you have a collection of pottery, vases or glass from that period, consider creating a suitable setting for it. There is no need to go all the way: pale walls, a stencilled frieze and a curved mirror would be sufficient to suggest this period, and would make an ideal background for some treasured possessions.

OTHER DECORATING STYLES

These three decorating styles – Victorian, Edwardian, Art Deco – are all instantly recognisable: to be more esoteric we could talk about others such as Elizabethan, Jacobean, Queen Anne, American Colonial, Shaker, Baroque, Gothic, Neo-Palladian and Post Modernist. However, although some people may, of course, be influenced to a certain degree by all these, many are only for the absolute purist. Instead, consider three of the best-loved styles which are all much in evidence today – the traditional, the country, and the modern; in fact the boundaries between these styles are fluid, but discussing them more fully should help you to form some ideas for the very personal look that you are perhaps trying to achieve.

TRADITIONAL STYLE

A traditionally furnished house would probably contain a collection of furniture from various periods – floral chintz fabrics, comfortable seating, shelves of books, an elegant fireplace, and lots of oriental rugs. The British in particular, with their long background of colonisation, exploration and trade, have been exposed to the cultural and domestic styles of other countries, and this has resulted in a comfortable blending of many styles which have been absorbed into our culture and now comprise the basis of traditional style.

The rooms of an eighteenth-century house probably epitomise this look more than any other, for it was during this period that proportions were particularly important, and high ceilings, moulded cornices, large sash windows and elegant fireplaces made a wonderful background for traditional furnishings. However, even if your house was not built during this period, if it has nicely proportioned rooms, think about adapting this style – it is easy to live with and furniture from many periods can meld and look comfortable together.

The fireplace, probably with an Adam-style surround in wood or marble, will be the focal point

A room furnished in traditional style. Note the balanced alcoves and sofas, as well as the colours which have been used so effectively

233

of the room and an important picture or large mirror placed directly above it will draw attention to its lines. A fender, perhaps with a padded leather top, would add a feeling of comfort, and during the summer large pots of hydrangeas or baskets of flowers sitting in the empty fireplace would complete the look. Balance is important in this type of room, and the walls on either side of the fireplace would probably have matching alcoves and be furnished with matching bookshelves, or a pair of pictures lit with brass-shaded lights.

A natural seating arrangement is to place sofas or chairs on each side of the fireplace, and a low table placed between them to hold books, magazines and a tea tray makes for comfort and ease. Sofas and chairs would most probably be of classic proportions and covered in chintz, floral linen union, striped materials, brocades or damasks; the curtains would be in the same materials or in something complementary, headed by swagged and tailed, ruched or frilled pelmets of some kind and probably held back by matching tie-backs or heavy cords and tassels.

Traditional wall treatments are subtle and discreet. Wallpaper in pale stripes or monotone toile de Jouey looks elegant, and most of the painting techniques such as ragging, dragging and sponging make an interesting background which will set off the rest of the furnishings. And rather than making a statement, the floor should also act as a backdrop for the furnishings – plain or barely patterned fitted carpets look good, as do polished floorboards and large traditional rugs.

Lighting, too, should be unobtrusive. Simple wall lights topped by silk shades, ceramic table lamps with either plain or oriental bases, and pleated silk lampshades or elegant brass-shaded task lights will blend together to provide a soft background lighting with interesting pools of light shining on polished furniture.

Traditional furniture ranges from the antique to good reproduction pieces, and the eighteenth-century styles of Chippendale, Hepplewhite and Sheraton seem particularly appropriate. Large carved or gilded mirrors are a feature of the traditional style and other accessories should include large bowls of flowers or houseplants, candlesticks, a collection of pictures, china or bronze ornaments, pieces of silver and other treasured possessions, with perhaps a large folding screen adding importance in a corner.

These are the basic elements of the traditional style, which seems equally at home in town or country. It can be made to look more masculine by using roomy, buttoned-leather chairs and chesterfields, writing desks and darker colours; or more feminine by the lavish use of chintz and floral patterns. The traditional look does not date, it always looks comfortable, and will not need constant refurbishment, particularly if the fabrics are wisely chosen.

COUNTRY STYLE

It could well be said that country style is also traditional, and this is true. But it is less formal and more eclectic than what is normally considered to be the traditional style of furnishing. It has an air of nostalgia, is comfortable and relaxing, and the matching of styles or colours need not be so relentlessly pursued as in some other styles; an integral part of country style is the profusion of colour and pattern mixed with natural materials.

When considering furniture, stripped pine perhaps immediately comes to mind and there is no doubt that original pieces are easy to live with, but of late the proliferation of brand new furniture with the so-called 'stripped pine look' has made rather a mockery of the original pieces. These were usually honestly made, plain, honey-coloured pieces of country furniture such as dressers, kitchen tables, splay-back chairs and corner cupboards, somewhat battered in appearance and bearing no resemblance to the polyurethane-coated pieces of yellow wood furniture which abound today. Of course, not all new pieces are horrid, but try to avoid those which have a coated finish as they will always retain that hard-edged look which is not at all what country style is about.

Most people would agree that a mixture of woods

A country style dining room, with stripped pine furniture and shutters, and dressers laden with a collection of pretty blue-and-white china

– plain or painted, wicker and cane – looks best of all, so hunt around for pieces that can be given a painted wash or some other soft finish which will blend with the rest of your furnishings. Large old sideboards, linen cupboards and chests will all come into their own, and the spare, simple lines of Shaker furniture, Windsor chairs and rocking chairs will also look good.

Country colours tend to be soft and earthy – soft greens, buttery yellows, misty blues, peaches and terracottas – and lovely schemes can be created by using a mixture of two or three of these colours. Country style does not mean 'twee' so do not be afraid to use quite strong designs. Wallpaper, for instance, does not have to be small floral sprigs, but could be stylised flowers in clean shapes, or geometrics. Matt-painted walls will also look good, perhaps decorated with a wallpaper or stencilled frieze at dado level. Tongue-and-groove panelling to dado level with a colour-washed or wallpapered wall

235

above it is also appropriate. It all depends on the size of the room and the condition of the walls.

Fabrics made from natural materials such as unbleached calico, muslin, gingham and mattress ticking may be humble, but they can look splendid when used with style. Other country fabrics include French patterned cottons, paisleys of all shades, Madras checks, batiks, patchworks and cotton lace – and combining a Madras check with, say, ticking can actually produce a rather sophisticated look. Crochet cloths of all sizes, crochet bedspreads, tapestry cushions on dining chairs or heaped on a bed will all emphasise the country look.

Country style decoration is often badly let down by insensitive lighting; it is best complemented by intimate areas of light, which can be achieved by using standard and table lamps, desk lamps and even candles in appropriate places. Old-fashioned oil lamps can still be found and traditional candlestick lamp bases also look particularly good. Rise-and-fall lights with soft shades work well over dining and kitchen tables, shedding an intimate light, but wherever shades are used they should be kept simple.

Natural floorboards or sisal matting covered with traditional rugs or dhurries work well with country furnishings, and curtains should be hung simply. They will look best gathered onto an unobtrusive curtain rail or hung from wooden poles.

Decorate the rooms with natural materials – baskets of all descriptions filled with fruit, dried flowers, fir cones or pot pourri. Hang collections of pretty plates on the walls together with tapestry samplers and a school clock. Make collections of country pieces which particularly appeal, such as decorative corn dollies, various jugs, cheese dishes or patchwork quilts – all will add character and interest.

Country style is perhaps the easiest of all looks to achieve. People nearly always have nostalgic feelings for the past and feel comfortable with things which help to recreate these warm feelings. There are no elaborate curtain treatments to think about, and floors can be given inexpensive treatments which are totally in keeping with the whole country aura. Collections of pretty china or needlework settle in happily, and most pieces of old furniture can be refurbished and given a useful new life. All in all it is an extremely comfortable way of living.

MODERN STYLE

Rather as the Edwardian era embraced the Aesthetic, the Arts and Crafts and the Art Nouveau Movements, modern style can come under the headings of Modernism, Post-Modernism and Minimalism.

From World War II until the middle of the 1970s there was only one main approach to the design of houses, furniture and interiors, and this evolved around the concept that design should simply look at functional needs. Decoration and ornamentation were considered to be irrelevant, even dishonest, and consistency in all things was made into a virtue. In housing terms this resulted in a lot of tidy little boxes totally without charm or character, whilst the office blocks, shops, multi-storey car parks and suchlike are now blots on the landscape. Of course simplicity can be desirable, but unless it is done with feeling it can look a great deal worse than something very ornate, and function alone does not always relate to good design.

Modernism is an abstract style which intentionally excludes the personal aspects, and towards the end of the 1970s people were beginning to complain bitterly about the sterile buildings which were being forced upon them by planners and architects. Naturally this included interiors and furniture too, and Post-Modernism was the architects' and designers' response to this reactionary feeling.

The new movement began in Italy and America, and set out to look deliberately representational and outrageous rather than abstract. It used colours in unconventional, frivolous ways, trying to inject humour into everyday objects such as tables and chairs, vacuum cleaners and telephones. In interiors the Post-Modernists preferred to create a series of small spaces rather than the large, open and unadorned spaces beloved of the Modernists. As public acceptance grew, the Post-Modernist designers calmed down and started producing serious designs for fabrics, furniture, glass and ceramics which influence practically everything we use today.

In the forefront of this new serious approach are people from all over the world known collectively as the Memphis Group. They began using startling colour combinations and old materials in new ways, overlaying traditional styling with their new approach. In broad terms it could fairly be said that Post-Modernists are trying to put back into all aspects of design the style which the Modernists took away in the name of function and mass-production.

Minimalists believe in reducing things to the barest minimum – no clutter, no decorative frills, nothing on the walls and no assertive pieces of furniture. A Minimalist employs only a very few pieces of furniture, and the placing of these is of paramount importance – their exact position in relation to a wall or window is critical. Although it has its place in modern decoration, this is a hard look to live up to and is probably best left to the modern aesthete.

So where does all this leave someone who would like to create a modern style at home? Basically, take all that is best from the ultra-modern designers, tone it down, mix it with ideas from the past and create a style that is easy to live with. In fact modern style can be hard- or soft-edged, the first being perhaps more suitable to city life and the second adaptable to all kinds of homes, both period and modern.

Hard-edged modern style is based on a totally monochromatic scheme, usually black, grey or

A room decorated in Post-Modernist style. Note the use of black and chrome furniture, accented with splashes of red, and the interesting wall and floor treatments

237

white, with chrome and glass adding to the clean lines. Furniture is usually quite angular in shape with minimal detailing and clearly defined outlines. Armchairs are made from tubular chrome with black leather or fabric seats and backs, and upholstery is confined to sofas only. Cabinets are either glass-fronted to show off a few elegant ceramics, or fully enclosed to hide away any suggestion of clutter. Tables and shelving may be either glass and chrome, or wood-stained in black or grey, but both will be absolutely plain.

Accessories are kept to a minimum, and are usually limited to modern pictures or posters, ceramics which rely purely on shape and texture, flowers with sculptural lines and green plants and trees. Sometimes one strong accent colour such as scarlet or vivid jade will be introduced to add excitement to the scheme. There are often no curtains at all, just narrow Venetian blinds, or tailored roller or Roman blinds.

Lighting is very important to this ultra-modern scheme, as some softness needs to be introduced, particularly at night, so that it does not look too stark. Rather surprisingly, Art Deco wall lights and freestanding lamps fit in well, as do some of the very modern cantilevered Italian designs.

Neutral colours predominate on both walls and floors, the walls and woodwork sometimes being given the same eggshell paint finish. If wallpaper is used it may be self-striped or have a very small geometric pattern, both of which would add texture rather than colour to the room. Floors can be left bare or covered with vinyl or studded rubber laid into draught-board patterns. Linoleum can also be laid in this way or cut to give a plain centre with a contrasting border.

This unfussy, elegant look which relies on clean, simple lines is easy to achieve and good shops dedicated to this style of furnishing are growing, so finding the right furniture and accessories is becoming much easier.

Soft-edged modern style also relies on streamlined, unfussy furniture and accessories but employs a whole host of colours, mostly pastel at the moment, to create a feeling of more warmth and comfort than the monochromatic hard-edged style.

Upholstered furniture is sometimes covered with soft, abstract designs or misty florals, often in the same tones so that they blend together well. A more tailored look may be achieved by using a plain, self-patterned fabric which is then piped with a contrasting colour, and this combination may be carried through onto Roman blinds beneath simply hung curtains. Other motifs such as trellises, checks and chevrons look good too, and may act in interesting counterpoint to both patterned and plain materials. Blond Scandinavian wood, elm and ash are often used as show-wood on upholstered furniture, and in simple shapes will be used for tables and chairs of all kinds.

Walls may be treated in a variety of subtle ways to provide a restful background. Painted finishes such as dragging, bagging, sponging and stippling are suitable, and if wallpaper is used then keep it pale, with perhaps a gentle, unstructured pattern to add texture. Woodwork should be kept pale and could be included in, say, the stippling treatment so that its lines sink into the overall background. To further increase the feeling of spaciousness and light the ceilings should be painted in pale colours. Floors should also increase the feeling of space, and are generally close-carpeted in plain shades or covered in sisal. Seating and dining areas may be emphasised by the use of patterned rugs and dhurries placed on top of the carpet.

Lighting should be warm and subtle. Lamp bases are mostly made from ceramics given a crackle-glazed finish and shades are plain and coolie-shaped or simply pleated. Pictures and framed posters abound, and green plants arranged in groups will further add to the feeling of freshness which this whole soft look imparts.

To summarise, the overall feeling of this look is softness. Gentle colours, smudged and dappled patterns and outlines, simple shapes which do not jar, plainly treated curtains perhaps swathed over a pole to add interest, pictures in simple frames, and fresh flowers and plants: all of these make this a look which anyone can achieve.

PROJECT PAPERS

Finding an individual style takes time and experience, and your tastes may cross all the boundaries of accepted styles. This is as it should be. Houses are meant to be loved and lived in and to grow with you; they are not museums, and only the purist would insist on having every detail correct in his or her given style. Besides, this does not necessarily make for comfortable living, so do not be afraid to mix styles or adapt ideas from various periods. The overall feeling should be harmonious and comfortable so do not feel that colours have to be matched too relentlessly, and do not be afraid to experiment.

PROJECT 27

From your growing reference library, select a prime example of a room decorated in the Arts and Crafts manner. Display this and write notes explaining, as if to the uninitiated, the things that went into its overall design and why it is so typical of its period. Go on to explain, with examples if you wish, how this movement still has an influence on today's interior design.

PROJECT 28

Illustrate, by photographs taken from magazines, the following furnishing styles:

- Victorian
- Art Deco
- Classical Edwardian
- Traditional
- Country
- Modern

Alongside each photograph note why it typifies its particular design style and what you personally like, or dislike, about this style of furnishing.

CHAPTER 15

FINISHING TOUCHES

By NOW, THIS BOOK and its projects should have succeeded in teaching its readers a great deal about the various aspects of interior design. Being able to draw up a scale plan, and with a new appreciation of how to plan everything from a lighting system to a kitchen, should prove invaluable assets in the future, whether for decorating one's own home or for advising others. And although there have been many suggestions on how to use the various elements which go into interior design, it is still worth mentioning a few of the finishing touches which can make all the difference.

FOCAL POINTS

Every room needs a focal point and the most obvious one is the fireplace. It is interesting that

builders of new houses are now reintroducing this feature, after years of ignoring it and saying that with central heating one did not need a fireplace. Even if people do not actually burn fuel in the fireplace they still prefer to have one in a sitting-room, as without it they find it difficult to focus attention on any arrangement of furniture.

During the winter months nothing can beat the feeling of comfort and warmth that a glowing fire can give. It need not bring dust and extra work in its wake, for today there are very realistic 'living flame' gas fires and glowing electric fires which will produce the same effect. New systems are being introduced all the time; for example, even if there is no mains gas, it is possible to have a gas fire by using a fuel pipe which leads directly through to gas cylinders sited on an outside wall. If gas is available but the house has no chimney, there is now a fire

Traditionally a space of 2 or 3in (5 to 7.6cm) was left between the bottom of the mirror and the mantelshelf so that the bottoms of candlesticks could tuck under and the lighted candles would reflect twice the light – an idea well worth remembering today.

A 'living flame' gas fire built into an outside wall, as there is no chimney breast. Focus has been added to the wall by the addition of a simple surround

which vents directly through an external wall, and this can be finished with a surround which is appropriate to the house or furnishing style.

During the summer months an empty fireplace can still be the focus of attention: fill it with lovely flowers, both fresh and dried, or green plants. Firescreens, too, are making a comeback and some can be commissioned, specially made so that they tone in with a particular colour scheme.

The wall above the fireplace should further focus attention; this can be done by hanging one important picture or a collection of smaller ones there, or even better, by placing a large mirror immediately above the mantelpiece as it will increase the size of the room by reflection and help lighten a dark room. Overmantels should never exceed the width of the mantelshelf and look best if they are the same width as the fire surround.

PICTURES AND MIRRORS

Pictures can make all the difference to any decorative scheme, but the way they are hung is important. A common mistake is to hang pictures too high on the wall – the ideal height is halfway between seated and standing eye level.

A picture, or group of pictures, should relate to other objects in the room, so place them above a table, a sofa, a desk or a fireplace so that they are anchored to something and have more impact. Placing pictures centrally is not always the best way of displaying them: consider hanging them off-centre, or in pairs. Groups of pictures can look very dramatic and work best if they all relate to one another in some way. For instance, they may be all shapes and sizes but their colours may be similar or they may have a common theme such as poppies. Even if the individual pictures are very different it helps if they are framed in the same way.

It is not particularly easy to work out a harmonious grouping for pictures of various sizes, but it helps to lay them all out on the floor first and play around with different arrangements until something results which works well – it also

ABOVE: *A four-fold firescreen with an Art Nouveau daisy design, coloured to pick up the shade of the other room furnishings*

LEFT: *Note how this picture has been 'anchored' to the chair below, and how the flowers and fruit have been carefully chosen to add further emphasis*

An ornate découpage screen
provides instant period feel

prevents too many holes in the wall! Groups of pictures do need a visual line of some kind – either they should appear to stand or hang from a horizontal line, or be grouped around a cross formed by a vertical and a horizontal line, or arranged symmetrically alongside a vertical line.

Mirrors are wonderful aids to the interior designer for not only are they decorative but they will also create space by deception. Entire walls can be mirrored, and this will double the apparent length or width of a room.

Always place mirrors so that they reflect something interesting. When they are placed opposite a window the garden comes inside, and if one is used in a firescreen behind a group of plants the display looks particularly extravagant. Mirrored alcoves can also deceive the eye, and look effective if lined with glass shelves displaying ornaments, as the pieces can then be seen on all sides.

RUGS AND SCREENS

Wonderful decorative effects can be achieved by using rugs and screens. Rugs can enliven floorboards and fitted carpets, and define a seating or dining area, and many also look wonderful when displayed on walls. They will certainly add focus and excitement to neutral colours, and many a designer has been inspired by the colours in a rug to create a truly unique decorative scheme. Also, when they were first imported they were displayed on large pieces of furniture such as settles and refectory tables or draped across couches: in the right setting, this is still an elegant way of displaying them.

Screens, too, are wonderfully versatile. They can literally screen off part of a room – perhaps a washbasin in a bedroom or an eating area in a living room – or they can hide objects such as a television set or ugly radiators which do not enhance the room. They can be purely decorative: use small ones in an empty fireplace, and tall ones to decorate a corner of a room or even as a bedhead; make them wonderfully ornate in the Eastern manner, covered in fabric to match the curtains or painted to suit a

particular colour scheme – always be alert to the possibility of using one in a special room.

PLANTS AND FLOWERS

A room cannot fail to be improved by introducing greenery of some kind, and a collection of houseplants is one of the fastest and most economical ways there is of bringing it to life. And anyone who uses plants will know how dead and empty it can look when they are removed.

So long as a plant is chosen and situated with regard to its natural growing conditions, it should thrive and last for many years. Some plants need plenty of sunlight, others need shade and some moisture – most good nurseries now label their plants, making it easier to select specimens for a particular position. Plants can be arranged individually or grouped together for dramatic effect. For instance, a common fern tends to be rather large and looks best when displayed alone, but large floor-level plants can be enhanced by having others grouped around their base, the whole arrangement probably being lit by an uplighter at night.

Unusual containers such as soup tureens, gravy boats and teapots can be used for flowering plants; providing there is gravel for drainage, they will thrive. Flowering plants such as the exuberant white marguerite will go on and on, and can be trained into rounded 'standard' shapes which contrast well with plain, modern furniture.

Use plants to draw the eye from one area to another – next to a window, for instance, so that the division between room and garden is blurred, or suspended in a stairwell so that the eye is drawn upwards and the shape of an elegant bannister or staircase is brought into focus. Some plants seem to lend themselves particularly well to certain styles. Who cannot immediately visualise the 'Palm Court' feeling of a room decorated in Art Deco style, where the sharp, angular shape of palm trees seems a natural extension of the whole look?

Fresh flowers always look good and they don't have to cost a fortune, particularly if you live in the

Why not create a wall rug by working one of the many tapestry rug designs now available?

245

This elegant palm-like plant suits this modern room very well

country and can call upon lots of greenery to bulk out a single bunch. Wild flowers in big jugs look wonderful in a country setting, whilst a few dramatic white lilies may be the only accent needed in a smart modern city room.

Dried flowers, too, play an increasing part in home decoration. The country look is emphasised by a variety of flowers hanging in large bunches from a ceiling clothes airer or from meat hooks, and in a formal room they can be beautifully arranged in baskets or elegant *jardinières*. Dried flowers can be twined around willow garlands or made into trees, and dishes filled with pot pourri made from dried flower heads mixed with herbs and aromatic oils will fill a room in both town and country with fragrance, recalling warm summer nights in flower-filled gardens.

COLLECTIONS

A collection can be used most effectively to form the basis of an interior design scheme; the mere fact that someone has bothered to collect certain items shows their strong appeal. Moreover many of us have possessions placed randomly around the house which might well form an attractive collection if they were all gathered together in one place – for example, items which despite being disparate all have a particular shade of blue in common; or a selection of similar items such as teapots or plates.

Use shelves, walls and table-tops to group them all together, and like pictures, try to achieve a certain balance in the way they are hung or displayed. Think about using a spotlight, a wall light or an uplighter to focus attention on the display at night, and remember it is attention to detail which marks the difference between a collection and a clutter.

MISCELLANEOUS

Small things can make a tremendous difference to a room – details such as the correct door furniture and

An uplighter at the base of this pretty niche and shining through the glass shelf will focus attention at night

knobs and handles generally can all affect its look, and should be thought about with care. Carefully managed, these will prove the designer.

Cover ugly radiators with a caned or trellis surround, or make a window seat in a reveal – this sort of attention shows that the overall appearance of the room has been carefully considered, to the last detail. This is the difference between merely decorating a room and designing it.

These finishing touches will be instinctive and very personal – but try not to get set into a particular mould. Adopt new ideas as they come along, continually adapt old ones, and above all else, develop your own particular style.

Finally, continue to collect and assemble ideas and examples you have seen, filing away any that are particularly appealing; even if they have no place in today's scheme, they may very well be useful one day.

This radiator cover not only looks elegant but makes a good display shelf as well

PROJECT PAPERS

And so to the final projects in this book. A great deal has been discussed concerning the foundations of interior design, and as you will now realise it is not all about putting pretty fabrics and elegant furniture together in a harmonious way; every aspect has to be given due consideration and the boring bits, such as plumbing, are quite as important as the final flourishes.

If you have managed to work through all the projects you will surely feel a great sense of achievement as you look at the room plans, the colour boards and the mass of coloured illustrations which have grown into such an impressive portfolio, a unique record of *your* home and *your* creativity.

The final projects are your chance to express everything you feel about interior design, so really go to town on them and finish with a flourish!

PROJECT 29

It is undoubtedly the finishing touches which bring an interior design scheme to life and win applause. From your collection of cuttings, select three items or themes which you particularly like, and note beside them how and where they could be used and why you like them so much.

PROJECT 30

This is the final project: let your mind roam free, and write down your ideas concerning the perfect home. It can be period, modern, a house or a flat, but try and illustrate with pictures or drawings the sizes and features of the sitting and dining rooms, the main bedroom, the kitchen and the bathroom.

Really let yourself go; submit the fullest possible details with perhaps an overall floor plan, and certainly fabric and paint swatches so that your design schemes can be fully appreciated.

Good luck for the future!

GLOSSARY

Accent lighting Lighting used to attract attention to an area or object.

Alive Used to describe a painted or varnished surface which is still wet and in a workable state.

Ambient light General light, such as that from a window.

Amorini Winged cupids or cherubs.

Appliqué Shaped pieces of fabric applied to another fabric to form a simple pattern.

Apron A shaped piece which is fixed between the legs of a chair or settee to mask the bottom. It is sometimes also used below the frieze rail of a cabinet or chest and may be decorated.

Arcading A series of ornamental arches.

Architrave The moulded frame around a door or window.

Art Deco Decorative art style of the 1920s and 1930s based on streamlined rounded, geometric and stepped *ziggurat* shapes. The hallmark of the style was decorative innovation.

Art Nouveau Decorative art style of the late nineteenth century personified by flowing designs based on the female form, flowers and leaves.

Bail A hanging shaped bar or pull for drawers.

Ball and claw A design for a foot on cabriole legs. Literally a claw holding a ball and thought to derive from a Chinese design.

Barley twist A spiral turning.

Baroque Extravagant and florid art style which flourished in the last half of the seventeenth century.

Base Colour The foundation colour of a design, not to be confused with base coat which is a paint on which other layers are applied.

Bauhaus A design style which evolved from a German institution where artists and architects were taught that there should be no separation between applied art, fine art and architecture.

Beading A narrow moulding, usually semicircular and sometimes in the style of a string of beads.

Beam Light, usually cone-shaped, emerging from a light fitting.

Bias binding Strips of material cut on the diagonal grain of fabric and used to bind raw fabric edges or to cover piping cord.

Blanket stitch A stitch used to neaten raw edges or to provide a decorative edging on scallops.

Blind stitch A stitch used to form invisible hems or to hold fillings and wadding in place.

Bow front A gentle curve on the front of furniture, usually chests of drawers.

Breakfront A piece of furniture on which the central section projects beyond the two side pieces.

Bulb The source of light, called a 'lamp' in the trade.

Bump A thick soft fabric made from waste cotton and used to interline curtains.

Bun foot A foot shaped like a large bun and mainly used on chests of drawers.

Cabriole A leg curving outwards from the top and tapering to a gentle arc at the foot. It sometimes ends in a ball and claw foot.

Candela A unit of luminous intensity.

Candlepower Luminous intensity expressed in candelas.

Carcase The basic frame of furniture before embellishment.

Casing A channel formed by two rows of machine stitching to take elastic or curtain wire. A casing can also be made by a row of stitching placed at a certain distance from a folded edge to take curtain poles etc.

Castors Small swivel wheels to ease the movement of furniture. They can be made from wood, metal, leather or porcelain.

Chinoiserie Chinese-inspired design.

Chip carving A simple form of carving to produce surface ornamentation.

Cornice Ornamental moulding around the wall of a room just below the ceiling.

Crown silver lamp An incandescent filament lamp with a mirror finish on the bottom half.

Cubism A revolutionary art movement created by Picasso and Braque during the years 1907–9 and heavily influenced by the artist Cézanne. The paintings reduced natural forms to geometric shapes and mathematical precision.

Dado A strip of moulding applied to the lower part of a wall when it is coloured differently from the upper part.

Dart A method of taking up fullness by tapering stitches from two points on an outer edge into a centre point.

Diaper Diamond-shaped.

Diffuse lighting Light which does not come from one direction.

Dimmer A switch used to regulate the intensity of light from a bulb/lamp.

Domette A curtain interlining made from a woollen weft and a cotton warp.

Dovetail A joint in which wedges interlock with corresponding wedges.

Eclectic Used to describe an interesting mixture of different styles which draws inspiration from many sources.

Escutcheon A protective plate surrounding a keyhole.

Facing A piece of fabric used to neaten a raw edge.

Fall front The writing surface of a bureau which is hinged to form a horizontal surface for writing. Sometimes known as a drop front.

Finial A terminal ornament which can be affixed to furniture to add further decoration. Sometimes shaped like an elongated knob or like a spear.

Flounce A fabric skirt around loose covers, bedspreads etc. It can be gathered or pleated.

Fly leg A table leg which swivels to support the top.

Gallery A miniature railing in metal or wood around the top of a table, tray or shelf.

General lighting A uniform level of lighting throughout an area.

Gesso A plaster used as a base for painted or gilded decoration.

Glare Brightness which is greater than the eye can take.

Gothic An architectural style popular in twelfth-century northern Europe. Pointed arches and traceried windows are particular features and it enjoyed a revival during the Victorian era.

Grain The direction in which fabric fibres run.

Gusset A piece of material placed between the top and bottom sections of a cushion to give depth, eg a sofa cushion.

HID lamps High-intensity discharge lamps.

High-tech A decorating style which leans heavily on industrial materials such as rubber flooring and metal shelving. Furniture and fittings are spare and functional.

Illuminance The density of light on a particular surface.

Indirect lighting Lighting in which most of the light being emitted is directed upwards and bounced back again.

Inlay Materials of all kinds laid into solid wood to form a design.

Kitsch An over-the-top, extremely pretentious decorating style of questionable taste.

Ladderback A chair back with horizontal rails like a ladder.

Linenfold Wood carved to resemble the folds of a piece of linen.

LPW Lumens per watt.

Lumen A unit of light energy.

Lux The number of lumens per square metre.

Marquetry Different veneers glued onto wood to produce a design.

Minimalism An extremely simple, totally uncluttered interior design style.

Mitre joint Two surfaces joined together usually at an angle of 45°.

Modernism An abstract style which considers decoration, ornamentation and personal aspects to be irrelevant, relying instead upon modern technology and scientifically developed materials.

Motif The most dominant part of a design.

Nap The raised surface on a fabric.

Neo-Palladian A revival of the neo-classical style of Italian architecture popular during the sixteenth century.

Ottoman A long upholstered seat, although Victorian variations include circular and octagonal shapes.

Patchwork The art of sewing small pieces of different material together to form attractive patterns. The pieces may be octagonal, square, diamond-shaped or rectangular.

Pendant light A light fitting hung from the ceiling.

Picture rail Horizontal bar of wood on upper part of wall, used to hang things on.

Piping A professional finish to loose covers and cushions etc. Bias-cut fabric is folded evenly over a piping cord, which should be pre-shrunk before use, and then inserted between two pieces of fabric.

Plank seat A seat made from a single piece of wood, sometimes shaped.

Post-Modernism A style which, like Minimalism, avoids clutter and fitted furniture but tries to make individual statements about design.

Quartering Four pieces of identical veneer opposed to each other to produce a mirror effect.

Quilting A method of joining and decorating two layers of fabric between which is a centre made from wadding material.

Rebate A groove cut to receive an edge.

Retro Any style which harks back to the past.

Runner A strip of wood on which drawers run easily.

Sabre leg A square-section leg curving outwards in a gentle arc.

Scallop A curved edge, sometimes finished with blanket stitch, which is used to decorate soft furnishings such as table linen, blinds and pelmets.

Screw eye A metal screw, sometimes covered with a plastic coating, which has a round eyelet at the head.

Scumble A ready-made oil-based glaze, ranging in colour from white to honey-coloured, which can be tinted with universal stainers or artists' oil colours.

Serpentine A long S-shape used for the fronts of chests and similar furniture.

Shaker Simply designed furniture with a purity of line made by the eighteenth-century Quaker community which fled to America to avoid religious persecution in England.

Skirting Board along bottom of room wall.

Surrealism A style of painting or decoration which seeks to shock by juxtaposing unreality with reality. In the art world Salvador Dali's paintings are the epitome of this style.

Swag A traditional way of draping fabric to form soft folds. Depending on where it is used the folds can be formal and regular or informal and loose.

Task lighting Light directed on a work surface.

Topstitching A decorative row of stitching on the right side of fabric.

Translucent Used to describe a colour which allows you to see another one beneath it.

Transparent Used to describe a colour which alters the shade beneath it but without obscuring it.

Under-toning Background colour tones on which top glazes are applied.

Valance A soft edge for bed linen or the top of curtains. It can be gathered to form a frill or pleated.

Wadding A padding made from cotton waste, synthetic fibres or wool. Available in different thicknesses and widths and used for quilting, soft furnishing and upholstery.

Warp Parallel strands of fibres running the length of a fabric.

Watt A unit of electrical energy.

Weft Horizontal strands of fibres running across the width of a fabric and interwoven with the warp threads.

Zigzag stitch A machine-made stitch which is used to neaten seams or decorate edges.

FURTHER READING

CHAPTER 2
Cavanagh, A. *Letter and Alphabets* (Dover Publications)
Gill, Robert *Basic Perspective* (Thames & Hudson)
Gill, Robert *Creative Perspective* (Thames & Hudson)
Wang, Thomas C. *Plan and Section Drawing* (Architectural Press)

CHAPTER 4
Cobb, Hubbard H. *How to Paint Anything* (Macmillan)
Hemming, Charles *Paint Finishes* (Macdonald)
Innes, Jocasta *Paint Magic* (Windward/Berger Paints)
Johnson, L. *The Decorator's Directory* (Michael Joseph)
Mayer, Ralph *The Artists' Handbook of Materials and Techniques* (Faber & Faber)
O'Neil, Isabel *The Art of the Painted Finish* (William Morrow)
Radford, Penny *Designer's Guide to Surfaces and Finishes* (Quill Publishing)

CHAPTER 5
Bishop, Adele & Lord, Cile *The Art of Decorative Stencilling* (Penguin Books)
Campbell, Sarah & More, Hilary *Soft Furnishings* (Macdonald)
Colvin, Maggie *Pure Fabrication* (Rainbird)
Plant, Tim *Painted Illusions* (Ward Lock)
Rogers Witsell, R. & Kittrel, S. *Authentic Stencil Patterns 1890–1930* (Designed Communications, 704 Boyle Building, 103 West Capitol, Little Rock, Arkansas, 72201, USA)
St George, Amelia *The Stencil Book* (Conran Octopus)
Seligman, Patricia *Painting Murals* (Macdonald Orbis)
Turner, Mark & Hoskins, Lesley *The Silver Studio of Design* (Webb & Bower)

CHAPTER 6
Argent, Jeanne *Home Sewing* (Orbis)
Campbell, Sarah & More, Hilary *Soft Furnishings* (Macdonald)
Curtains & Soft Furnishings (Ward Lock)
Designers Guild, The *Soft Furnishings* (Pan Books)
Dickson, Elizabeth & Colvin, Margaret *The Laura Ashley Book of Home Decorating* (Octopus)
Watkins, Charmian *Fabric Liberty Style* (Ebury Press)

CHAPTER 7
Ferguson, Pamela *The Complete Book of the Home* (Quarto)
Gilliat, Mary *The Decorating Book* (Michael Joseph)
Johnson, Lorraine *The Decorator's Directory* (Michael Joseph)
Reader's Digest Repair Manual (Reader's Digest Association)
Riley, Noel *Tile Art – A History of Decorative Ceramic Tiles* (The Apple Press)
The Manufacture of Ceramic Tiles (British Ceramic Tile Council)

CHAPTER 8
Billcliffe, Roger *Mackintosh Furniture* (David & Charles)
Bly, John *Discovering English Furniture* (Shire Publications)
Fastnedge, Ralph *English Furniture Styles* (Penguin Books)
Haslam, Malcolm *Art Deco – A Buyer's Guide* (Macdonald Orbis)
Oughton, Frederick *Grinling Gibbons and the British Woodcarving Tradition* (Stobart & Son)
Pearsall, Ronald *The Joy of Antiques* (David & Charles)
Taylor, V. J. *The Antique Furniture Trail* (David & Charles)
Woodforde, John *The Observer's Book of Furniture* (Frederick Warne)

CHAPTER 9

Campbell, Sarah & More, Hilary *Soft Furnishings* (Macdonald)
Curtains and Soft Furnishings (Ward Lock)
Denton, Susan & Macey, Barbara *Quiltmaking* (David & Charles)
Designers Guild, The *Soft Furnishings* (Pan Books)
McCalls Sewing in Colour (Paul Hamlyn)
McNeill, Moyra *Quilting* (Treasure Press)
Rolfe, Margaret *Patchwork Quilts* (David & Charles)

CHAPTER 10

Butler, H. *Home Decorating Using Light* (Marshall Cavendish)
Effron, Edward *Planning and Designing Lighting* (Windward)
Freeth, Richard *Plan Your Home Lighting* (Studio Vista)
Grosslight, Jane *Light – Effective Use of Daylight and Electric Lighting* (Prentice Hall)
Interior Lighting Design (The Electricity Council)
Kalff, Louis C. *Creative Light* (Van Nostrand)
Kellogg, Fran & Bertolene, F. *Bringing Interiors to Light* (Whitney Library of Design)
Phillips, Barty *Christopher Wray's Guide to Decorative Lighting* (Webb & Bower)
Phillips, Derek *Planning your Lighting* (Design Council)
Szenasy, Susan S. *Light: The Complete Handbook of Lighting Design* (Columbus Books)

CHAPTER 11

'Bathroom Style' (*Ideal Home*, February 1990)
Conran, Terence *The New House Book* (Conran Octopus)
Designing and Planning Bathrooms (Ward Lock)
Ferguson, Pamela *The Complete Home Book* (Quarto)
Gilliat, Mary *The Decorating Book* (Michael Joseph)
'Ideas for Bathrooms' (*Homes & Gardens*, April 1990)
Planning Your New Bathroom (Armitage Shanks)

CHAPTER 12

'Creating a Special Look' (*Ideal Home*, November 1989)
Designing and Planning Bedrooms (Ward Lock)
House Style (Holt, Rinehart & Winston)
Phipps, Diana *Affordable Splendour* (Weidenfeld & Nicolson)
The House & Garden Book of Romantic Rooms (Collins)

CHAPTER 13

'Beautiful Living' (*Ideal Home*, October 1989)
Gibberd, V. & Phillips, B. *Planning and Designing Kitchens* (Windward)
Planning a Better Kitchen (Ward Lock)
The National Home Improvement Guide Issue No 10 (National Home Improvement Council)

CHAPTER 14

Adams, Steven *The Arts and Crafts Movement* (The Apple Press)
Buffet Challie, Laurence *Art Nouveau Style* (Academy Editions)
Garner, Philippe (ed) *Encyclopedia of Decorative Arts 1890–1940* (Phaidon)
Garner, Philippe *The World of Edwardiana* (Hamlyn)
Gilliat, Mary *English Country Style* (Orbis)
Horsham, Michael *The Art of the Shakers* (The Apple Press)
Hudson, Malcolm *Art Deco – A Buyer's Guide* (Macdonald Orbis)
Kemp, Jim *Victorian Revival in Interior Design* (Columbus Books)
Miller, Judith & Martin *Period Style* (Mitchell Beazley)
Moffat, Alistair *Remembering Charles Rennie Mackintosh* (Colin Baxter)
Morris, Barbara *Liberty Design* (Pyramid Books)
Turner, M. & Hoskins, L. *Silver Studio of Design* (Webb & Bower)

ACKNOWLEDGEMENTS

Wren Loasby and the publishers would like to extend their grateful thanks to the following people and companies who have been of immense help in supplying photographs and illustrations included in this book:

The Amtico Company Limited, 17 St George Street, London W1R 9DE

Aristocast Originals Limited, Bold Street, Sheffield S9 2LR

Armitage Shanks Limited, Rugeley, Staffordshire

Caradon Twyford Limited, P.O. Box 23, Stoke-on-Trent ST4 7AL

G. P. & J. Baker Limited, P. O. Box 30, West End Road, High Wycombe HP11 2QD

Chelsom Limited, Heritage House, Clifton Road, Blackpool, Lancashire FY4 4QA

Crown Berger Europe Limited, P. O. Box 37, Darwen, Lancashire BB3 0BG

Crucial Trading, 77 Westbourne Park Road, London W2

Davies, Keeling Trowbridge Ltd, 3 Charterhouse Works, Eltringham Street, London SW18 1TD

Hill & Knowles, 133 Kew Road, Richmond, Surrey TW9 2PN

ICI Paints, Wexham Road, Slough, Berkshire SL2 5DS

Ideal Home, King's Reach Tower, Stamford Street, London SE1 9LS

Miele Company Limited, Fairacres, Marcham Road, Abingdon OX14 1TW

Monkwell Limited, 10–12 Wharfdale Road, Bournemouth, Dorset BH4 9BT

Ornamenta Limited, 23 South Terrace, London SW7 2TB

Original Bathrooms Limited, 143–145 Kew Road, Richmond, Surrey TW9 2PN

The Original Tile Company, 23a Howe Street, Edinburgh, Scotland

Ramus Tile Company Limited, Palace Road, Bounds Green, London N11 2PX

J. R. Ratcliffe & Company Limited, 135a Linaker Street, Southport PR8 5DF

Redland Plasterboard Limited, Redland House, Reigate, Surrey RH2 0SJ

Sacuisine, 63 Chobham Road, Sunningdale, Berkshire SL5 0DT

Arthur Sanderson & Sons Limited, 52/53 Berners Street, London W1P 3AD

B. C. Sanitan Limited, Unit 12, Nimrod Way, Elgar Road, Reading, Berkshire RG2 0EB

Stevensons of Norwich Limited, Roundtree Way, Norwich, Norfolk NR7 8SH

Top Knobs, 4 Brunel Buildings, Newton Abbot, Devon TQ12 4PB

Jennie Jones, Southlands, Stoke Gabriel, Paignton, South Devon

Paul Biddle, St James, Capton, Nr Dartmouth, TQ6 0JE

Old Pine, 594 Kings Road, London SW6

Nice Irma's, Spring House, Spring Place, London NW5 3BH

Dragon of Walton Street, 23 Walton Street, London SW3 2HX

Leisure, Meadow Lane, Long Eaton, Notts NG10 2AT

Poppy Ltd, 44 High Street, Yarn, Cleveland TS15 9AE

Johnny Grey Design, Hampshire Farm, South Harting, Petersfield, Hants GU31 5LP

We would also like to thank the following for the loan of items included in the chapter opening photographs:

Sitting Rooms, Foss Street, Dartmouth

Simon Drew, Foss Street, Dartmouth

Arcadian Tiles, Palladium Arcade, Dartmouth

Diana Austin, 61 High Street, Totnes

Jenny Jones Interiors, Southlands, Stoke Gabriel, Paignton

The Kitchen Shop, Foss Street, Dartmouth

Bogan House Antiques, 43 High Street, Totnes

Bernard & Wright, 8 Lower Street, Dartmouth

George Gildersleve Antiques, 49 Victoria Road, Dartmouth

Painted backgrounds by:

Jane Darby Designs, Jopes Mill, Trebrownbridge, Cornwall

Fabric samples from:

Osborne & Little, King's Road, London SW6

Anna French, 108 Shakespeare Road, London SE2

Designers Guild, King's Road, London SW6

INDEX